Influencer Boot Camp

A Guide to Building a Successful Social Media Business

John Biggs
Jessa Moore

Influencer Boot Camp: A Guide to Building a Successful Social Media Business

John Biggs	Jessa Moore
Brooklyn, NY, USA	New York City, NY, USA

ISBN-13 (pbk): 979-8-8688-1391-7   ISBN-13 (electronic): 979-8-8688-1389-4
https://doi.org/10.1007/979-8-8688-1389-4

Copyright © 2025 by John Biggs, Jessa Moore

This work is subject to copyright. All rights are reserved by the Publisher, whether the whole or part of the material is concerned, specifically the rights of translation, reprinting, reuse of illustrations, recitation, broadcasting, reproduction on microfilms or in any other physical way, and transmission or information storage and retrieval, electronic adaptation, computer software, or by similar or dissimilar methodology now known or hereafter developed.

Trademarked names, logos, and images may appear in this book. Rather than use a trademark symbol with every occurrence of a trademarked name, logo, or image we use the names, logos, and images only in an editorial fashion and to the benefit of the trademark owner, with no intention of infringement of the trademark.

The use in this publication of trade names, trademarks, service marks, and similar terms, even if they are not identified as such, is not to be taken as an expression of opinion as to whether or not they are subject to proprietary rights.

While the advice and information in this book are believed to be true and accurate at the date of publication, neither the authors nor the editors nor the publisher can accept any legal responsibility for any errors or omissions that may be made. The publisher makes no warranty, express or implied, with respect to the material contained herein.

> Managing Director, Apress Media LLC: Welmoed Spahr
> Acquisitions Editor: Shivangi Ramachandran
> Development Editor: Jim Markham
> Project Manager: Jessica Vakili

Cover credit by eStudioCalamar

Distributed to the book trade worldwide by Springer Science+Business Media New York, 1 New York Plaza, New York, NY 10004. Phone 1-800-SPRINGER, fax (201) 348-4505, e-mail orders-ny@springer-sbm.com, or visit www.springeronline.com. Apress Media, LLC is a Delaware LLC and the sole member (owner) is Springer Science + Business Media Finance Inc (SSBM Finance Inc). SSBM Finance Inc is a **Delaware** corporation.

For information on translations, please e-mail booktranslations@springernature.com; for reprint, paperback, or audio rights, please e-mail bookpermissions@springernature.com.

Apress titles may be purchased in bulk for academic, corporate, or promotional use. eBook versions and licenses are also available for most titles. For more information, reference our Print and eBook Bulk Sales web page at http://www.apress.com/bulk-sales.

If disposing of this product, please recycle the paper

Table of Contents

About the Authors..**xvii**

Chapter 1: Introduction to Influence: Understanding the Power and Reach of Influencers..**1**

Traditional Media Experts vs. the Rise of the Everyday Expert 6

The Metrics of Influence 7

Pop Culture Trendsetters 8

Authenticity Matters 10

The Responsibility of Influence 11

    Empowered Consumers 13

    Key Takeaways 14

Chapter 2: The Evolution of Influencer Marketing.......................**15**

The Evolution of Influencer Marketing: From Ancient Times to Social Media Stardom 16

Ancient Beginnings: Influencers of Antiquity 17

The Rise of Print: Celebrities and Endorsements 18

The Birth of Mass Media: Hollywood and Beyond 20

The Digital Revolution: Enter the Social Media Influencer 21

Key Takeaways 22

Today and Beyond: The Future of Influence 23

Key Takeaways 31

TABLE OF CONTENTS

Chapter 3: Defining Your Niche: Identifying Your Passion and Expertise 33

Prepare Yourself 35
    The Rules of Content Creation 37
The Influencer's Checklist 39
    Evolving with the Audience 41
More Niche Advice 42
    Self-Discovery and Passion 43
    Market Research and Analysis 44
    Niche Specialization 44
    Content Creation and Consistency 45
Influencer Insider: Huda Kattan—From Beauty Blogger to Beauty Empire 46
    Early Days: Beauty Blogger 46
    Pivot 1: Product Creation 46
    Pivot 2: Expanding Product Line 47
    Pivot 3: Content Expansion 47
    Pivot 4: Building a Beauty Community 47
    Pivot 5: Global Expansion 47
Key Takeaways 48

Chapter 4: Influencer Ethics: What You Can and Can't Do 51

Libel and Slander 53
Private Information and NDAs 55
Transparency and Accountability 56
Managing Sponsored Trips and Brand Perks 57
Review Units and Product Samples 58
FTC Guidelines and Legal Requirements 59
Trust, Leaks, and Confidential Information 60

TABLE OF CONTENTS

Avoiding Conflicts of Interest 61
Long-Term Ethical Success As an Influencer 61
Key Takeaways 62

Chapter 5: Crafting Your Personal Brand: Building a Unique Identity in a Crowded Space 65

Crafting Quality Content 66
    Infusing Authenticity into Your Influencer Content 67
    Building Strong Connections 69
    Responding to Comments and Messages 73
    Asking Questions 74
    Tracking Metrics 74
    Analyzing Trends 74
    Gathering Direct Feedback 75
    Participating in Discussions 75
    One-on-One Interactions 76
    Meeting Fans 76
    Collabs 76
Creating "Less Edited" Content 78
    Establishing Clear Community Guidelines 80
    Case Studies 85
    Key Takeaways 88

Chapter 6: Content Creation 101: Strategies for Captivating Your Audience 91

Influencer Insider: Lindsay Adler 93
    Master Lighting Techniques 94
    Use the Golden Hour 95
    Use Composition Techniques to Guide the Viewer's Eye 97
    Prioritize Sharp Focus and Use Depth of Field Creatively 99

TABLE OF CONTENTS

    Enhance Your Storytelling Through Visual Style 100
    Utilize Movement in Video for Dynamic Shots 101
    Make the Most of Post-production 102

Practice, Patience, and Experimentation 109

Crafting Compelling Social Media Content: A Visual and Copywriting Guide 110
    Social Media Terms 111
    Visuals: The Core of Engagement 113
    The Power of Words 115

The Influencer Creation Process 116
    1. Planning and Ideation 116
    2. Content Creation 117
    3. Testing and Optimization 118
    4. Promotion and Engagement 119

Crafting a Content Calendar: Influencer Strategies 119

How Content Performs on Different Platforms: A Quick Overview 122
    Instagram 122
    TikTok 122
    Facebook 123
    X (Formerly Twitter) 123
    YouTube 124
    Key Considerations for Content Performance 124

Key Takeaways 125

Chapter 7: Growing Your Audience: Techniques for Increasing Followers and Engagement 127

Growing Your Audience: Techniques for Increasing Followers and Engagement 130
    Direct Engagement 130
    Data Analysis Tools 131

TABLE OF CONTENTS

Content Creation and Optimization 131
Engagement Strategies 132
Platform-Specific Tactics 133
Community Building 133
Hashtag Optimization 133
Paid Advertising 134
Drew Barrymore's Influential Community 134
Early Beginnings on YouTube 137
Transition to Social Media 138
Building a Personal Brand 138
Leveraging Social Media Features 138
Community Building Initiatives 139
Key Takeaways 139
Ballerina Farm: A Community Built on Homesteading 140
Building a Community 140
Key Values and Goals 141
Ballerina Farm's Social Media Engagement 141
Key Takeaways 142
Content Optimization and Algorithm Insights 145
Platform-Specific Strategies 146
The Cultural Landscape of Social Media Platforms 146
1. Communication and Social Interaction 147
2. News and Information Consumption 147
3. Entertainment and Pop Culture 147
4. Politics and Social Movements 148
5. Ecommerce and Consumer Culture 148

TABLE OF CONTENTS

A Deeper Dive into Social Media's Cultural Impact 149
    Communication and Social Interaction 149
    News and Information Consumption 150
    Entertainment and Pop Culture 150
    Politics and Social Movements 151
    Ecommerce and Consumer Culture 152
Becoming an Influencer: Tips for the Ordinary Person 152
    1. Niche Down and Find Your Voice 152
    2. Create High-Quality Content Consistently 153
    3. Engage with Your Audience 153
    4. Utilize Different Platforms 154
    5. Build Relationships 154
    6. Be Patient and Persistent 154
Expanding Your Reach and Building a Loyal Fan Base 157
A Comprehensive Hashtag Strategy for Social Media 158
    Instagram 158
    Twitter 159
    TikTok 159
    Facebook 160
    LinkedIn 160
    General Hashtag Tips 160
    Leverage Relevant Hashtags 161
    Collaborate with Other Creators 161
    Utilize Social Media Features 162
    Run Contests and Giveaways 162
    Analyze Your Performance 162
Key Takeaways 163

TABLE OF CONTENTS

Chapter 8: Surviving the Influencer Life 165
    Structured Routines 167
        Sample Daily Schedule 167
        Tips for Flexibility 169
    Time Blocking 169
        Example Time Blocking Schedule 169
        Key Tips for Effective Time Blocking 171
    Digital Detox 171
        Weekend Digital Detox Plan 172
    Mindfulness Practices 174
    Physical Activity 174
    Healthy Boundaries 174
    Support Systems 176
    Self-Reflection 177
    Key Takeaways 177

Chapter 9: Monetization Methods: Turning Influence into Income ... 179
    Social Media and Your Wallet 179
        Sponsored Content 180
        Affiliate Marketing 180
        Product Collaborations/Brand Ambassadorships 180
        Selling Digital Products or Services 181
        Merchandise Sales 181
        Crowdfunding or Donations 181
        Ad Revenue (YouTube, TikTok, etc.) 182
        Paid Appearances/Speaking Engagements 182
        Licensing Content 182
        Selling Physical Products 182

TABLE OF CONTENTS

    Consulting/Coaching 183
    Licensing or Selling Intellectual Property 183
    Summary 183

How Do Sponsors Judge You? 183
    1. Classification of Influencers 184
    2. Compensation Models for Influencers 186
    3. Factors Influencing Compensation 190
    Summary 191

Finding Your Niche 191
    1. Nano-influencers 191
    2. Micro-influencers 192
    3. Mid-tier Influencers 193
    4. Macro-influencers 195
    5. Mega-influencers (Celebrities) 196
    Summary of Compensation by Influencer Tier 198

Building Engagement, Reaping the Benefits 199
    Example: Kristin Johns on Monetizing Social Media 199
    Kristin's Advice for Aspiring Influencers 202

Key Takeaways 203

Chapter 10: The Importance of Authenticity: Maintaining Trust with Your Audience 205

Why Authenticity Matters 206
    1. Trust Is Everything 206
    2. Building Long-Term Relationships 206
    3. Your Reputation Is Your Brand 206
    4. Loyalty Over Numbers 206

TABLE OF CONTENTS

How to Stay Authentic While Working with Brands 207
    1. Know What You Stand For..207
    2. Be Transparent..207
    3. Only Promote What You Truly Use 207
    4. Engage Meaningfully with Your Audience...208
    5. Stick to Your Style and Voice 208
    6. Don't Overwhelm with Promotions..208
    7. Be Honest About Your Journey 208
    8. Choose Partnerships That Fit..209
The Big Picture: Why Authenticity Is Crucial for Your Personal Brand 209
    1. Know Your Values and Stick to Them 210
    2. Be Transparent About Sponsored Content 210
    3. Promote What You Truly Believe In 210
    4. Engage with Your Audience Genuinely 211
    5. Avoid Over-promotion 211
    6. Share Your Personal Journey..211
    7. Stay Consistent in Your Message 212
    8. Set Boundaries with Brands..212
    9. Maintain a Clear Brand Identity 213
    10. Be Patient and Take Your Time 213
    11. Don't Be Afraid to Evolve 213
A Spotlight on Authenticity...214
    1. Emma Chamberlain: The Queen of Relatable, Unpolished Content.........214
    2. Zoe Sugg (Zoella): The Power of Consistency and Self-Branding...........215
    3. Alexandria Ocasio-Cortez (AOC): Authenticity in Politics and Activism....217
Final Thoughts...218
Key Takeaways..218

TABLE OF CONTENTS

Chapter 11: Handling Challenges: Dealing with Criticism, Burnout, and Changes in Algorithms 221

Influencer Exhaustion 221
    Dealing with Criticism 222
    Managing Burnout 222
    Adapting to Algorithm Changes 223

How to Handle Critics 228
    1. Stay Calm and Don't Respond Immediately 228
    2. Don't Engage with Trolls 228
    3. Address the Crisis Professionally 229
    4. Use "The Power of the Delete Button" 230
    5. Use Humor (When Appropriate) 230
    6. Take the High Road 231
    7. Engage with Your Supportive Community 231
    8. Take Care of Your Mental Health 232
    9. Learn from the Experience 232

Dealing With Online Hate 233
    1. Don't Take It Personally 233
    2. Don't Engage with Hate 233
    3. Block or Mute Haters 234
    4. Delete Hateful Comments 234
    5. Report Abusive Behavior 235
    6. Take a Step Back 235
    7. Focus on the Positive 236
    8. Respond Thoughtfully (When Necessary) 236
    9. Set Boundaries 237
    10. Consider Professional Help 237

11. Educate and Advocate 238
12. Keep Perspective 238
    Conclusion 239
Case Study: Chrissy Teigen's Response to Past Tweets and
Cyberbullying Controversy 239
    The Crisis 239
    Chrissy Teigen's Response: How She Handled the Crisis 240
    Key Strategies That Contributed to Her Successful Crisis Management 243
    Outcome and Public Perception 244
    Conclusion 244
Key Takeaways 244

Chapter 12: Looking Ahead: Trends and Opportunities in the Influencer Industry 247

The Rise of New Platforms and Digital Spaces 247
    TikTok and Short-Form Video Domination 247
    New Platforms and Communities 248
Evolving Consumer Behaviors 249
    Authenticity and Relatability 249
    Purpose-Driven Influence 249
The Growth of the Creator Economy 250
    Monetization Beyond Sponsorships 250
    Virtual and Augmented Reality (AR/VR) Experiences 251
Shifting Marketing Budgets and Brand Expectations 252
    Increased Investment in Micro- and Nano-influencers 252
    Long-Term Partnerships Over One-Off Campaigns 252
The Impact of Artificial Intelligence and Data Analytics 253
    AI-Powered Content Creation and Personalization 253
    Influencer Marketing Platforms and Data Tracking 254

TABLE OF CONTENTS

Preparing for the Future..254
    1. Increased Focus on Authenticity and Niche Communities 255
    2. Shift Toward Long-Term Partnerships Over One-Off Campaigns.............256
    3. Emergence of Virtual Influencers and AI Integration 256
    4. Integration of the Metaverse and Augmented Reality (AR).....................257
    5. Greater Integration of Ecommerce and Social Commerce 258
    6. Data-Driven and Performance-Based Campaigns..................................258
    7. Rise of Purpose-Driven Influencer Marketing...259
    8. Personalized and Interactive Content..259
    9. Expansion of Influencer Marketing into New Industries.........................260

A More Integrated, Immersive, and Data-Driven Future...................................261
    1. Authenticity and Transparency in Content 261
    2. Building Long-Term Relationships Rather Than One-Off Campaigns 262
    3. Audience Involvement and Interaction 263
    4. Leveraging Technology and Data for Personalization.............................264
    5. Sustainability and Social Responsibility...265
    6. Trust via User-Generated and Peer Reviews..266
    7. Authentic Storytelling and Content That Adds Value..............................267
    8. Privacy and Data Protection 268

The Future of Trust in Influencer Marketing...268
    1. Increased Demand for Authenticity and Transparency 269
    2. More Direct Interaction with Brands and Products 270
    3. More Active Participation in Campaigns..271
    4. Shift Toward Ethical and Purpose-Driven Purchasing 272
    5. Influencer-Driven Ecommerce (Social Commerce).................................273
    6. Increased Demand for Privacy and Data Control....................................274
    7. Preference for Virtual and Digital Influencers...274
    8. Hyper-personalization and Predictive Shopping.....................................275

TABLE OF CONTENTS

The Evolution of Consumer Behavior with Influencer Marketing 276

Key Takeaways 276

Chapter 13: The Future of Influence: Predictions and Insights into the Next Era of Influencer Marketing 279

The Evolution of Influence 279

    1. The Rise of AI-Driven Influencer Marketing 280

    2. Increased Focus on Micro- and Nano-influencers 280

    3. The Integration of Virtual Influencers and Digital Avatars 281

    4. Expansion into New Platforms and Technologies 282

    5. The Convergence of Influencer Marketing with Consumer Activism 283

    6. Influencers as Content Creators and Brand Entrepreneurs 284

    7. Greater Scrutiny on Transparency and Ethics 284

    8. The Importance of Data Privacy and Consumer Control 285

The Next Era of Influence Is Data-Driven, Authentic, and Immersive 285

    1. The Importance of Authenticity and Transparency 286

    2. The Consequences of Overselling and Misleading Claims 287

    3. The Power of Cancel Culture and Consumer Backlash 288

    4. The Impact of Mental Health on Influencers 289

    5. Ethical Concerns Around Sponsored Content and Brand Ambassadorships 289

    6. The Limits of Social Media Influence and "Influencer Fatigue" 290

    7. The Power of Algorithms and Data Privacy Concerns 291

The Path Forward 292

Index **293**

About the Authors

John Biggs is an entrepreneur, consultant, writer, and maker. He spent 15 years as an editor for Gizmodo, CrunchGear, and TechCrunch and has a deep background in hardware startups, 3D printing, and blockchain. His work has appeared in *Men's Health*, *Wired*, and *The New York Times*.

He has written nine books including the best book on blogging, *Bloggers Boot Camp*, and a book about the most expensive timepiece ever made, *Marie Antoinette's Watch*. He lives in Brooklyn, New York. He runs the Keep Going podcast, a podcast about failure. His goal is to share how even the most confident and successful people had to face adversity.

Jessa Moore is a media expert and the owner of Jessa Moore Media. With a diverse background spanning journalism, digital strategy, branding, social media marketing, and influencer marketing, she brings a unique and insightful perspective to the media landscape.

Based in New York City, Jessa is known for her strategic thinking, creative problem-solving, and ability to analyze complex media trends. Her expertise extends to understanding digital behavior, political analysis, developing effective branding strategies, and navigating the evolving world of influencer marketing.

ABOUT THE AUTHORS

Jessa's approach to branding is particularly noteworthy. She takes a holistic view, combining her knowledge of digital strategy, social media, and marketing, including influencer marketing strategies, to create well-rounded and impactful brand identities. Her focus on understanding and leveraging digital behavior, including the influence of key influencers, sets her apart, allowing her to develop data-driven and innovative branding solutions.

Jessa has worked with a wide range of clients, from startups and entrepreneurs to established organizations like the USC Shoah Foundation and the Hague, demonstrating her adaptability and ability to tailor her approach to diverse needs. Her commitment to helping individuals and organizations achieve their full potential through effective branding, including leveraging the power of influencers, makes her a highly sought-after media consultant.

CHAPTER 1

Introduction to Influence: Understanding the Power and Reach of Influencers

They're relaxing by the pool, holding cans of a new sparkling energy drink that quickly became popular on TikTok. They're in matching pajamas under a Christmas tree (link to the pajamas in bio). They're smiling at a fashion event that none of us could ever hope to be invited to.

They're young, perfectly toned, and well-dressed. Sometimes they're in bikinis and swimsuits or lounging in white dress shirts and jeans. They're trying on makeup, opening shopping bags, and talking about meditation and juice cleanses. They're showing off fancy watches and new gadgets, convincing you that their lifestyle can be yours for the low, low price of "Tap to Like" or "Subscribe Now."

They're playing music you'll soon love, sharing animations you'll spread to your friends, and writing long posts about their pets that you'll read at lunch. They're filming reviews of cars, guitars, hats, and watches.

CHAPTER 1 INTRODUCTION TO INFLUENCE: UNDERSTANDING THE POWER AND REACH OF INFLUENCERS

They're hosting game shows and showing off videos of squirrel obstacle courses. They're producing an endless stream of content for one purpose: to keep you from scrolling past them and to keep you coming back, no matter how hard it is to game the algorithms that are intent on thwarting them at every turn.

They're influencers and they're everywhere. And what you see regularly, the stuff that percolates to the top of your Instagram feed or TikTok river, is only the tip of the iceberg. Influencers have a wide and deep range of skills. At this point in history, they are producing more media in a way that is both new and familiar. Like bloggers before them, they are destroying old forms of media. In 2023, children spent an average of 84 minutes a day on YouTube and a mere 49 minutes on "traditional" Netflix. This move from longform video to shorts and community-generated content is probably the biggest shift in media in the past decade, and it's become a wildly lucrative way to market, sell, and entertain.

But what are influencers? Do they make any money? Are they as popular and successful as they seem? And are they vital to modern culture and business in the same way a good blog article or Vogue photo shoot is? The answers to those questions are yes, maybe, and yes.

Influencers are the new celebrities. While it might not seem like they often cross the Internet barrier between the online and the real world, they are as popular as many movie stars and definitely have more reach on the aggregate. Some YouTube videos get more views than some popular TV shows. Many stars who are trying to become influencers find themselves playing second fiddle to people who have been online longer. If follower counts are any guide, many random influencers are hitting millions of viewers, while many popular stars—current and past—are barely breaking the million mark.

If you're interested in media or marketing at all, you need to be aware of influencers, their tactics, and how you can use their tricks to increase engagement. Maybe you want to sell something online or offer services to people in need. Maybe you want to review products and share your

CHAPTER 1 INTRODUCTION TO INFLUENCE: UNDERSTANDING THE POWER AND REACH OF INFLUENCERS

opinion. Maybe you're a journalist who has been left behind by social media editors. Maybe you're an extrovert who wants to share their thoughts with a wide audience. Whatever your goal, influencer tactics will help you achieve it.

This book will tell you how to become an influencer. We can't promise you one million followers or even one follower. But we can promise you that these tactics have helped ourselves and our clients reach millions of people globally. Your co-authors, Jessa Moore and John Biggs, have worked in marketing and media for many years. We were there when many of the biggest online platforms were created, including X (formerly Twitter), Instagram, and Facebook. We have seen it all and have used and abused social media for decades.

The Power of Influencers

In early 2024, McDonald's faced a challenge. Financial reports showed poor results, largely due to negative customer perceptions. Many customers were unhappy with high prices and declining food quality, prompting some to switch to Chick-fil-A. The backlash gained traction online, where people shared photos of unappealing McDonald's burgers and hefty receipts, fueling a perception that the chain was falling short. Influencers added to the narrative by comparing McDonald's and Chick-fil-A's offerings and suggesting that McDonald's had allegedly copied Chick-fil-A's sauce.

The story took off after Chef Mike Haracz, a former McDonald's developmental chef, posted on TikTok, accusing the chain of copying Chick-fil-A's chicken sandwich style and ingredients. This claim, reported in the poultry industry publication WATTPoultry, led to widespread criticism. Whether the claim was true didn't seem to matter; viewers were quick to believe it.

Here's a snippet from the article:

McDonald's chose to release a Chick-fil-A chicken sandwich "knockoff" over alternative recipes following owner-operator pressure, former McDonald's chef, Mike Haracz, claimed on a now-viral TikTok video.

CHAPTER 1 INTRODUCTION TO INFLUENCE: UNDERSTANDING THE POWER AND REACH OF INFLUENCERS

"You might notice that the chicken sandwich [McDonald's] launched was in a foil pouch," Haracz said in the video. *"It had butter, it had two pickles, it had a bunch of that MSG-type flavor, and it was a knock-off of Chick-fil-A. Do you think McDonald's can out Chick-fil-A, Chick-fil-A? No, they cannot."*

Haracz served as manager of culinary innovation for McDonald's from 2015-19, according to his LinkedIn page. According to the TikTok video, he was a part of the McDonald's team that was focused on developing a new chicken sandwich.

The sandwich video went almost viral, maxing out at 35,600 views and over 2,900 comments. But even with those numbers, McDonald's got lucky. Other viral influencer posts can hit millions of views and have a tangible effect on stock prices, political parties, and even real lives. Essentially, influencers bring the Internet into real life.

McDonald's is still cleaning up the perception mess. Recent videos have shown the brand's burgers covered in slime, and some viral posts feature receipts from the early 2000s compared with today. This kind of attack—uncoordinated, seemingly ridiculous, and impossible to quell—is exactly what companies have to deal with daily in this weird new world.

Just as bloggers once exposed corporate controversies, influencers now wield similar power, challenging brands and drawing attention. The result? Companies are increasingly trying to manage these influencers and preempt potential backlash from smaller influencers who can quickly post critical commentary on trending topics.

Social media has become a dominant force in shaping consumer behavior and has a wider reach than most traditional media. Platforms and content creators are reshaping consumer culture, enabling small brands to compete with large advertisers. Though it's challenging, those who understand social media's potential have seen significant rewards.

Consider the beauty industry: Ulta and Sephora are now stocked with indie brands designed to cater to short consumer attention spans. Beauty influencers are also launching their own brands, tailored to niche audiences. Some succeed, others don't, but this shift reflects a broader change in how people spend their time. Rather than watching TV ads, consumers now engage directly with creators and brands through their phones. Brand loyalty is increasingly tied to the influencer or community rather than the product itself—a major shift. Where trusted brands were once names like Charmin or Tollhouse, today, trust lies with creators.

Traditional media refers to non-digital channels of communication like newspapers, television, radio, and magazines. The digital landscape encompasses online platforms, social media, websites, blogs, and streaming services. Traditional media often has a fixed distribution structure and limited interaction with the audience, whereas digital media allows for instant access, interactivity, and real-time feedback. Social media and digital media in general are more agile, with direct access to the audience in real time. This is an important component to understanding how social acts and how to use it.

The way we consume information and make decisions has undeniably shifted in the digital age. Social media platforms and online content creators have become a powerful force, shaping trends, opinions, and even purchasing habits. But with this influence comes a responsibility— both for creators and for the consumers of their content.

A quirk of social media is the fact that it has a sense of intimacy that hides its power. Meanwhile, social media platforms and online content creators have become a powerful force, changing trends, opinions, and even purchasing power. Traditional ways of reaching people have also ignored the needs of people outside the groups that big advertising agencies want. This has caused social media to create whole new categories of brands. Rihanna's Fenty is a good example. It was started by a woman of color, but it has become one of the most inclusive beauty brands in the world. It is known for its wide range of foundation colors and sophisticated products. This is a huge driver of sales. Influencer campaigns and feedback from social media helped create and launch the line.

So how do we harness this power? By learning how others have used it and taking online influence and social media seriously. By understanding the behavior associated not just with the consumers but the brands and platforms.

Traditional Media Experts vs. the Rise of the Everyday Expert

Influencers have been around for a long time, but the job was only for the very few people who were famous or liked. Think royalty and celebrities. Evangelists on late-night TV and church leaders. Political figures and rock stars. Persuasion is an art, and the successful were widely imitated, often creating fashions along the way.

Then, as newspapers developed, we had society articles, actors, and P. T. Barnum's bunkum. For decades, celebrities and established media outlets held sway in pop culture and news consumption. News anchors and journalists delivered information, shaping public perception of current events. The trusted voices were baked into the media and news. The pervasive idea was that "If it's on television, it must be good." Earned media—so-called because it can't be bought—is still the most prized source of trust from consumers. The idea that a product is endorsed with no payment or product changing hands is very powerful. But what if you could simulate that trust and hide the pay-for-play aspect under a wrap of intimacy?

The rise of social media led to this new intimacy. The immediacy of, say, X or Instagram has created a normalization of parasocial relationships. Creators talk to their followers, sometimes making real friends and relationships. But the breaking of the fourth wall has also created a bond that can be very helpful for people who like to buy things. All you need is a simple smartphone, and anyone with a camera and an Internet connection could become a content creator.

CHAPTER 1   INTRODUCTION TO INFLUENCE: UNDERSTANDING THE POWER AND REACH OF INFLUENCERS

This democratization of the media gave rise to the "influencer"—individuals who have amassed a dedicated community online. Creators are part of this group, but not all creators are part of the group called influencers. This term is a bit controversial in the field. Influencers can focus on specific niches, from beauty tutorials and fashion styling to gaming, news, personal coaching, and financial advice. They connect with their audience on a more personal level, fostering a sense of trust and community. A creator's community is their money, the social value they bring. Trust in them is usually built over years, when they use their content to become an expert in their field. The actual niches are as endless as the communities you have globally—while Kim Kardashian is often considered the gold standard, the real beauty and value in communities are the specific niches creators have built based on their interests, say, birdwatching. Or medieval art. For our purposes here, we will use all kinds of creators to demonstrate the power of social media.

The Metrics of Influence

An influencer's power is often measured by their follower count and engagement rate. The number of "likes," comments, and shares their content receives shows how effectively they engage their audience. However, the actual art of a good influencer campaign means understanding that smaller creators often have more conversion with their communities—especially as consumers become more sophisticated. Brands have taken notice, partnering with influencers to promote products and services directly to their target demographics. Influencer marketing is now a billion-dollar industry. Companies know that these people can influence others. There is a lot more than just these basic metrics, however, that goes into a successful campaign. There is an art that is rarely discussed. Taste is a huge driver of conversion. Social media is a way to share ideas. Not everyone is stylish, but they know what makes people happy and want to share their own style. These are the hardest aspects to conquer.

CHAPTER 1   INTRODUCTION TO INFLUENCE: UNDERSTANDING THE POWER
            AND REACH OF INFLUENCERS

What are "good" numbers? First, understand that most influencers pay for their followers. Likes, views, and subscribers can be bought online in minutes, resulting in a massively skewed perception of popularity. We'll talk more about this—and the ethical challenges associated with this kind of thing—later in the book.

Ultimately, any numbers are good. What an influencer must have is an audience. In turn, this audience can be monetized through affiliate marketing or advertising. Some sites like X will pay you for popularity, but that rarely works without a huge audience and an immensely viral focus. That said, it's not impossible to make money from sites like TikTok and YouTube—it's just very hard.

Let's assume you want to either tell a story, market a product, or explore a passion. Numbers for these kinds of things are low, but as long as you have repeat visitors and plenty of content, you'll be doing exactly what you set out to do. In short, influencing happens on any scale. It's important for beginners to accept that numbers will be low or views and subscribers will have to be paid for.

Pop Culture Trendsetters

The impact of influencers is undeniable in the realm of pop culture. A fashion blogger sporting a new outfit can spark a trend, leading to increased sales for the featured brand. The Kardashians are masters at this. Look at Skims, their lounge line. The Kardashians as a unit are the queens of beauty and fashion—with each sister cornering a market. Kim is known for her beauty and fashion. Kylie for her beauty, Khloe for her home and fashion, and Kourtney for selling organic wellness gummies. Kourtney sells these products, as well as nutrition and parenting. Kendall is the traditional editorial sister, and her business is the only one that combines traditional media and fashion.

CHAPTER 1 INTRODUCTION TO INFLUENCE: UNDERSTANDING THE POWER AND REACH OF INFLUENCERS

Beauty tutorials can turn unknown makeup artists into household names, with their product recommendations driving consumer choices. We see this endlessly online. Charlotte Tilbury is a luxury beauty brand selling the top lipstick, Pillow Talk. Her entire line is based on online and social branding, but celebrities use it on the red carpet, turning an online brand into a real-world powerhouse. This is a key marketing channel for her. According to Forbes, the brand reported that one Pillow Talk product is sold every ten seconds globally. It doesn't hurt that the brand, which launched in 2013, has 6.5 million followers on Instagram and 1.4 million followers on TikTok.

Food bloggers can influence restaurant choices and even culinary trends. We see everyone from home chefs to cordon bleu types vying for views on Instagram. The meal delivery service RealEats used real chefs to show off their pre-made dishes. The company used influencers to show that organic food was tasty and easy to get. While the service is no longer available, you can still see the same marketing techniques as today. For example, meal delivery service CookUnity in New York City features chefs that cook meals online to show their customers. The company then sends those meals across the country. Clients get to experience amazing meals in their home; famous chefs can get even more famous, and CookUnity builds a fanatical audience with its cooking demos. In this specific case, influencers are offering access or even the perception of access.

In fact, access is a huge deal in digital, and brands are refining their use of relationships in nontraditional ways. Segmenting in different areas can be broken down to reach your own group to build. There is a beauty in being able to find not just your tribe but your vibe. Why build nationally if you are a mom-and-pop restaurant in a small town in Texas? Why not just convince the world to come to you, either through delivery or through tourism?

CHAPTER 1   INTRODUCTION TO INFLUENCE: UNDERSTANDING THE POWER
              AND REACH OF INFLUENCERS

Tapping into pop culture is the most important aspect of strategy. It doesn't mean stealing content—it means reading the room. Nothing sinks a brand like tone deafness. For example, we have had several celebrities setting up GoFundMes for themselves or staff. While it is true not everyone who is an influencer is wealthy, the assumption is enough to create a backlash.

Authenticity Matters

Digital media moves at the speed of light, so the only constant with successful brands is authenticity. Audiences crave real connections with the creators they follow. Influencers who come across as relatable, transparent, and true to themselves are more likely to build a loyal following. Consumers are more and more aware of sponsored content. Influencers who balance showing products and staying true to their own brand are most popular.

One of the largest beauty creators, Tati Westbrook, talks a lot about which products are PR and which she buys. Her viewership values that transparency highly. She covers everything from cheap to expensive and shows off her makeup artistry skills and opinions while talking about her relationship with her husband. The creation of a compelling online persona and branding isn't just about curating perfection; it's about weaving a narrative that resonates with your audience on a profoundly human level.

For example, influencers like Jenna Kutcher, a coaching mentor, are attractive because they combine the inspiring with the relatable. They show both the best and most honest parts of their lives, showing both the good and the bad moments. Their authenticity isn't a marketing tactic—it's in their DNA. While carefully curated, their work reads as open and vulnerable.

CHAPTER 1   INTRODUCTION TO INFLUENCE: UNDERSTANDING THE POWER AND REACH OF INFLUENCERS

In the realm of branding, companies like Patagonia have set a gold standard by aligning their values with their actions. Their commitment to environmental activism isn't just a slogan; it's part of every part of their business. This makes them not just customers but very loyal supporters. After Covid, consumers have changed their expectations. They have been mistrustful online as misinformation changes the world. There is no PR crisis like a social-good company not living up to their values, and these can include some fairly ordinary missteps. The breaking of the fourth wall works both ways, positive and negative. Online comments have a brutality that is seeping into everyday life.

Navigating the digital landscape requires a delicate balance of vulnerability and strategic positioning. It's about how people relate to imperfection. Consumers who are interested "read" brands for "vibes" and decide if they will buy yours.

The Responsibility of Influence

With great influence comes great responsibility. Influencers should be honest about sponsored content and partnerships. They should make sure the information they share is correct and well-researched, especially when talking about sensitive topics like health or money. Audiences need to be empowered with critical thinking skills to discern real recommendations from paid promotions.

As technology continues to evolve, so too will the landscape of influence. The rise of short-form video platforms like TikTok and the increasing popularity of live streaming offer new ways for creators to connect with audiences. The lines between traditional media and social media influencers will likely continue to blur, creating a more dynamic and interconnected media landscape. Other issues, like the Congressional hearings and fate of TikTok, will also dictate partly where creators and communities land. But the real deciding factor is where the users decide to be.

CHAPTER 1 INTRODUCTION TO INFLUENCE: UNDERSTANDING THE POWER AND REACH OF INFLUENCERS

Generations all use social media differently, and each platform has its own personality. Social platforms often have unique personalities based on their features, user demographics, and the types of content they prioritize. Here's a general overview:

1. **Facebook**: It was first for friends and family. Over time, it has become the most popular place where people meet and talk about their personal lives and opinions. It was originally the most personal, but has evolved into a heavily older crowd, but with a versatility in both niches, reach, and community.

2. **Instagram**: Facebook's younger, hipper visually focused platform is focused on photos and videos. It's popular among younger users and influencers who share lifestyle, fashion, travel, and artistic content. The platform encourages creativity and aesthetic presentation. It is the equivalent of reading a magazine—with an interactive component.

3. **X, a.k.a. Twitter**: X is a platform that updates people in real time. It has short messages (tweets) and fast-moving conversations. It's often used for news, discussions, and sharing thoughts or opinions. Its feed supports photos, but the content is usually between the community and written. Very popular with business/tech.

4. **LinkedIn**: The "Professional Network," LinkedIn is used for job searching, career development, and business networking. Content on LinkedIn often revolves around industry news, career advice, and professional achievements, as well as hobbies common to users.

5. **TikTok:** TikTok is all about short-form video content. It's highly interactive, with users often engaging through likes, comments, and duets. TikTok appeals to a younger audience and thrives on creativity and entertainment. While mainly a younger demographic, its addictive algorithms are building a more diverse base, as it distances itself from its "dance app" roots.

These are just generalizations, and each platform has a diverse user base with various interests and behaviors. Platforms change over time, so their personalities may change as new features are added or user groups change.

Empowered Consumers

In this quickly changing world, the main asset is information and media literacy. Knowing how powerful influence is and looking at online content with a critical eye helps consumers make smart choices. Look for diverse voices, fact-check information, and be mindful of the motivations behind the content you consume. There's a lot of shiny, pretty things online.

We are in the Golden Age of Influencers. By recognizing their power and understanding the dynamics at play, we can navigate the media landscape with both awareness and appreciation for the voices shaping our world. Community is the strength of social media.

So let's dive into the *why's* and *how's* of becoming an online influencer.

CHAPTER 1   INTRODUCTION TO INFLUENCE: UNDERSTANDING THE POWER
           AND REACH OF INFLUENCERS

Key Takeaways

- An influencer is a modern microcelebrity.

- The industry is not new, but it has only come into its own in the last few years.

- Creating a personal brand is difficult but vital. Modern business success requires much more than showing up. Using influencer tactics can supercharge your career.

CHAPTER 2

The Evolution of Influencer Marketing

From the early days of traditional celebrities endorsing products to the rise of social media personalities, influencers have reshaped how brands connect with audiences. Their journey reflects the power shift away from publishers and toward individual content creators. It is the story of democratization of influence itself.

"People do not buy goods and services. They buy relations, stories, and magic," said marketer Seth Godin. He is correct: influencers do not sell goods and services either. They sell stories, experiences, and lifestyles and then meld these things with products that they like or, more likely, are paid to advertise.

Influencer marketing's roots stretch far deeper than social media, with Wedgwood pottery pioneering the strategy in 1760. The company's founder, Josiah Wedgwood, cleverly used royal connections to market his ceramics, earning the title "Potter to Her Majesty" from Queen Charlotte. This royal endorsement transformed Wedgwood from a local pottery maker into a luxury brand, setting a pattern that marketers follow today. By displaying his royal warrant and creating special pieces for aristocratic customers, Wedgwood established the fundamental principle that still drives influencer marketing: social proof from respected figures can shape consumer behavior. The strategy that began with royal seals has evolved into today's $16.4 billion industry, where digital creators hold influence once reserved for nobility. Modern influencers, like their royal predecessors, continue to bridge the gap between brands and consumers, though now through smartphones rather than royal courts.

We could say that the first truly modern, electronic influencer marketing came in the form of soap operas. The programs originated on radio in the 1930s, with programs like *Guiding Light*, all of which eventually transitioned to television. The term "soap opera" was coined because these serialized dramas were often sponsored by soap manufacturers, targeting homemakers who were the primary audience during the daytime. These shows featured melodramatic storylines focused on personal relationships and emotional conflicts, designed to captivate audiences with ongoing, episodic content that encouraged regular viewing. Just as a modern Instagrammer posts snippets of their glamorous life, soap operas allow harried homemakers the ability to slip away into a fantasy world, even if just for a moment. Like a posed shot next to a pool in Bali, consumers simultaneously understand that these influencers are likely faking their wealth and leisure, and yet they suspend their disbelief for the fun of it.

Influencers' power will keep changing. This is because of technology, changing consumer behavior, and the ongoing search for authenticity in digital communication. Platforms also go in and out of style—we saw Vine be absorbed into larger platforms, and we see the changes in our favorites, like Facebook and Instagram. The immediacy of connecting with your favorite influencer creates a real bond, and influencers are often followed and given credence over a period of years, creating a parasocial relationship that mimics that of a trusted friend.

The Evolution of Influencer Marketing: From Ancient Times to Social Media Stardom

Influencer marketing seems like something that only popped up recently. But its roots stretch far back into history, weaving through cultures and

CHAPTER 2   THE EVOLUTION OF INFLUENCER MARKETING

technologies. Join us on a journey through time as we learn about the interesting history of influencer marketing.

Ancient Beginnings: Influencers of Antiquity

Our story begins in ancient times, where influential figures held sway over the masses long before Instagram and YouTube. Think back to the court jesters of medieval Europe, who used their wit and charm to sway the opinions of kings and nobles. These jesters weren't just entertainers; they were the original influencers, wielding their influence to shape public perception and promote ideas.

Often seen as mere entertainers in medieval courts, jesters actually played a significant role as the first influencers, wielding considerable power through their unique position. One notable example is Archibald Armstrong, who served King James VI and I of Scotland and England. Armstrong's sharp wit and humor allowed him to influence court politics and public opinion. Despite his humble—and hilarious—beginnings as a sheep thief, Armstrong gained prominence and even managed to sway royal decisions with his jokes. His ability to speak freely, mock the high and mighty, and offer critiques without facing severe repercussions made him a crucial figure in the court.

Moving east, we meet the teachers and scholars of ancient China. Their wisdom and teachings spread through word of mouth, just like viral content does today. Confucius himself could be considered an early influencer, whose ideas shaped Chinese society for centuries. Similarly, Shen Jiangao, a jester for the Southern Tang emperor in tenth-century China, demonstrated the profound impact jesters could have. During a drought, Jiangao humorously remarked that even the rain feared being taxed, prompting the emperor to lower taxes.

CHAPTER 2   THE EVOLUTION OF INFLUENCER MARKETING

The Rise of Print: Celebrities and Endorsements

Fast forward to the Renaissance and the dawn of print media. Here, we find the precursors to modern celebrity endorsements. Picture a bustling London marketplace, where vendors touted the latest pamphlets featuring endorsements from literary giants like Shakespeare. These endorsements weren't just about selling products; they were about associating brands with cultural authority and prestige.

In the Middle Ages, writers, artists, and manufacturers played pivotal roles as influencers, using their works and products to convey messages and shape societal norms. Writers like Geoffrey Chaucer and Dante Alighieri used their literary talents to comment on social issues and critique the political landscape. Chaucer's *The Canterbury Tales* provided a satirical view of English society, highlighting the vices and virtues of its various classes. Dante's *Divine Comedy*, particularly its portrayal of hell in "Inferno," was a powerful commentary on morality and the state of the Church.

Artists like Giotto di Bondone and Jan van Eyck also wielded significant influence through their works. Giotto's frescoes, which depicted religious scenes with unprecedented realism and emotion, helped shape the visual language of Christian art, reinforcing religious messages and narratives. van Eyck's detailed oil paintings often contained complex iconography and symbolism, which conveyed moral and spiritual lessons to viewers. These dual meanings—both artistic and cultural—helped spread science, education, and innovation across the known world through simple but effective artistic endeavors.

Further, manufacturers, particularly those involved in the production of textiles and manuscripts, played a crucial role in disseminating ideas. The production of illuminated manuscripts, for example, was a highly influential industry. These manuscripts, often commissioned by the

Church or nobility, not only contained religious texts but also intricate illustrations that conveyed theological and philosophical messages. The spread of such manuscripts facilitated the dissemination of religious and cultural ideas across Europe.

Finally, the creators of luxury goods, like tapestries and stained glass windows, used their craftsmanship to tell stories and propagate values. These items were often commissioned by wealthy patrons who sought to display their piety, wealth, and social status. The imagery and symbolism in these works communicated messages about power, faith, and the social order to all who viewed them. Interestingly, many of the popular brands we know and love were advertised as being sold to royalty, meaning kings and queens were some of the first influencers, which also suggests that maybe the vendors might have slipped some free product to Her Royal Majesty to get the endorsement needed to sell a few more jars of tea.

As the printing press revolutionized communication, so too did the concept of influence evolve. Enter the nineteenth century, where the rise of newspapers and magazines brought forth a new breed of influencers: writers, artists, and performers whose work captured the public imagination. Charles Dickens wasn't just a novelist; he was a cultural icon whose endorsement could make or break a product. His serialized novels, published in popular magazines, reached vast audiences and often highlighted social injustices, allowing him to also influence public opinion and policy.

Another example is Victor Hugo, whose works not only entertained but also carried powerful social and political messages. Hugo's novel *Les Misérables* did more than tell a gripping story. It also shined a light on the struggles of the poor and the injustices of the legal system in France. His vivid portrayal of societal issues spurred public discourse and inspired reforms. Hugo's influence extended beyond literature; he was actively involved in politics and used his platform to advocate for causes like the abolition of the death penalty and the improvement of living conditions for the poor.

CHAPTER 2   THE EVOLUTION OF INFLUENCER MARKETING

The Birth of Mass Media: Hollywood and Beyond

The twentieth century ushered in the age of mass media, with Hollywood leading the charge. Movie stars like Charlie Chaplin and Marilyn Monroe became icons of style and glamor. Their endorsements were sought after by advertisers eager to capitalize on their star power. This era marked the birth of celebrity endorsements as we know them today, where the image and charisma of a public figure could sell anything from cigarettes to cars.

In addition to Hollywood stars, writers like Ernest Hemingway also emerged as influential cultural figures. Hemingway's rugged persona and adventurous lifestyle made him a symbol of masculinity and resilience. His endorsement of products like Ballantine Ale and Parker Pens not only boosted sales but also shaped consumer perceptions, aligning the products with his personal brand of toughness and sophistication.

Artists like Pablo Picasso further illustrate the power of cultural influencers in the twentieth century. Picasso's revolutionary art and distinctive style made him a central figure in modern art. His influence extended beyond the art world; his unique approach and avant-garde aesthetics influenced fashion, design, and popular culture. Picasso's collaborations with brands, like his iconic design for the Vallauris ceramics, showcased how an artist's endorsement could elevate a product's cultural cachet.

Performers like Elvis Presley also played a significant role in shaping cultural trends and consumer behavior. Presley's music, style, and charisma captivated audiences worldwide. His endorsement deals, like those with RCA Victor and Pepsi, demonstrated how a performer's popularity could be leveraged to sell products, reinforcing the idea that celebrity endorsements were a powerful marketing tool.

The Digital Revolution: Enter the Social Media Influencer

Fast forward to the late twentieth and early twenty-first centuries, where the digital revolution changed the landscape once again. The rise of the Internet and social media platforms like Facebook, Instagram, and YouTube democratized influence, allowing everyday individuals to amass followings in the millions. Suddenly, influencers weren't just movie stars or athletes; they were beauty gurus, gamers, travel enthusiasts, and more.

If anything defined the previous generation of influencers, it was the concept of broadcasting. In most cases, every one of our examples was a one-to-many, one-way form of influence, be it via a published book or a television show. Modern influencers now offer two-way communications with their fans, something impossible (and unwanted) in the era of the film and TV stars. This two-way communication creates an odd dynamic, encouraging a more personal relationship with people who, on the aggregate, want nothing to do with the fans. But influencing is all about the personal touch, and therefore this back-and-forth is vital to growth.

There are two kinds of interaction—paid and unpaid. OnlyFans models, for example, will simulate relationships with fans in order to encourage them to buy products they produce. This communication comes in the form of chats, many of them canned and created by bots. Other creators, presumably those with smaller audiences, will offer a more intimate form of interaction. The OnlyFans model has also expanded out into health, wellness, finance, and music influencers. Sites like Patreon also allow creators to make money and interact with fans, although Patreon is less focused on interaction.

Not every platform forces fans to pay for access. Many influencers make money by charging advertisers for access to the fan base. Platforms like Instagram became virtual marketplaces where brands and influencers could collaborate to reach highly targeted audiences. Influencer marketing

CHAPTER 2 THE EVOLUTION OF INFLUENCER MARKETING

exploded as brands realized the power of authentic, peer-to-peer recommendations over traditional advertising. For example, beauty influencers like Huda Kattan and James Charles built massive followings by sharing makeup tutorials and reviews, which led to lucrative brand partnerships and even their own product lines. Gamers like PewDiePie and Ninja leveraged platforms like YouTube and Twitch to reach millions of viewers, influencing game sales and the popularity of gaming culture.

Travel enthusiasts like Jack Morris and Lauren Bullen turned their wanderlust into influential careers by showcasing picturesque destinations and partnering with travel brands and tourism boards. Their visually stunning content and personal narratives inspired followers to visit new places, significantly impacting travel trends and preferences.

The democratization of influence also extended to fashion and lifestyle influencers. Chiara Ferragni, founder of The Blonde Salad, started as a fashion blogger and evolved into a global influencer with a successful fashion line. Her journey exemplifies how digital platforms can transform individuals into powerful brand ambassadors and trendsetters.

No longer confined to Hollywood elites, influencers have become the new tastemakers, shaping trends and driving consumer behavior in real time. Brands have embraced this shift, recognizing that influencers' authentic connections with their audiences can drive engagement and sales more effectively than traditional advertising methods. This evolution underscores the significant role of digital media in reshaping the dynamics of influence and marketing in the contemporary world.

Key Takeaways

- Anyone can leverage influence via communities.
- People respond to "people like them," which can convert to sales or clients.

CHAPTER 2   THE EVOLUTION OF INFLUENCER MARKETING

- Everyone has a niche of their own.
- Social media is the new "TV," in which commercials began. Influencers are the new brand partners.

Today and Beyond: The Future of Influence

As we look to the future, influencer marketing shows no signs of slowing down. It keeps changing with new technology like virtual reality (VR) and artificial intelligence (AI). Influencers are no longer just individuals; they're digital avatars, AI personalities, and virtual influencers blurring the lines between reality and fiction.

The landscape may change, but one thing remains constant: the power of influence. From ancient storytellers to today's social media stars, the art of persuasion keeps changing our world. It connects people and ideas across time and space.

So, the next time you scroll through your Instagram feed or watch a YouTube video, remember that you're witnessing the latest chapter in a long history of influence and marketing. Who knows what the future holds? One thing is certain: wherever there are people, there will be influencers shaping the world around them.

The future of influencers is likely to continue evolving in several directions:

1. **Platform Expansion**: Influencers will likely be on many platforms, not just Instagram and YouTube. Emerging platforms, including TikTok, Clubhouse, and others, will offer new opportunities and challenges.

2. **Niche Creation**: As the market becomes more competitive, influencers may become more focused on specific niches to stand out. This could include

everything from highly technical areas like AI or biotech to lifestyle niches like sustainability or minimalism. Or birdwatching. If there's a niche, there's a channel.

3. **Regulation and Transparency**: There may be increased scrutiny and regulation, especially around advertising disclosures and authenticity. Influencers may need to be more transparent about sponsored content and partnerships. The Federal Trade Commission (FTC) has been cracking down, notably on crypto influencers—whose channels can wipe out the savings of followers.

4. **Virtual Influencers and AI**: The rise of virtual influencers (computer-generated characters) and AI-generated content may continue to blur the lines between what is real and what is not.

5. **Long-Term Brand Partnerships**: Influencers might move toward more sustainable, long-term partnerships with brands rather than short-term sponsorships. This could involve deeper collaborations and brand ambassadorships.

6. **Impact on Consumer Behavior**: Influencers will likely continue to have a significant impact on consumer behavior, influencing purchasing decisions and trends.

7. **Professionalism**: Influencers may become more professional, with more focus on contracts, legal protections, and business plans.

8. **Globalization**: Influencers from different regions and cultures may gain prominence, offering a broader spectrum of content and perspectives.

While the world may change, influencers will probably stay in some form. They will still have to adapt to new technologies, rules, and consumer behavior. There will always be the aspect of human interaction, as well as direct marketing, which jumps across the fourth wall—but that interaction is also what creates the magic of influencer marketing.

HISTORIC CAMPAIGNS

Historic influencer campaigns often involve influential figures or celebrities promoting products or ideas, often before the digital age. Here are a few notable examples:

1. **Santa Claus and Coke**: In the 1930s, Coca-Cola asked Haddon Sundblom to make pictures of Santa Claus drinking Coke. This helped create the modern image of Santa Claus as a happy, cola-drinking figure.

2. **Michael Jordan and Nike**: Nike's collaboration with Michael Jordan in the 1980s revolutionized sports marketing. The "Air Jordan" line of basketball shoes became iconic, using Jordan's status as a basketball superstar to create a highly successful influencer-driven campaign.

3. **Marlboro Man**: In the 1950s and 1960s, Marlboro rebranded from a women's cigarette to a masculine product with the introduction of the Marlboro Man. This rugged cowboy became a symbol of masculinity and outdoor adventure, significantly boosting Marlboro's sales.

CHAPTER 2   THE EVOLUTION OF INFLUENCER MARKETING

4. **Oprah and Authors**: Oprah Winfrey's Book Club, started in 1996, has been very important in promoting books and authors. A recommendation from Oprah could skyrocket a book to the top of bestseller lists, demonstrating her power as an influencer in the literary world.

5. **Got Milk? Campaign**: Launched in 1993, this campaign featured celebrities with milk mustaches, aiming to promote the consumption of milk. It became a cultural phenomenon and successfully increased milk sales.

6. **Pepsi and Michael Jackson**: Pepsi's endorsement deal with Michael Jackson in the 1980s, culminating in the ill-fated commercial shoot where Jackson's hair caught fire, was a landmark in celebrity endorsements, though not entirely positive. It showed the power of using a celebrity for promotion.

These campaigns illustrate how influential figures, whether celebrities or cultural icons, have been used to effectively promote products, ideas, or behaviors throughout history.

Influencer Spotlight: Estée Lauder

One historic beauty influencer campaign involving Estée Lauder was the collaboration with model Karen Graham in the 1970s. Karen Graham became the face of Estée Lauder during this time and played a significant role in transforming the company's image and market presence. Here are some details about this influential campaign:

- **Background**: Karen Graham, a Canadian model, became the primary model for Estée Lauder in the early 1970s. Estée Lauder, a cosmetics company started by Estée Lauder herself, wanted to change its image and appeal to younger people.

CHAPTER 2   THE EVOLUTION OF INFLUENCER MARKETING

- **Impact**: Karen Graham's partnership with Estée Lauder was groundbreaking because it marked one of the first times a cosmetics company used a single model consistently across all its advertising campaigns. This consistency helped create a brand that people could recognize and helped the company grow during the 1970s.

- **Glamor**: Estée Lauder's campaign with Karen Graham focused on natural beauty and elegance, matching the current cultural trends. The advertisements stressed sophisticated yet accessible beauty, which resonated well with consumers.

- **Legacy**: Karen Graham's tenure as the face of Estée Lauder helped solidify the brand's reputation as a prestigious and aspirational beauty company. Her influence extended beyond traditional advertising, shaping perceptions of beauty and style during that era.

- **Longevity**: Karen Graham's partnership with Estée Lauder lasted for several years, contributing to the company's expansion into global markets and its continued success in the beauty industry.

This important beauty influencer campaign with Karen Graham shows how Estée Lauder used a well-known model to change its brand identity and reach more people. It is a big step forward in beauty marketing history.
There are several key aspects about digital influencers that are important for people to understand as we move forward, especially for brands wanting to use influencer marketing:

1. **Influence and Authenticity**: Not all influencers are the same. Audiences increasingly value genuine authenticity and credibility. Influencers who are transparent about sponsorships and partnerships tend to maintain trust better than those who are not.

CHAPTER 2   THE EVOLUTION OF INFLUENCER MARKETING

2. **Evolution of Platforms**: Platforms rise and fall in popularity. Influencers who adapt to new platforms and changes in algorithms tend to stay relevant. It's not just about Instagram anymore; platforms like TikTok, YouTube, and even emerging platforms will shape influencer dynamics. These shifts are day-to-day, and the dynamics are partly why brands need to be hands-on.

3. **Diverse Content Formats**: Successful influencers diversify their content. It's not just about still images anymore. Video, interactive content, and even immersive experiences (like VR) are becoming more common. Events are also important, bringing branding to life in person.

4. **Data and Analytics**: Influencer marketing is increasingly data-driven. Understanding audience demographics, engagement metrics, and return on investment (ROI) is crucial for brands and influencers alike. It's not just about follower count but about how engaged and active those followers are. Kim Kardashian has millions of followers, but smaller influencers are the ones converting.

5. **Longevity and Sustainability**: Building a sustainable career as an influencer, or a brand, requires planning for the long term. This includes building a personal brand, investing in skills beyond social media, and diversifying income streams.

6. **Regulations and Ethics**: There are growing regulations around influencer marketing, particularly regarding disclosures and transparency. Understanding these regulations is crucial for both influencers and brands to avoid legal issues and maintain trust.

7. **Impact and Responsibility**: Influencers have a significant impact on their audiences. Influencers are becoming more aware of their role in spreading good messages, being inclusive, and acting ethically.

8. **Community and Engagement**: Successful influencers build strong communities around their content. Engagement and interaction with followers are key factors that contribute to long-term success.

9. **Risks and Challenges**: The influencer landscape can be volatile. Influencers can face problems because of changes in algorithms, platform rules, and changes in how people like to watch videos.

10. **Collaborations and Partnerships**: Collaborations between influencers and brands are becoming more sophisticated. Brands are looking for real alignment with influencers' values and narratives rather than just reaching a large audience. "Authenticity" is the current buzzword, and influencers, as well as their audiences, can sniff out fakes quickly—which risks trust.

Understanding these aspects can provide a more nuanced view of digital influencers and their role in the future of media and marketing.

Political Influence

Political influencers are important in government. They often have a lot of power over public opinion, policy decisions, and even election results. Here are several ways in which political influencers impact government:

1. **Political Action:** Influencers can change how people think about political issues. They can do this through traditional media, social media, or other ways. Their ability to reach and resonate with large audiences gives them significant power to sway public sentiment in favor of or against specific policies or politicians.

2. **Policy Advocacy**: Influencers often advocate for specific policies or legislative changes. They may use their platform to promote certain agendas, lobby lawmakers, or mobilize public

CHAPTER 2   THE EVOLUTION OF INFLUENCER MARKETING

support for particular causes. This advocacy can directly affect the lawmaking process and the creation of government policies.

3. **Election Campaigns**: Political influencers can be pivotal during election campaigns. Their endorsements, public support, and ability to mobilize voters can sway election outcomes at various levels, from local to national elections. Politicians often seek endorsements from influencers to boost their credibility and appeal to a broader audience.

4. **Access to Decision-Makers**: Influencers may have direct access to government officials and policymakers. This access lets them directly affect decision-making by giving ideas, suggestions, and feedback on policy issues. In some cases, influencers may even serve as informal advisors to political leaders.

5. **Media and Public Relations**: Many political influencers are skilled communicators who can effectively manage media relations and public perception for politicians and government agencies. They can help craft messages, manage crises, and improve the public image of political figures.

6. **Agenda Setting**: Influencers often set the agenda for public discourse by highlighting specific issues or topics. They can bring attention to things that are not being talked about or make people's worries stronger. This can change what policymakers focus on and what is on the political agenda.

7. **Checks and Balances**: Influencers sometimes serve as a check on government power by scrutinizing policies, exposing corruption or misconduct, and holding elected officials accountable. Their scrutiny can lead to increased transparency and accountability within government institutions.

CHAPTER 2   THE EVOLUTION OF INFLUENCER MARKETING

Overall, the role of political influencers in government is multifaceted and can have profound implication6s for governance, public policy, and democratic processes. Their power can help make people more involved and accountable in the democratic process. But it can also cause worries about too much influence, division, and the power being concentrated in people who are not elected.

Key Takeaways

- The first modern influencer marketing campaign was launched in 1760 by Wedgwood pottery, using royal endorsements to boost their brand. Today's influencer marketing industry has grown to over $16.4 billion in 2022.

- Studies show that micro-influencers (10,000–50,000 followers) typically generate 60% higher engagement rates than macro-influencers, despite having smaller audiences. This demonstrates why metrics beyond follower count matter.

- Platforms like Instagram and TikTok have transformed individual users into media entities—the average successful influencer now reaches more people daily than many traditional media outlets. For example, Charli D'Amelio's TikTok posts regularly reach 150 million followers.

- Research indicates that 92% of consumers trust influencer recommendations over traditional advertising. This behavior pattern has led to the development of specific engagement metrics like EMV (earned media value), which measures the impact of influencer content vs. paid advertising.

CHAPTER 3

Defining Your Niche: Identifying Your Passion and Expertise

Crafting a successful influencer strategy hinges on deep research within your chosen niche. A niche is quite simply your focus. Your niche can be health, fitness, food, psychedelics, gadgets, toys, or movies. The more precise the niche, the better, however. If you like movies, why not focus on sci-fi or horror? If you like books, why not focus on history or fantasy? This goes beyond monetization goals, because it's largely a creative endeavor. Influencers who thrive eat, sleep, and breathe their niche.

The reason you need to create a focused niche is because your first followers will be those who are very specifically interested in a small subset of information, be it fashion blunders or funny animals. In short, don't try to drink the whole firehose of, say, books or yoga, when you can focus on your own specific journey in that world.

The diversity of niches is staggering. There is literally a community for everything. The essence of influence, however, lies not just in identifying one's niche but in connecting with like-minded individuals. This communal aspect forms the platform upon which influence flourishes, demanding constant nurturing. Influencer work is not "set it and forget it."

Central to this idea is discovering one's unique voice—authenticity reads as accessibility. In an age tainted by social media controversies, the gravest insult for an influencer is the label of a "clout chaser," perceived as sacrificing authenticity for fleeting gains. People want to see you as a close friend they can trust regarding one of their favorite things.

The path to finding one's niche, therefore, lies in embracing authenticity and forging relationships. People are much savvier now than in days past. Lose trust, and you lose your followers. A good example, if extreme, is the Jaclyn Hill case. She was once a highly influential beauty YouTuber, but her star tarnished badly after a scandal.

The failure impacted her reputation so badly she never recovered. What was the scandal? Lipstick Gate.

Hill was a beauty influencer who faced significant backlash and online cancellation following several controversies, most notably the failed launch of her cosmetics line in 2019. Many customers reported receiving lipsticks that were defective, containing strange textures, particles, and even mold.

Hill initially downplayed the complaints, blaming the issues on production inconsistencies, but as more customers came forward, the situation spiraled. The lack of transparency and delayed response fueled further criticism. This, combined with prior business controversies and accusations of dishonesty, led to widespread calls for her to be "canceled," as trust between her and her audience was damaged.

In addition to the lipstick debacle, other factors contributed to her decline:

- **Business Challenges**: Her cosmetics brand, Jaclyn Cosmetics, faced financial difficulties and ultimately shut down.

- **Changing Beauty Landscape**: The beauty industry is highly competitive, and new influencers have emerged. She was too slow to keep up with her broad and growing niche.

CHAPTER 3   DEFINING YOUR NICHE: IDENTIFYING YOUR PASSION AND EXPERTISE

It's not enough to just grow. You need to understand that your personal brand is a living thing that needs to be nourished and nurtured. It is a cross between a digital Tamagotchi—one of those little devices kids used to play with that required constant attention or the little alien inside died—and one of those egg babies given to teenagers to show them the trials of childrearing. On one hand, the influencer's phone is a chittering device dedicated to creating dopamine in both the influencer and the reader, and on the other hand the influencer's online life is a burden akin to carrying around a bag of flour in a high school for a week.

It is, in a word, difficult.

Remember: influencers are humans. We are all used to being marketed to by faceless corporations. Therefore, the influencer is a refreshing change. They seem to tell people what they really think about things they're interested in, and in most cases they aren't selling something. When you are selling something, however, you need to be as authentic as possible. If you lose any of that authenticity, you're toast.

Ultimately, the journey of becoming an influencer is not just about garnering followers, but about caring for a community built on shared passions and genuine engagement. It is a testament to the evolving landscape of digital influence, where authenticity and passion remain the guiding stars amid the ever-changing currents of social media.

So how do you start? It's about diving into what you love, engaging authentically, and building a community that values your passion. Becoming an influencer isn't just about numbers—it's about creating genuine connections in a digital world that's constantly evolving.

Prepare Yourself

Before stepping into the world of being an influencer, you need to reflect on a few important questions. These questions aren't just about your brand, but about what drives you and how you'll sustain that energy.

The answers will shape how you interact with your audience, and they will help you maintain your identity in a competitive space.

First, think about who you are. It's not just about what you present to your audience, but how well you know yourself. As an influencer, you are your brand. The content you create should align with your personality, values, and the image you want to project. Followers can sense authenticity, and that's what keeps them engaged. If you're entering this space for the first time, prepare for criticism—often from people who don't know you personally. Thick skin is a requirement. The Internet can be a harsh place, and you will need to handle criticism, trolls, and disagreement while keeping your composure. Can you stay motivated despite negativity? Can you consistently create content and engage with your audience, day in and day out?

Next, consider what expertise you bring to the table. In the influencer space, your knowledge or skill in a particular area will help you stand out. The more you know about your subject, the more value you bring to your followers. People come to influencers for advice, recommendations, or simply because they trust their opinion on a certain topic. Whether you're into fashion, tech, fitness, or food, understanding your niche well will help you connect with your audience on a deeper level. And if you're still learning, that's okay too. Be transparent about it. People appreciate seeing your growth, and it builds a stronger connection.

Passion plays a huge role in long-term success. As an influencer, it's not just about having content ideas, but about having the passion to pursue them consistently. **Creating content is demanding, and without a real love for what you're doing, burnout is almost inevitable**. Your followers will pick up on whether you're genuinely invested in the topic or if you're just going through the motions. If you're passionate about what you're sharing, it shows, and that's what draws people in. Passion keeps the content fresh and keeps you energized to push through the challenging days.

Finally, think about your focus. What specific content are you going to create? While being passionate is essential, narrowing your focus helps you find your audience. A niche allows you to build a loyal following by providing them with the content they're looking for, rather than trying to appeal to everyone. If you try to cover too much, you'll lose the attention of those who could have become your core followers. Choosing a focus early on also makes it easier to maintain a clear and consistent message. You can always expand later, but in the beginning, it's important to define what your influence will center around.

Becoming an influencer isn't just about posting pictures or videos. It's about building a community, creating content that resonates, and continually refining your voice in a way that makes people want to come back for more. Keep these questions in mind, and you'll have a solid foundation to begin your journey.

The Rules of Content Creation

When stepping into the role of an influencer, there are a couple of essential rules to keep in mind. Influencing is not just about posting content when you feel like it. It's about consistent effort, a strategy, and the long game. If your goal is to make a career out of it or even just grow your influence as part of your personal brand, understanding these rules is key.

The first rule is simple: stay active. The digital world moves quickly, and your audience expects regular content. If you go silent for too long, they'll move on to someone else. You have to maintain a presence. This doesn't mean you need to churn out content every hour, but regular updates are a must. Many will tell you that daily content isn't absolutely necessary, but we've found that the more you post, the better your chances of gaining an audience. **Content production is the low hanging fruit for growth in all forms of media. The more content on your page, the better.** The trick is finding a balance that works for both you and your audience. Whether it's daily posts, weekly videos, or frequent

CHAPTER 3   DEFINING YOUR NICHE: IDENTIFYING YOUR PASSION AND EXPERTISE

stories, keeping your content fresh is essential to staying relevant. Your followers come to you for insight, opinions, or entertainment, and that's a relationship you need to nurture by consistently delivering.

There will be days when you feel stuck or when inspiration is nowhere to be found. That's normal, but it doesn't mean you can take a break. Content doesn't always have to be groundbreaking. It can be personal anecdotes, reactions to current events, or shout-outs to other creators. What matters is showing up. Even if it feels like you have nothing new to say, find ways to engage with your community. Keep conversations going. In the world of influencing, disappearing for long stretches means losing momentum, and that's hard to get back.

The second rule is consistency in your voice and style. Your followers are drawn to you because of how you express yourself and the unique perspective you offer. Whether you prefer longer, in-depth content or quick, daily updates, pick a style that feels natural and stick with it. Consistency builds familiarity, and familiarity fosters trust.

Your style doesn't have to fit a particular mold. You might lean toward a lighthearted, humorous tone or take a more serious, informative approach. What's important is making sure that your content reflects who you are and remains consistent in its delivery. Over time, this helps you stand out. People come to know what to expect from you and your posts, and that builds loyalty. However, be careful not to confuse consistency with rigidity. Your style can evolve, but it should feel authentic at every stage.

Personal touches matter. Don't shy away from showing your personality. Injecting your experiences and opinions into your content helps create a connection with your audience. What big media outlets can't offer is personal insight. This is where you have an edge as an influencer. People are drawn to authenticity, and by opening up, even in small ways, you allow your followers to relate to you.

These rules—staying active and maintaining a consistent voice—are what keep influencers successful over time. It's not easy, and it requires dedication, but with focus and effort, you can build something lasting.

CHAPTER 3   DEFINING YOUR NICHE: IDENTIFYING YOUR PASSION AND EXPERTISE

The small, daily efforts build into something bigger, and eventually, they pay off in ways you might not expect.

The Influencer's Checklist

What do you love? This is the first question and the only question that really matters. You need to answer this question before doing anything else.

What do you love? What do you love to do? Who are you? What defines your viewpoint, your attitude, and your morality? To begin, decide who you are: a teacher? A writer? A singer? A photographer?

This will help define what you will create. If you love to teach and love to cook, you should focus on dining or cuisine. If you love to shoot photos and exercise, you can become a fitness influencer. If you want to heal people and support psychedelics, you need to focus on mind expansion and growth.

You must create things that you love. This is the bottom line. If you do not love your chosen focus, you will fail. Sure, there are people to totter along for years, producing things they don't care about, but they're usually found out eventually. To influence is to share love with an audience, big or small. If you wouldn't wake up every morning preaching the value of good health, fine food, or good books, then you have to find something different to do.

Understand your audience. What tribe do you want to reach? Why? Find your base through research—the who, what, where, when, and why of the targets. Notice we used the word "tribe" here. Tribes are the equivalent of your family, your friends, and folks you want to eventually reach. Target your first influencer work to people you know: what will they want to see? If people know you for your political views, reinforce that with some information on rallies and debates. If people know you as a knitter, show off your creations, explore your yarn box, or just film yourself doing some ASMR needle clacking. Have fun and watch to see what people respond to.

Analyze your tribe's needs. Conduct thorough research within your niche's landscape to identify trends, competitor strategies, and preferences. Identify gaps or untapped segments where you can deliver value. This is especially important in organic society.

How do you do this? Send out Google Forms surveys to your friends and family. Hold a focus group or group class. Ask people what they'd like to see from you on Instagram or Twitter. Create a newsletter that you send out weekly to friends and family to create a testbed for content. Remember: you need to talk to people. This is not a "build it and they will come" process. It is a give and take, a process of communication that helps you and your tribe grow.

Know your competitors. Examine competitor influencer partnerships and marketing methodologies. Scrutinize the niches they target and the influencers they engage with to glean insights into promising areas that resonate with potential followers.

Follow other influencers in the space. Understand what they post, what works best for them, and how many likes and comments they get. If this is to be your job or even a dedicated pastime, you need to study the world in which you're operating.

Leverage feedback and data. Harness feedback from existing customers garnered through surveys, reviews, and social media interactions. Uncover patterns in likes, interests, and niche preferences. Analyze data from your website, email list, and other social media platforms.

One of the easiest things to do to investigate your niche is to try tools like Google Analytics on your websites.

Explore keyword research. Conduct comprehensive keyword research pertinent to your niche and related industries. Identify popular keywords, hashtags, and trending topics to gain insights into actively searched niches. Never underestimate chatter or environment.

Experiment with influencer partnerships. Explore partnerships with influencers across various niches on a smaller scale to evaluate impact and resonance with both your and their target audiences. Track performance metrics and engagement levels to identify high-yield niche opportunities.

Seek advice from mentors. Never underestimate the value of experience. Reading books is one thing; field experience is another. Cultivate a support network; be generous with your own knowledge.

Can't seem to find a mentor? Reach out to other influencers online and ask them for ten minutes of their time. Go to events focused on your particular niche and talk to creators there. Visit a convention or seminar focused on your niche or even reach out to university professors or other professionals. Explain what you are doing, be it explaining historical costumes to a wider audience or talking about anime, and ask a few focused questions. Don't waste their time, but don't be afraid to reach out either. People love to talk about what they're working on.

Understand your current assets. Do you have email lists? Current social media accounts? A newsletter or a meetup that you run? These are your assets, and they are integral to boosting your audience. By focusing on these you can create a seed crystal from which your influencer empire can grow.

Evolving with the Audience

- **Staying Authentic**: While adapting to trends, it's crucial to maintain authenticity. Influencers who remain true to their core values resonate better with their audience.

- **Understanding Audience Insights**: By closely monitoring analytics and audience engagement, influencers can identify shifting preferences. This helps them tailor content accordingly.

CHAPTER 3   DEFINING YOUR NICHE: IDENTIFYING YOUR PASSION AND EXPERTISE

- **Experimenting with New Formats**: Influencers who diversify their content formats (e.g., short-form videos, podcasts, live streams) can reach a wider audience and stay relevant.

- **Collaborating with Others**: Partnerships with other influencers or brands can introduce new audiences and perspectives.

- **Embracing Challenges**: Addressing current events or social issues can demonstrate an influencer's relevance.

More Niche Advice

Influencers, much like any successful entrepreneur, have honed in on their unique selling proposition (USP) to carve out a specific niche. Here's a breakdown of how some famous influencers found their footing and adapted to their audience's changing needs:

- **Passion and Expertise**: Most influencers started with a genuine interest or expertise in a particular area. For instance, beauty gurus like Huda Kattan and Kylie Jenner had a deep-rooted passion for makeup and skincare.

- **Identifying a Gap**: Many influencers saw an opportunity in a specific underserved market. For example, body positivity advocates like Jameela Jamil filled a void by promoting self-love and acceptance.

- **Leveraging Personal Brand**: Some influencers built their niche around their personality. Comedians like Lilly Singh and MrBeast have cultivated strong personal brands based on humor and entertainment.

CHAPTER 3 DEFINING YOUR NICHE: IDENTIFYING YOUR PASSION AND EXPERTISE

In the X (formerly known as Twitter) world of social media, finding your unique niche as an influencer is paramount. It's not just about collecting followers; it's about cultivating a loyal audience that resonates with your content.

Here's how to identify and capitalize on your niche.

Self-Discovery and Passion

- **Introspection**: What are you naturally drawn to? What topics ignite your curiosity and make you want to share your knowledge? What can you talk about for hours? What do you collect? What facts do you know that no one else does?

- **Interests and Hobbies**: Explore your passions. Your personal interests can be a goldmine for content ideas. What do you love to do in your spare time? Can you teach basic guitar and talk about your favorite bands? Can you show off your carpentry skills or technical prowess? Are you well-versed in the lore of a favorite show? Anything is fodder for your future as an influencer.

- **Values and Beliefs**: Align your content with your values. Authenticity is key to building a genuine connection with your audience. If you're religious, focus on communicating to religious or spiritual people. Are you grumpy? Cultivate grumpuses! Do you believe the glass is always half full? Focus on that optimism and bring it to the forefront.

CHAPTER 3   DEFINING YOUR NICHE: IDENTIFYING YOUR PASSION AND EXPERTISE

Market Research and Analysis

- **Identify Gaps**: Look for underserved niches or areas where there's a lack of quality content. This is actually harder than it sounds. The world is literally full of content at this point, and to find something that is popular, interesting, and not completely saturated is quite difficult. Our rule of thumb? If *The New York Times* would cover it, it's probably too mainstream already.

- **Competitor Analysis**: Study successful influencers in your desired niche. Learn from their strategies, but don't simply imitate.

- **Audience Research**: Understand your target audience's needs, preferences, and pain points.

Niche Specialization

- **Define Your Niche**: Narrow down your focus to a specific area within your broader interest. For example, instead of "fitness," you could specialize in "plant-based fitness."

- **Unique Selling Proposition (USP)**: What sets you apart from others in your niche? Highlight your unique perspective or expertise.

Content Creation and Consistency

- **Quality**: Prioritize creating high-quality content that adds value to your audience.

- **Consistency**: Establish a regular posting schedule to keep your audience engaged.

- **Experimentation**: Try different content formats (e.g., videos, blog posts, podcasts) to see what resonates best with your audience.

Unusual Cases: Nontraditional Niches

While many influencers find success in traditional niches like beauty, fashion, and travel, there are also opportunities in more unusual or niche areas. Here are a few examples:

- **Hyper-specific Hobbies:** Consider niches like "crochet for beginners" or "urban beekeeping." Our favorite accounts are the really geeky ones that focus on obscure topics, like "how to make mead."

- **Unique Skills or Talents**: If you have a rare skill, like juggling or tightrope walking, you could build a following around it.

- **Controversial Topics**: While it's important to approach controversial topics with sensitivity, there can be a market for thought-provoking content. Political influencers are often quite popular, but you may find yourself pigeonholed if you become too polarizing. Tread carefully when it comes to focusing on something that isn't seen as typical.

Influencer Insider: Huda Kattan—From Beauty Blogger to Beauty Empire

Huda Kattan is a prime example of an influencer who successfully transformed from a beauty blogger into a global beauty mogul. Her journey, marked by strategic pivots and innovation, offers valuable insights into the evolution of influencer marketing.

Kattan is an American-Iraqi beauty entrepreneur, makeup artist, and founder of the cosmetics brand Huda Beauty. Born in Oklahoma in 1983 to Iraqi immigrant parents, she later moved to Dubai, where she gained fame through her beauty blog and social media presence.

Early Days: Beauty Blogger

Huda started her career in the early 2000s as a beauty blogger, sharing makeup tutorials and product reviews on her personal blog. Her candid approach and expert knowledge quickly garnered a loyal following. Recognizing the potential of visual content, she transitioned to YouTube, where her engaging personality and detailed tutorials catapulted her to fame.

Pivot 1: Product Creation

Capitalizing on her growing influence and deep understanding of consumer preferences, Huda launched her own beauty brand, Huda Beauty, in 2013. The brand's initial focus was on false eyelashes, a product category she had mastered and was passionate about. The success of Huda Beauty's lashes was phenomenal, solidifying her position as a beauty entrepreneur. The content she shared focused on beauty and, obviously, her lush lashes. This is an example of creating a focused product around a specific niche and then expanding your focus from there.

Pivot 2: Expanding Product Line

Building on the success of her lash line, Huda expanded Huda Beauty's product range to include eyeshadow palettes, liquid lipsticks, and skincare. Each product launch was met with immense anticipation and sold out quickly, demonstrating the power of her personal brand. Huda's ability to identify beauty trends and translate them into successful products showcased her keen business acumen.

Huda took special care to tease each launch in order to maximize the effect of every release. By building anticipation, she was able to sell more of her own products to an audience that clearly enjoyed what she had to offer.

Pivot 3: Content Expansion

While product creation became a core focus, Huda continued to produce engaging content. She expanded her YouTube channel to include beauty challenges, product reviews, and collaborations with other influencers. Additionally, she launched a successful beauty blog and a popular Instagram account, maintaining a strong connection with her audience.

Pivot 4: Building a Beauty Community

Huda recognized the importance of fostering a community around her brand. She launched the #HudaBeauty hashtag, encouraging fans to share their makeup looks and experiences. She also created online and offline events, bringing together beauty enthusiasts and building a loyal fanbase.

Pivot 5: Global Expansion

With Huda Beauty becoming a global phenomenon, Huda expanded her business beyond makeup. She launched a skincare line, Kay Beauty, catering to the Middle Eastern market. This move demonstrated her ability to adapt to different cultural preferences and expand her brand's reach. She used her entire persona to spin off multiple projects while seamlessly blending community with her personal brand. Today, Sephora carries her entire brand, which is in effect a beauty lifestyle brand, which includes perfume. In her case, her connection to both beauty and her community successfully translated to a highly successful beauty brand available outside her community.

This case study seems nearly impossible to someone just starting out. How do you go from a beauty blogger to a global CEO? As you noticed, each step of Huda's journey was calculated to expand her audience into a new direction or social media endeavor. Further, Huda was very specifically focused on YouTube for a long time before expanding out into more general products. By bringing your goal into focus—I will talk about my niche on Instagram—you are able to reduce the area of influence to a smaller audience. Once that audience is big enough, however, you'll want to connect with other audience sources including social media, blogs, and newsletters. Don't try to do too much at once and accept that this is a long, fun, and winding road.

Key Takeaways

- Authenticity is the key to influencer success, demonstrated by cases like Jaclyn Hill's downfall after her lipstick scandal. When influencers lose trust through dishonesty or poor product quality, they rarely recover their reputation in the digital space.

- Finding your niche requires deep introspection and market research. Instead of targeting broad categories like "books" or "fitness," successful influencers focus on specific segments where they have genuine expertise or passion, making their content more valuable to a dedicated audience.

- Regular content creation is essential for maintaining influence. The influencer's life needs constant attention to stay afloat. While daily posts aren't mandatory, consistent activity keeps audiences engaged and prevents loss of momentum.

- Building an influencer career requires preparation beyond content creation. This includes developing thick skin for criticism, understanding your expertise level, maintaining genuine passion for your subject matter, and having a clear focus that helps you connect with your target audience.

- Organic social's secret sauce is individuality. Don't be afraid to make content in your niche your way.

CHAPTER 4

Influencer Ethics: What You Can and Can't Do

In the influencer space, maintaining transparency and credibility can be challenging. Audiences are drawn to influencers because of the trust and authenticity they provide, but as partnerships with brands grow, balancing that authenticity with commercial interests becomes difficult. Followers want to feel that influencers are genuine, that their recommendations and opinions are sincere, and that they aren't simply being swayed by financial incentives or free products. When transparency is lacking or when an influencer fails to disclose partnerships, it undermines trust, and that damage can be difficult to repair.

The commercial side of influencing—brand deals, sponsorships, and gifted products—adds another layer of complexity. As an influencer's platform grows, so does the pressure to align with brands. While working with brands is a key revenue stream for many influencers, it also presents ethical questions. Can you be objective if you've received something for free? How do you ensure your content reflects your genuine opinion and not just the demands of a sponsor? And, aside from vague FCC issues, does it really matter? These are questions every influencer needs to consider.

CHAPTER 4   INFLUENCER ETHICS: WHAT YOU CAN AND CAN'T DO

Establishing personal ethical guidelines before entering these partnerships is crucial. Without clear standards in place, it's easy to fall into gray areas where choices become more about pleasing brands than being honest with your audience. Ethical guidelines serve as a framework for making decisions, helping influencers navigate the pressures of commercial opportunities while maintaining the integrity that built their audience in the first place.

We come at these ethical considerations from the standpoint of journalists. While influencers might not feel that they are offering a public good or participating in the media landscape, they very much are. They are telling the truth (or their truth) to a large audience, and they are trying to make money based on that truth. By all means you can produce only fiction, but your audience will notice and leave you.

Note that many of our concerns come from an older mode of doing business. Modern influencers often have no qualms about faking airplane crashes and taking—and talking about—free products. If that last sentence gave you pause, let's talk about what not to do as an influencer in regard to airplanes—or anything, really.

In 2022, YouTuber Trevor Jacob crashed his plane for the sake of creating content. Jacob, who had around 133,000 subscribers at the time, posted a video called "I Crashed My Plane," where he claimed his plane experienced engine failure while flying over the Los Padres National Forest in California. He parachuted out of the aircraft before it crashed, with dramatic effect. After the video went up, aviators noticed plenty of holes in Jacob's story and reported him to the FAA.

Finally, the FAA expressed concerns about his actions during the flight, noting that he made no effort to restart the engine, contact air traffic control, or look for a safe place to land, despite there being multiple options. The agency also pointed out the unusual fact that Jacob was already wearing a parachute before the alleged engine failure occurred. After the crash, Jacob is said to have recovered and disposed of the wreckage, which further raised doubts about the incident's legitimacy.

CHAPTER 4   INFLUENCER ETHICS: WHAT YOU CAN AND CAN'T DO

In short, he crashed his plane for the 'gram.

The FAA revoked his pilot's license. Then something worse happened. In 2023 he wrote on his Instagram:

Two years ago I jumped out of a perfectly good airplane and let it crash into the ground, took some bad advice, and decided to remove the wreckage. Today I was sentenced to 6 months in Federal Prison. Thank you to my unconditional loving family and friends. You know who you are, and who you aren't :) My incredible lawyer, and Federal Judge Walter, for understanding the truth of the situation, and giving me a second chance at life. This situation could have been a lot worse, and I am extremely grateful I am here to talk about it. I look forward to teaching our youth from my mistake, and the lessons I have learned from this, it has changed me as a person forever, and therefore, I am so excited for this next chapter of implementing those changes into society for the better. I made a video about this on my YouTube channel if you'd like to watch it.

His last video went up on December 4, 2023, and he hasn't posted anything since, leading us to believe that he was finally cured of his attention-seeking influencer behavior.

Don't be like Jacob. That said, let's dig in.

Libel and Slander

Libel and slander are serious concerns for influencers who frequently share opinions and information with their audiences. Libel refers to false statements made in writing that harm someone's reputation, while slander covers spoken statements. Both can lead to significant legal consequences if the information shared is untrue and damaging. For influencers, who often engage with a wide range of topics and individuals, the risk of unintentionally spreading false information is very real.

The fast pace of social media can tempt influencers to post content quickly, but verifying facts is essential. Whether discussing a brand,

CHAPTER 4   INFLUENCER ETHICS: WHAT YOU CAN AND CAN'T DO

another influencer, or public figures, the accuracy of the information must always be a priority. Failing to confirm details before posting can result in not only reputational harm but also potential lawsuits. Brands and individuals have the legal right to defend themselves against false claims, and influencers can be held liable if they spread misinformation.

Remember the McDonald's chicken sandwich problem we talked about a few chapters ago? The TikToker who produced it could have been sued for slandering the company. That said, there are very few slander or libel cases brought to bear against influencers because the law is very new and still forming around the industry. But the warning stands: do you want to be the first influencer to be successfully sued by Nike or Burger King?

To minimize the risk of facing a defamation suit, influencers should focus on accuracy and documentation. Keeping detailed records of sources, whether it's data from a reliable website, an interview, or official statements, is important for backing up claims. If an influencer chooses to share opinions or speculations, they should clearly distinguish these from facts. This approach not only protects influencers from legal repercussions but also maintains the credibility that is essential to their relationships with their audience. This is especially important when your niche is true crime, history, politics, or health.

If you accuse any real person of anything in your work, you must use the word "alleged" to preface any negative things. This is the absolute least you can do to maintain any legal protection as an influencer. That said, as a rule of thumb, avoid calling out individuals or companies at all costs. While outrage clicks can be addictive, the results can be devastating.

One example in the blogosphere happened during Steve Jobs' last years before he succumbed to cancer. A blogger, Robert Scoble, took pictures of Jobs during the last months of his life. The Apple CEO had lost weight, and he was in the final stages of cancer. Scoble allegedly took pictures of Jobs and posted them to early social media. The result was an immediate ban in Silicon Valley. His entire livelihood as an early influencer was truncated, and it took years to rebuild his reputation. Sometimes the story might not be worth it, especially if it concerns the private lives of powerful people especially if you aren't protected by journalistic privilege.

Private Information and NDAs

Non-disclosure agreements (NDAs) have become a common tool in the media industry, especially when brands want to share new products or campaigns ahead of their public release. By signing an NDA, an influencer agrees to keep specific information confidential until a set date, often called an embargo. These agreements allow influencers to prepare content in advance, giving them time to thoroughly explore a product or message before sharing it with their audience. However, NDAs come with the responsibility to respect the terms of confidentiality, and breaking those terms can lead to legal consequences and damage to professional relationships.

Balancing the desire to respect an embargo with the competitive nature of the influencer space can be tricky. There's often pressure to be the first to share new information, especially in industries where being early can significantly boost engagement. But breaking an embargo—even if others have—risks losing trust with the brand and missing out on future opportunities. In a fast-moving digital world, it may feel tempting to post early when others do, but doing so can undermine your long-term credibility.

Knowing when to sign an NDA is critical. If the brand is offering something valuable, like exclusive access to a product or event, and the terms of the NDA are reasonable, it may be worthwhile. However, influencers should avoid signing NDAs that feel too restrictive or unnecessary, especially if the information is not particularly sensitive. If others break the embargo, it's essential to maintain your commitment to the NDA. While it may feel unfair when others release content early, honoring the agreement builds trust with the brand and sets you apart as a professional who can be relied upon.

CHAPTER 4   INFLUENCER ETHICS: WHAT YOU CAN AND CAN'T DO

Remember: your goal as an influencer is to give your audience access. Therefore, brands might give you early access to products your audience is interested in. If you abuse that trust, you can be banned from news events or even press releases, and you will definitely stop getting free products and the like.

Transparency and Accountability

Transparency is the foundation of trust between influencers and their audience. Followers expect honesty, especially when it comes to partnerships with brands. Being open about sponsorships, gifted products, or any form of compensation helps maintain credibility. When an influencer is transparent about their relationships with brands, it signals to the audience that their opinions are still authentic, even if compensation is involved. This openness helps prevent skepticism and allows followers to trust that the influencer's recommendations are based on genuine beliefs rather than purely financial gain.

To maintain this trust, influencers must clearly disclose any brand deals, gifted products, or sponsored content. This can be done directly in posts, videos, or captions, ensuring that followers know when content is part of a paid partnership. Simple statements like "sponsored by," "in partnership with," or even "gifted" make it clear that there is a commercial element to the content. Transparency doesn't diminish the value of the content—in fact, it often strengthens the relationship with the audience by showing that the influencer values honesty.

Mistakes happen, and how influencers handle them is critical. If an error is made—whether it's misinformation, a poor brand partnership, or an oversight—it's important to address it publicly. Admitting mistakes shows accountability and reinforces trust. Publicly acknowledging and correcting the issue, whether by updating posts or adding clarifications, ensures that followers feel respected. Influencers can maintain transparency by openly discussing changes, edits, or updates to their content, demonstrating that they are committed to providing accurate, trustworthy information.

Managing Sponsored Trips and Brand Perks

All-expense-paid trips, luxurious events, and exclusive brand experiences are enticing perks for influencers. However, these benefits come with ethical considerations. Accepting these offers without disclosing them can lead to a loss of credibility with the audience, as followers may question the objectivity of the content created during these trips. Transparency is key when influencers accept sponsored travel—followers need to know that a brand covered the costs, so they can understand the context of the content.

To maintain credibility, influencers should clearly disclose sponsored travel, just as they would with any brand deal. This can be as simple as stating in a post or video that a brand sponsored the trip. It's also important to ensure that the content produced from these trips remains honest and reflective of the influencer's true experiences, rather than skewed by the luxury or exclusivity of the event. Being clear about the nature of the partnership allows influencers to maintain their audience's trust while still benefiting from these opportunities.

Sponsored trips can sometimes lead to a conflict between access and honest reviews. Brands often expect positive coverage in exchange for these experiences, which can put pressure on influencers to deliver glowing reviews, even if their experience wasn't entirely positive. The challenge is to strike a balance—providing an honest review while maintaining a professional relationship with the brand. Ultimately, the influencer's responsibility is to their audience, and any content should reflect genuine opinions. If an influencer feels that a trip or gift could compromise their objectivity, it may be best to decline the offer or communicate those concerns directly to the brand.

Accepting gifts and trips can enhance an influencer's content, providing unique experiences and insights for their audience. However, it's crucial to handle these perks responsibly. Disclosure, honesty, and transparency must guide how influencers talk about these experiences, ensuring that their content remains trustworthy and authentic. By being up-front about the nature of these perks, influencers can continue to provide value to their audience without sacrificing credibility.

Review Units and Product Samples

When influencers receive free products for review, they have ethical obligations to uphold. These products are provided to give influencers firsthand experience with the item, but accepting them comes with the responsibility of being transparent and impartial in the review process. Just because something is free doesn't mean it should automatically receive a positive review. The influencer's duty is to their audience, and providing honest feedback ensures trust remains intact.

In some cases, brands allow influencers to keep review units after the evaluation period, while in others, the expectation is that the product will be returned. It's important to clarify these terms up front with the brand. Keeping a product may be acceptable if the brand explicitly offers it or if extended use is necessary for a thorough review. However, influencers should not assume they can keep a product without confirmation. If there's any doubt, it's best to ask the brand or simply return the item once the review is complete.

Disclosure is essential, especially when reviewing products over an extended period. Whether it's a short-term loan or a product that's been kept for further use, influencers need to make their relationship with the product clear to their audience. The audience should always know if the influencer received the product for free or if there are ongoing collaborations with the brand. Transparency in these situations helps maintain the influencer's integrity and the trust of their followers.

Influencers may also face subtle or direct pressure from brands to provide favorable reviews. This pressure can be difficult to navigate, especially for those looking to build long-term partnerships. However, maintaining impartiality is critical. An honest review, even if it's not entirely positive, builds credibility with the audience. If a brand expects only positive coverage, it may not be the right partnership. Ultimately, an influencer's value lies in their authenticity, and that should never be compromised for the sake of pleasing a brand.

FTC Guidelines and Legal Requirements

The Federal Trade Commission (FTC) has clear guidelines regarding endorsements and affiliations for influencers. These rules are designed to ensure that followers are aware of any material connections between influencers and brands. Whether it's a paid partnership, a gifted product, or a sponsored post, influencers are required to disclose these relationships to their audience. The aim is to prevent any confusion about the influencer's motivations and ensure that consumers can make informed decisions based on the content they are viewing.

To comply with FTC rules, influencers need to be up-front about their brand relationships in every post, video, or story that features sponsored content or gifted items. These disclosures should be clear, conspicuous, and placed where the audience can easily see them. Terms like "sponsored," "paid partnership," or "gifted" work well to let the audience know there's a financial or material connection. It's not enough to bury disclosures in hashtags or in hard-to-find sections of the post; they need to be easily visible and understandable to all viewers.

Ensuring compliance while maintaining audience trust is straightforward if approached correctly. Transparency doesn't harm credibility—if anything, it strengthens it. Audiences appreciate honesty, and disclosing partnerships demonstrates that the influencer values their trust. By following the FTC's guidelines and being open about brand affiliations, influencers can avoid legal issues while continuing to build genuine connections with their followers.

Trust, Leaks, and Confidential Information

As influencers grow in popularity, they may be entrusted with insider information from brands or PR representatives. This information, whether it's about upcoming product launches, marketing strategies, or unreleased features, is often shared under strict confidentiality agreements, like non-disclosure agreements (NDAs). Handling this information with care is crucial, as leaking confidential details can have serious consequences.

Leaking insider information not only damages trust with the brand but can also have legal repercussions. Brands invest significant time and resources into product launches and marketing strategies, and leaking information prematurely can harm their business. Furthermore, once an influencer is known for breaking confidentiality, it becomes difficult for other brands to trust them in the future. This can harm long-term relationships and limit access to exclusive opportunities.

Influencers must balance the desire to be first with their ethical responsibilities. While it's tempting to break a story or be the first to reveal new information, honoring confidentiality agreements is essential for maintaining professional integrity. Even if rumors or leaks appear on other platforms, sticking to the agreed-upon embargoes or NDAs reinforces the influencer's reliability. In the end, building a reputation as a trustworthy partner will create more opportunities for exclusive information and collaborations down the line.

Avoiding Conflicts of Interest

When working with multiple brands, influencers must be vigilant in recognizing and managing potential conflicts of interest. A conflict of interest can arise when an influencer promotes products or services from competing brands or when financial incentives clash with their ability to provide honest feedback. It's crucial to maintain a clear boundary between partnerships to ensure that content remains unbiased and authentic.

The first step in avoiding conflicts of interest is to be transparent with all parties involved. If you're working with two brands that might overlap in terms of their products or services, it's essential to disclose this to both brands and your audience. It's equally important to consider whether promoting competing brands would dilute the value of your endorsements or confuse your followers. If there's any chance that working with multiple brands will compromise your authenticity or credibility, it may be best to choose a single partnership or space out the timing of the collaborations.

Financial incentives and personal relationships can also blur the lines between honest content creation and biased promotion. While it's normal for influencers to develop strong ties with certain brands or benefit financially from partnerships, it's critical to ensure that these relationships don't interfere with the honesty of your content. An influencer's success relies heavily on the trust of their audience, and once that trust is broken, it can be challenging to regain. Prioritizing transparency and staying true to your values will help maintain credibility and keep your content authentic, regardless of financial or personal pressures.

Long-Term Ethical Success As an Influencer

Maintaining transparency and integrity is not only essential for building trust but also for achieving long-term success as an influencer. As the industry becomes more competitive and saturated, those who consistently demonstrate honesty and accountability will stand out. An influencer's relationship with their audience is built on trust, and that trust is the foundation for sustainable growth, future partnerships, and continued relevance.

Being up-front and honest with followers, brands, and peers benefits everyone involved. For followers, it fosters a sense of loyalty and connection, as they know they can rely on your authenticity. For brands, it establishes a foundation of respect, making it clear that your endorsements are genuine and well-considered. For peers in the industry, it sets a standard of professionalism and ethical behavior, encouraging a community where trust is valued.

New influencers entering the industry should take the time to establish personal ethical standards from the start. By deciding early on how to approach brand partnerships, product reviews, and transparency with their audience, influencers can avoid the pitfalls that arise from conflicts of interest or compromising integrity for short-term gains. Sticking to these standards will ensure long-term success and help create a more honest, respected, and thriving influencer community.

Key Takeaways

- Legal and ethical consequences in influencer marketing can be severe, highlighted by cases like Trevor Jacob's airplane crash stunt that led to prison time. Authenticity and honesty are critical, not just for maintaining audience trust but for avoiding serious legal issues.

- Transparency in brand deals and sponsorships is both a legal requirement and ethical necessity. The FTC requires clear disclosure of material connections

CHAPTER 4   INFLUENCER ETHICS: WHAT YOU CAN AND CAN'T DO

between influencers and brands, including paid partnerships, gifted products, and sponsored posts. These disclosures should be easily visible, not hidden in hashtags.

- Managing confidential information and NDAs is crucial for long-term success. Breaking embargoes or leaking information might provide short-term attention but can permanently damage relationships with brands and limit future opportunities.

- Conflicts of interest need careful management, particularly when working with multiple brands or receiving sponsored perks. Influencers must balance commercial opportunities with honest reviews and maintain transparency with their audience about paid partnerships, gifted products, and sponsored trips. The focus should be on providing genuine value to followers while being clear about brand relationships.

CHAPTER 5

Crafting Your Personal Brand: Building a Unique Identity in a Crowded Space

A strong personal brand can help you stand out from the crowd, build credibility, and attract opportunities. For this chapter, you may want to sit down and brainstorm where you want your accounts to go, as well as your goals. Is it to bring awareness to a certain topic? Is it to lure beauty brand sponsorships? Is it to break into travel writing? Also, look at your organic posts. They can absolutely be a roadmap to branding. A journal, vision board, or whiteboard can be helpful—it can get you used to getting your ideas on paper.

First, let's define personal branding. Personal branding is the practice of consciously creating and managing the image and identity you present to the world. It involves defining your values, skills, and unique qualities in a way that sets you apart from others. Personal branding is not just about what you do, but also how you communicate to others, both in person and online. It includes everything from your professional presence on

CHAPTER 5 CRAFTING YOUR PERSONAL BRAND: BUILDING A UNIQUE IDENTITY IN A CROWDED SPACE

social media to the way you network and interact with others. Essentially, personal branding is about shaping how people perceive you, helping to build trust and establish your reputation in your field or industry.

You need to create a personal brand because, in a world full of noise, you need to make yourself and your personal product stand out. This might seem difficult at first, but you already create a personal brand on a daily basis in the form of what you wear, what you say, and how you look. You can even redefine yourself daily, and that can be part of your personal brand. In the end, your goal is to tell the world something about you that is different and important. That's not easy, but it's vital.

Crafting Quality Content

In social media, quality content reigns supreme. As an influencer, your ability to consistently produce engaging, valuable, and authentic material will directly impact your success. Here are some key strategies to help you craft content that resonates with your audience.

Understanding your audience is key to success. By identifying their pain points, desires, and interests, you can tailor your content to address their specific concerns and provide solutions that resonate with them. The better you understand your audience, the more relevant and engaging your content will be.

You wouldn't open a restaurant without understanding what the people who live in your neighborhood like to eat or drink. The same can be said of an influencer's focus. You must become an expert in your audience. Ask them questions, learn from them, and build your content to suit.

Further, your content needs to look great. You don't have to be the most handsome or beautiful influencer on the block, but your quality must be impeccable. One influencer, Dimitra Neonaki, calls herself the Culture Muse. She shoots videos of various Roman ruins, walking us through Pompeii and Pisa while talking in detail about what we're seeing. Her videos are surprisingly simple: just a handheld phone and voiceover, but her audio is crisp and video clear and it's obvious she understands her topic and audience. Watching her videos is like walking these cities with a capable and compelling tour guide, something most of us will never experience.

Authenticity is at the heart of building meaningful connections. Let your true personality come through in your content, as being genuine helps to build trust with your audience. Authenticity creates a strong, lasting bond with followers, fostering loyalty and engagement. Neonaki speaks simply and clearly and makes it seem like she's actually interested in sharing her expertise with you.

Producing high-quality content is essential. While you don't need expensive equipment, it's important to ensure your shots are steady, the audio is clear, and the lighting is good. New devices make creating quality content easier than ever, but investing in good gear, when possible, can make a noticeable difference. Additionally, watching content from other creators can provide valuable insights and inspiration, helping you stay informed and continuously improve your own work.

Infusing Authenticity into Your Influencer Content

Authenticity is the cornerstone of a successful influencer career. It fosters trust, loyalty, and genuine connections with your audience.

Here are some strategies to infuse your content with authenticity.

Be Yourself

- **Share Personal Experiences:** Share personal stories and experiences relevant to your topics. Writer Ryan Holiday, for instance, often weaves in stories from his life in Texas when discussing Stoicism. In one example, he shared how he ignored his own advice about slowing down, which led to a running injury—showing that even a self-proclaimed Stoic can struggle with his own teachings. These well-chosen, authentic stories are crucial because they help your audience see you as a real person, not just a marketer.

- **Express Your Opinions:** Don't be afraid to share your thoughts and perspectives, even if they're controversial. But be prepared to lose followers if you are going against the grain. Remember: most social media fans skew younger and are probably more progressive. If you want to enter the world of far-right social media, you need to be prepared to grow an entirely different kind of audience.

- **Don't Worry About Being Vain:** A friend recently told us that they felt posting on social media was vain. If you're doing it wrong, then you can definitely come across as vain, but if you're genuine and kind, you can guarantee that you'll be seen as helpful, not harmful.

Be Consistent

- **Maintain a Brand Voice:** Develop a consistent tone and style that reflects your personality. Think about MrBeast. He has turned influence into an art, creating teaser images for each of his videos that show him smiling brightly. This kind of brand focus allows him to spread seamlessly from social site to social site and from fan to fan. McDonald's doesn't change the color of its logo to match a whim. Neither should you.

- **Stay True to Your Values:** Ensure your content aligns with your beliefs and principles. If you're a religious person, don't do anything you'd find immoral. If you feel strongly about an unpopular topic, you should talk about it with your audience. This kind of honesty is vital online, especially in an era of misinformation and canned outrage.

- **Post on a Schedule**: You don't need to post five times a day, but you do need to be posting at least once a day. There are services that you can use to help you cut up video clips and schedule posts, but before you use those, please do things by hand. This teaches discipline and gets you ready for when you'll be building a bigger audience on multiple sites.

Building Strong Connections

Community is the heart and soul of influencer marketing. By cultivating a strong and engaged community, you can amplify your reach, foster loyalty, and create lasting relationships with your audience. Here are some strategies to leverage community as an influencer.

Engage Actively

- **Respond to Comments:** Show that you value your followers' input by responding to their comments and questions. Have conversations about your personal experience.

- **Start Conversations:** Initiate discussions and ask open-ended questions to encourage engagement. The goal of an engaged community is to foster relationships with each other, as well as you, the influencer.

- **Don't Charge for Authenticity:** Many influencers eventually decide that their time is too valuable to chat back and forth with fans. OnlyFans folks—those who are focusing on deeply personal content—tend to charge for interactions, but if you're producing beauty regimens or posting hauls perhaps, it's better to connect with people without asking for cash. You can absolutely offer consulting contracts with brands and even customers, but this will come later in your career.

Create a Sense of Belonging

- **Use Inclusive Language:** Inclusive language makes everyone feel heard and comfortable. Every community has their "jargon"—which they use—but it should be your priority to invite viewers into your world without confusing them or offering non-inclusive experience. You want the people who happen upon your content to stay and your fans to appreciate your honest and understandable products. Instead of going deep into minutiae, become the person fans will send to their inexperienced friends for further clarity.

- **Run Contests and Challenges:** Encourage your followers to create content related to your brand or niche. One social media marketer we spoke to ran a pumpkin carving contest for its fans, asking them to send in their best branded pumpkins. While this is often a proverbial crapshoot—even accounts with large followings might not create enough engagement to make these things interesting—it's an opportunity to suss out true fans and understand their aesthetic.

- **Feature User-Generated Content:** Share and promote the best submissions to give your followers a sense of recognition. When you have enough fans, it's helpful to feature their videos and remixes on your own channels. Again, the goal for any influencer is to create a two-way discussion between your fans and yourself. While this may be difficult for larger accounts, early influencers must cultivate these relationships. Remember, however, that this back-and-forth can be potentially dangerous. Share only as much as you're comfortable and share only things that are in earnest and are potentially beneficial to your fan and yourself.

- **Listen to the Noise:** Influencers "listen" to their audience through a variety of methods. This practice is often referred to as social listening. Early influencers would send their fan base to attack other Instagram or YouTube stars, creating small wars between specific fandoms. At this point in the influencer economy, there is no need to react or attempt to attack other like-minded folks. To paraphrase an old adage, it's far easier to build an audience with honey than vinegar.

Keep Track of Fan Sentiment

There are a few very specific ways to keep your finger on the pulse of your audience:

- **Social Media Tracking Tools:** Managers can use these tools to monitor mentions of their brand, competitors, and relevant industry topics across platforms. These tools allow for filtering and analysis, helping to spot trends, gauge sentiment, and flag potential issues. Tools like TweetHunter.io, for instance, can help identify content that aligns with a manager's interests, making it easier to engage with the broader conversation. Other platforms, like Sprout and TweetDeck, enable real-time tracking of specific topics. LinkedIn offers opportunities to build expertise by asking and answering questions on industry-related subjects. These tools can help broaden reach and authority in the field.

- **Hashtag Monitoring:** Following certain hashtags is another way managers can track conversations tied to their industry, products, or ongoing campaigns. Hashtags often center on topics like startups, brands, and events, and tapping into trending ones can occasionally boost content visibility. However, hashtag effectiveness has waned in recent years, and their impact is now considered limited.

- **Keyword-Based Searches:** Searching relevant keywords allows managers to find discussions connected to their brand or area of interest. When relevant conversations are found, joining in can help build authority. On LinkedIn, for example, responding to questions within the timeline can establish a professional presence and highlight expertise.

- **Sentiment Analysis:** This approach uses algorithms to assess the emotional tone in social media posts, enabling managers to get a sense of how audiences feel about their brand or products. Sentiment analysis sometimes uses natural language processing (NLP) and machine learning algorithms to assess the emotional tone of social media posts, reviews, and other user-generated content. This approach enables managers to understand whether the general sentiment around their brand, products, or specific topics is positive, negative, or neutral.

By effectively listening to social media chatter, influencers can gain insights into their audience, identify potential branding opportunities, and address community concerns proactively. This is actually one of the most important aspects of branding. It's a way of figuring out the context of the landscape you are playing in.

One other quick and easy way to stay abreast of news in your niche is to create a Google alert. To start, visit the Google Alerts website at google.com/alerts. In the search bar at the top of the page, enter the keyword or phrase you want to track. You'll see a preview of the types of results you might receive based on your keyword. You can customize the alert by clicking "Show Options" to choose how often you want to receive updates, the types of sources (news, blogs, etc.), and the region or language. Once you're satisfied with your settings, click the "Create Alert" button. Google will then send email notifications whenever new content containing your chosen keyword is published online.

Responding to Comments and Messages

Managing an influencer's audience goes beyond simply posting content—it requires active engagement. Responding to comments and messages is crucial to building strong relationships with followers. Tools like Instagram's Direct Message and Comments Manager, Facebook's Creator Studio, and TikTok's inbox feature help streamline this process by allowing influencers to respond quickly and efficiently. There are also third-party tools, like Hootsuite and Sprout Social, which consolidate comments and messages across multiple platforms. Actively engaging with followers

CHAPTER 5   CRAFTING YOUR PERSONAL BRAND: BUILDING A UNIQUE IDENTITY IN A CROWDED SPACE

fosters loyalty and helps create a community around the influencer's content. It shows that the influencer values their audience's input, which can drive higher engagement over time.

Asking Questions

Encouraging open dialogue by asking questions is a key method for increasing engagement and understanding audience preferences. Tools like Instagram Stories' question stickers or Twitter polls allow influencers to ask their followers for feedback in real time. These features enable followers to share their thoughts easily, making them feel more connected to the influencer. Influencers can use these insights to fine-tune their content strategy and ensure they're addressing the topics and issues their audience cares about. Asking questions also invites ongoing interaction, turning passive followers into active participants in the conversation.

Tracking Metrics

Influencers need to keep a close eye on key metrics to measure the success of their content. These include engagement rates, impressions, reach, follower growth, and click-through rates. Most social media platforms offer built-in analytics tools, but influencers can also use external tools like Metricool, Iconosquare, or Social Blade for a more comprehensive view. Monitoring these metrics helps influencers understand what type of content works best, identify their most engaged followers, and spot trends in their audience's behavior. This data-driven approach is essential for refining content strategy and growing a loyal audience over time.

Analyzing Trends

Staying on top of trends is crucial for remaining relevant in the fast-paced world of social media. Influencers can use tools like Google Trends,

BuzzSumo, and Exploding Topics to identify popular content ideas and stay ahead of the curve. Participating in viral challenges, like TikTok dances or meme formats, allows influencers to tap into trending conversations and increase their visibility. Understanding trends in audience behavior and preferences also helps influencers know when to post certain types of content, ensuring that they align with the mood of the moment and meet audience expectations.

Gathering Direct Feedback

To gain a deeper understanding of their audience, influencers can use tools to create polls, surveys, and Q&A sessions. Instagram's poll and question stickers, Facebook polls, and Google Forms are great ways to gather direct feedback from followers. This allows influencers to ask their audience specific questions about what they like, what they need, and what they want to see more of. Gathering this data helps influencers stay in tune with their followers' evolving interests and ensures that their content remains relevant and engaging.

Participating in Discussions

Joining online communities and forums related to their niche is another way for influencers to stay connected with their audience. Platforms like Reddit, Discord, and Faccbook Groups are great places to see what topics are trending and what people in their audience are talking about. Tools like Feedly and Pocket can help influencers curate and track content from niche communities and discussions. Actively participating in these conversations not only gives influencers insight into audience interests but also positions them as thought leaders within their community.

One-on-One Interactions

Direct, personal interactions with followers can make an audience feel special and valued. Tools like Instagram Direct, personalized video messages on Cameo, or live Q&A sessions on platforms like YouTube or Instagram Live foster a sense of intimacy and connection. These one-on-one interactions help influencers build deeper relationships with their followers, making them feel seen and appreciated. By taking the time to interact personally with fans, influencers create loyal, engaged communities that are more likely to support and share their content.

Meeting Fans

In-person interactions are powerful for deepening audience connections. Influencers can attend events like VidCon, which brings together thousands of creators and fans, or host smaller, more intimate meet-and-greets. Tools like Eventbrite or Facebook Events can help organize these gatherings. Meeting followers face-to-face solidifies relationships and often leads to lifelong supporters. Even smaller events, like local meetups or workshops, allow influencers to engage with their audience in a personal, meaningful way, fostering a community around their content.

By actively listening to their audience, influencers can tailor their content to better meet their followers' needs and expectations, fostering stronger connections and building a loyal community. The personal connection can also be the real magic in a community—followers want to engage with their favorite influencers and community.

Collabs

Teaming up with other influencers in your niche or related fields can expand your reach and introduce your content to a broader audience. Collaborations can take many forms: joint livestreams, co-hosted podcasts, shared videos, or even mutual Q&A sessions. Collaborating in this way not only brings fresh ideas to your content but also allows both you and your partner to benefit from each other's unique audience insights and engagement styles. One tip? Collaborate "down" by finding smaller influencers who can benefit from your mentorship, audience, and experience. While this might seem counterintuitive, some of your strongest allies will be folks that you helped on their way up.

Support Each Other Authentically: Build a community of mutual support with other influencers by promoting each other's work when it resonates with your brand. This approach isn't about artificially boosting numbers; rather, it's about organically engaging with content that you genuinely enjoy and find valuable. For instance, if another influencer's insights are relevant to your audience, sharing that can enhance your followers' experience and help establish a network of trusted peers.

Be Transparent and Open-Minded: Transparency is essential to build credibility and trust. Share your thoughts, experiences, and even challenges honestly, and consider engaging with influencers who may have different viewpoints. Working with those who bring diverse perspectives can add depth to your content and foster a dynamic environment where both of your audiences benefit. When followers see influencers engaging in real, open dialogue, it builds a sense of authenticity and attracts fans who value these genuine exchanges.

Build Relationships Over Time: Cultivating lasting relationships in the influencer space relies on consistency and authenticity. People follow influencers not just for their content, but also for the personal connection and life updates. Sharing your journey and growth—whether it's career milestones, lessons learned, or personal stories—helps followers feel they're part of your story. Gary Vaynerchuk is a prime example of this, sharing his entrepreneurial journey in a relatable and grounded way that keeps his followers invested over time.

Focus on Community Building: Ultimately, success in influencing is about building a loyal and engaged community. This means valuing each follower as a unique individual who trusts your voice and values your insights. By engaging meaningfully and treating your audience with respect, you can cultivate a supportive base that goes beyond numbers and supports you for the long haul.

Creating "Less Edited" Content

In today's digital age, oversaturated with polished and perfect content, authenticity has become increasingly valuable. Less edited content can foster a deeper connection with your audience. Here's how to achieve it:

Embracing imperfection means letting your personality and quirks show, rather than striving for perfection. Being yourself and allowing your raw, unfiltered side to come through—whether through behind-the-scenes footage or candid moments—creates a more personal connection with your audience. People appreciate vulnerability and respond to authenticity.

CHAPTER 5 CRAFTING YOUR PERSONAL BRAND: BUILDING A UNIQUE IDENTITY IN A CROWDED SPACE

Limiting editing can also enhance authenticity. While basic post-production can help improve audio and video quality, avoid over-editing. Rely on natural lighting and sound whenever possible, focusing on substance rather than appearance. This approach keeps the emphasis on the message itself, making it strong enough to stand alone. Sharing personal stories and meaningful anecdotes can help resonate with your audience on a deeper level.

Maintaining quality is still important, even with less edited content. While aiming for a natural and raw feel, ensure your content is visually and audibly appealing. Balancing authenticity with professionalism helps you present an image that aligns with your story without compromising quality. Less edited content feels genuine, builds trust, and deepens connections, leading to more meaningful engagement.

Take risks and allow your unique voice to shine, including unpolished moments or behind-the-scenes footage. This approach helps you stand out and makes your content resonate more strongly. Collaborating with like-minded influencers who align with your values is also important. Avoid forced partnerships, as authenticity in collaboration is crucial for growth and reputation. Building trust with followers, who often feel personally invested in their influencers, is essential, especially as transparency in sponsorships becomes more expected.

Being mindful of tone on social media is also key. Mistakes and unpopular opinions happen, and having a plan to apologize when needed is part of managing your online presence. Followers are quick to notice missteps, so thoughtful responses go a long way in maintaining trust.

Finally, embrace vulnerability by sharing your struggles and honest thoughts. Opening up without fear of judgment strengthens your connection with your audience and enhances the authenticity of your content.

Remember, authenticity is a journey, not a destination. Stay true to yourself and your values, and you'll build a loyal and engaged following. Building an inclusive online community requires a conscious effort to create a welcoming and supportive environment for everyone. Here are some strategies to consider.

Establishing Clear Community Guidelines

The world has enough hatred and vitriol. As influencers, we're encouraged to share the truth but also express our positivity and desire for growth. For example, we don't like to "work blue," as it were, when producing content. Working blue is an old comedian's term for cursing on stage or talking about unpleasant things in a way that is not constructive. Working blue, in the influencer's context, is akin to insulting your audience. Choose your words and your views carefully.

This goes for your audience as well. We recommend having clear rules and examples for interaction that you either state outright on your profile or work into your posts over time.

Clearly define acceptable behavior, including respectful communication, avoiding discrimination, and promoting inclusivity. Ensure that guidelines are consistently enforced to maintain a safe and welcoming space. Or maintain moderation to suit the mood of your community. Elon Musk and X have a much different idea of moderation than, say, Threads. Enforcing doesn't mean more than deciding what your community boundaries are.

> **Encourage Representation**: Actively seek and promote content that includes diverse perspectives. One-sided narratives limit engagement and interest, so strive to bring multiple viewpoints into your work. For example, if you're posting about books, consider expanding beyond your usual authors and exploring voices from different backgrounds or cultures. When it comes to food, try diving into global cuisines and discussing how they influence

CHAPTER 5 CRAFTING YOUR PERSONAL BRAND: BUILDING A UNIQUE IDENTITY IN A CROWDED SPACE

your tastes and understanding of the world. Reaction videos are a popular way to explore diverse perspectives—one influencer, for instance, saw a video about "wine pie" online. Instead of dismissing it, another influencer tried the recipe, shared the results, and sparked a new dialogue around it. Consider doing a similar reaction video yourself, perhaps by exploring recipes or ideas from other cultures. Such content not only diversifies your feed but also shows your audience that you're open to new experiences and perspectives.

Celebrate Differences: Showcase the unique experiences and contributions of all community members, whether your group is united around a hobby, shared experience, or even a favorite historical figure. Inclusivity doesn't mean catering to everyone but rather creating a space where people feel accepted for who they are. For example, your community might be a gathering place for fans of a specific president or political figure, and that's okay too. In the often uncivil world of online communities, managing civility becomes essential. Strong moderation and setting clear boundaries, such as using the block button judiciously, can go a long way in maintaining a respectful space.

Create Safe Spaces: Encourage your community members to share their thoughts and experiences openly, without fear of judgment. Creating a safe and supportive environment can build deep connections, as people feel more at ease when they know their opinions and stories are welcomed.

CHAPTER 5   CRAFTING YOUR PERSONAL BRAND: BUILDING A UNIQUE IDENTITY IN A CROWDED SPACE

Direct messages (DMs) can serve as a powerful tool to strengthen these relationships. Engage in one-on-one interactions, giving each member a chance to feel valued and understood within your community.

Listen Actively: Take feedback seriously and address concerns as they arise. Active listening not only strengthens your community but also fosters trust, as people feel heard and respected. Responding promptly to feedback, especially around sensitive topics, demonstrates your commitment to an inclusive and positive environment. Listening goes beyond merely hearing words; it's about understanding and acknowledging the needs and concerns of your audience.

Right now, the social media world is filled with bad actors. Here are some ways of controlling negative energy, which can chase people away and ding your brand:

Model Inclusive Behavior: Lead by example by treating everyone in your community with respect and empathy. Inclusivity starts at the top, and your behavior sets the standard. When you engage with others kindly and listen openly, you create a tone that others will follow. Show others that everyone's contributions are valued, and be open to a variety of viewpoints. Modeling this behavior encourages others to do the same, helping to build a community that feels safe and respectful for all members.

Encourage Positive Interactions: Foster a culture of kindness, encouragement, and support. When members interact positively, it strengthens the community and makes it a place where people want to stay and engage. Set guidelines that promote kindness and discourage negativity, and acknowledge members who contribute in supportive ways. Recognize that a community built on respect and positive engagement is more likely to thrive, as people feel valued and uplifted by the experience.

Consider Accessibility: Make sure your community platform is accessible to people with disabilities. Accessibility isn't just about technology; it's a critical part of inclusivity. Social media is a vital platform within the disability community, particularly for social activism and advocacy. Making your platform accessible not only broadens your audience but also supports your brand or community's role in amplifying important conversations. When your space is accessible, you send a message that everyone is welcome and that your community values diverse voices and experiences.

Continuously Evaluate and Improve: Regularly gather feedback from community members to understand what's working and what could be better. Feedback is invaluable in helping you identify areas for improvement and keeping your community relevant. Be willing to adapt and evolve as needed to ensure that your space remains inclusive and welcoming. Effective moderation, such as blocking disruptive members, can also help maintain harmony. Assessing whether followers "mesh" well with other members helps ensure

CHAPTER 5 CRAFTING YOUR PERSONAL BRAND: BUILDING A UNIQUE IDENTITY IN A CROWDED SPACE

that the community maintains a positive, cohesive environment. Adaptability and openness to change are essential in creating a dynamic, inclusive space where everyone feels they belong.

By implementing these strategies, you can create an online community where everyone feels valued, respected, and included. Remember, building an inclusive community is an ongoing process that requires constant attention and effort.

Don't hesitate to try out different content formats and styles to see what resonates best with your audience. Experimentation allows you to discover fresh approaches that could engage your followers in new ways. After launching different types of content, analyze the results to track which pieces perform well and draw the most engagement. Understanding these patterns will help you refine your content strategy and focus on what works best.

High-quality images and videos are essential for capturing attention and making a strong impression. Visual appeal can often be the difference between a quick scroll past and a viewer stopping to engage. Consider using graphics such as infographics, memes, or other visual aids to convey information in a concise, engaging way. Visual content is not only eye-catching but also makes complex information more digestible for your audience.

Connect with your audience on an emotional level by sharing relatable narratives and personal anecdotes. Storytelling adds depth and makes your content memorable, as people tend to resonate more with authentic, human experiences. Use effective storytelling techniques, like setting the scene or adding a narrative arc, to keep your audience engaged and invested in your message. A strong story can turn casual viewers into loyal followers who feel connected to you and your journey.

Keep up with the latest trends and developments in your niche to ensure your content stays relevant. Knowing what's popular or timely allows you to create content that aligns with current interests and conversations. Be flexible and willing to adjust your content strategy as needed, incorporating new topics or formats to stay fresh. Adaptability is key in a constantly evolving online landscape, helping you maintain relevance and engagement with your audience.

By following these guidelines, you can create content that not only attracts and retains followers but also establishes you as a trusted authority in your field. Remember, quality over quantity is key. Focus on producing meaningful content that truly resonates with your audience, and you'll be well on your way to influencer success.

Be patient. Building a successful personal brand takes time and effort. Don't get discouraged if you don't see results overnight. Many of the accounts with millions of people are both long-term and have large budgets. Stay consistent within your goals.

Case Studies

Here are a few case studies of successful influencers who have built strong personal brands by honing distinct voices, connecting deeply with their audiences, and staying consistent in their messaging:

> **Gary Vaynerchuk**: Gary Vaynerchuk, also known as "Gary Vee," is a serial entrepreneur, author, and renowned social media influencer. His no-nonsense, energetic style is instantly recognizable, as he frequently shares advice on entrepreneurship, marketing, and digital media through platforms like Instagram, TikTok, and YouTube. Vaynerchuk's success stems from his authenticity and the way he shares personal stories, hardships, and lessons learned in business. His brand is built around "hustle culture," where he emphasizes hard work,

CHAPTER 5   CRAFTING YOUR PERSONAL BRAND: BUILDING A UNIQUE IDENTITY IN A CROWDED SPACE

patience, and resilience. He connects with his audience by responding to comments, offering real-time advice, and even doing live Q&A sessions to address their questions and concerns directly. Vaynerchuk's approach has not only made him a sought-after speaker but also a trusted figure for aspiring entrepreneurs and marketers.

What He Does Right: Gary is a blunt speaker. All of his videos feature him saying things you probably wouldn't hear in business school. This endears him to his audience. He also has excellent production quality. He runs multiple video podcasts that feature different topics, and he sells books and courses based on his experience.

Marie Forleo: Marie Forleo is a business coach, author, and popular online influencer known for her uplifting and empowering messages. Her personal brand, often represented by the slogan "Everything is Figureoutable," focuses on inspiring people to overcome self-doubt and achieve their life and business goals. Forleo has built a multimedia empire that includes a YouTube show, *MarieTV*, online courses, and best-selling books. Her content on personal development, entrepreneurship, and creativity is both practical and motivational, giving her audience actionable steps and mindset shifts to make progress. She often shares success stories from her clients and followers, creating a community atmosphere that resonates with those seeking both business and personal growth. Forleo's positive and relatable personality has made her a go-to voice in the self-help and business coaching industry.

What She Does Right: Marie has created multiple routes into viewers' hearts and minds. By producing multiple streams, including courses and books, she has expanded from the traditional influencer role into a multimedia organization. This is often the best route for CEOs and other highly skilled people—by telling your story multiple times and in multiple ways, you expand your reach considerably.

Michelle Khare: Michelle Khare is a YouTuber and travel influencer who captures her adventures with an enthusiasm and curiosity that attracts viewers looking for authentic travel experiences. Known for her adventurous spirit, Khare immerses herself in local cultures, sharing destination guides, cultural insights, and travel tips that go beyond typical tourism content. Her "Challenge Accepted" series on YouTube, where she tries out demanding jobs and lifestyles (from astronaut training to firefighter boot camps), has expanded her brand beyond travel into personal challenge and growth content. This combination has allowed her to create a relatable, adventurous brand that resonates with a broad audience. Khare's willingness to step outside her comfort zone and bring her followers along for the journey has cultivated a loyal fan base who look up to her as a relatable and courageous content creator.

What She Does Right: Khare puts herself into uncomfortable situations, including trying to perform one of Houdini's most difficult tricks or trying out for Secret Service training. This fish-out-of-water style of content is popular with younger viewers who might be trying to escape the humdrum of daily life. Further, she pivoted many times and has moved from travel content to something decidedly more exciting.

These influencers have built strong personal brands by remaining true to their unique styles, engaging with their audiences, and consistently delivering value through diverse yet focused content. By learning from these case studies, you can develop a strong personal brand that resonates with people and positions you as a trusted, inspiring voice in your field.

Key Takeaways

- Personal branding must align with authenticity and genuine passion. Influencers like Gary Vaynerchuk and Marie Forleo built their brands by staying true to their personalities while delivering consistent value through multiple channels like books, courses, and social media.

- Quality content production requires understanding your audience deeply and maintaining high production standards. Even simple content like Dimitra Neonaki's Roman ruin tours succeeds through clear audio, steady video, and expert knowledge rather than fancy equipment or overproduction.

CHAPTER 5   CRAFTING YOUR PERSONAL BRAND: BUILDING A UNIQUE IDENTITY IN A CROWDED SPACE

- Community building happens through active engagement and genuine interaction. Responding to comments, participating in discussions, and creating opportunities for direct feedback are crucial for building a loyal following.

- Personal brand development requires patience and strategic planning. Start with clear goals, understanding your niche thoroughly, and accept that building a successful influence takes time. Top influencers often took years to build their current followings, and many invested significant resources to reach their level of success.

CHAPTER 6

Content Creation 101: Strategies for Captivating Your Audience

Content creation is the key to a successful social media strategy.

This is the work that represents you publicly, attracts your audience, and ultimately explains why people follow influencers. Content comes in countless forms, and people follow accounts for a range of reasons: for knowledge, community, entertainment, networking, or even a sense of personal connection with creators. This process of creating is also highly creative. Whether someone is documenting a journey, seeking to connect with like-minded individuals, or establishing expertise in a field, social media's dynamic nature offers endless opportunities. Platforms and creators constantly evolve, driven by trends and community shifts. For example, while TikTok started as a lip-syncing app, it's now a hub for everything from cooking and beauty to fashion and education, even functioning as a search engine for younger users.

Content trends evolve rapidly, yet one thing stays consistent: people want authentic connections with creators. High-profile influencers like Kim Kardashian attract millions with polished, aspirational content, but

CHAPTER 6   CONTENT CREATION 101: STRATEGIES FOR CAPTIVATING YOUR AUDIENCE

millions more seek out creators whose unique perspectives resonate with them personally. Influencers today come in endless varieties, each offering something distinctive. For example, fashion might include Kim Kardashian's sleek brand, but it also includes smaller creators who specialize in vintage fashion and whose loyal followers eagerly await every haul. While large accounts have massive reach and resources, they also require significant overhead and large production teams. Meanwhile, smaller creators are gaining traction and can make an impact with fewer resources. Trends increasingly favor smaller, more engaged accounts and the more authentic, individualized styles they offer. Audiences now look for what makes a creator's voice unique rather than fitting a single aesthetic mold.

Agility is another key to successful content creation. Today, you'll find creators capturing and editing high-quality content on an iPhone just as often as you'll see a full-scale production team. What matters most is that content tells *your* story. While high-quality editing has its place, over-editing can be a turn-off; many creators use tools like Canva, which are simple yet effective. This ease of use is essential because platforms reward consistency and genuine effort over heavily polished content. Creators can set their own style and aesthetic, with countless tools at their disposal, and social media thrives on this creative freedom. The most effective content creation is fun, interactive, and quick-moving. Great content creators understand that social media is a relationship—a space where knowledge, stories, and ideas are shared in real time. The best accounts build trust and community; while virality can't be guaranteed, quality can be.

Content creators can use a range of formats tailored to their audience and topics. These formats include videos, images, audio content, and written works, each contributing to a well-rounded, engaging online presence.

All of this isn't easy. Content creators must now be

- Videographers
- Email experts
- HTML coders
- Social media managers
- Copywriters
- Designers
- Photographers
- Educators
- Explorers

If that sounds difficult, that's because it is. But it also means you can become one of the most amazing content creators out there with just a little effort.

Influencer Insider: Lindsay Adler

Lindsay Adler is a prominent New York City–based fashion and portrait photographer whose influence extends far beyond her commercial success. Known for her dramatic, high-contrast style, Adler's work has graced the pages of *Marie Claire*, *InStyle*, and *Elle*, and she has collaborated with major brands like Canon, Adobe, and Profoto. This high-profile work initially helped her gain visibility, but her journey to becoming an influencer was driven largely by her dedication to teaching and sharing her craft with aspiring photographers.

Adler stands out in the industry for her commitment to education. She has created a wealth of instructional content on platforms like CreativeLive and KelbyOne, where her practical, hands-on approach has earned her a loyal following of photographers eager to learn her techniques. Her book, *The Linked Photographers' Guide to Online Marketing and Social Media*, was one of the first in the field to guide photographers through the complexities of online branding and social media, helping professionals navigate these new channels to build their businesses. This focus on accessible education has cemented her as a trusted authority.

Her industry recognitions, including being named a Canon Explorer of Light and a Profoto Legend of Light, further amplified her influence. These titles are awarded to elite photographers who demonstrate both technical mastery and a passion for inspiring others, solidifying her role as a mentor and role model in the field. Adler's influence is not only about her striking images but also about her ability to blend technical skill with accessible education, making her a go-to resource for photographers around the world seeking inspiration and practical guidance.

Lindsay Adler's approach to photography and education provides specific insights and practical advice that can help anyone elevate their photo and video skills, regardless of their experience level. Here are some top strategies inspired by her for taking better photos and videos.

Master Lighting Techniques

Natural Light: Photographers often emphasize the power of natural light for beginners. Start by practicing in areas with abundant, soft natural light, such as near a large window. Use sheer curtains as diffusers to soften harsh light, which can help eliminate shadows and give a more polished look to your photos.

Artificial Lighting: Experimenting with different light sources like LED panels, strobes, or softboxes allows more control. Equipment like Profoto lighting is versatile, and positioning lights at a 45-degree angle can create flattering, natural-looking shadows.

Lighting Ratios: Adjusting lighting ratios can add depth and mood to images. For example, a one-to-two lighting ratio can bring a dramatic, high-contrast look to portraits, while soft backlighting creates a warm, glowing effect.

Use the Golden Hour

The golden hour (Figure 6-1) in videography and photography is the period shortly after sunrise or just before sunset when the sun is low on the horizon, casting warm, diffused light that enhances images and footage. During this time, sunlight takes on a soft, golden hue that can add warmth and depth to scenes, often resulting in more flattering, natural lighting that brings out colors, textures, and contours. Here's why the golden hour works so well:

- **Soft, Diffused Light**: Because the sun is low, its light is scattered across a larger area, reducing harsh shadows and minimizing the intensity of highlights. This soft light is especially flattering for portraits as it reduces blemishes and adds a gentle glow to the skin.

- **Warm Tones**: The color temperature of golden-hour light is warmer than midday light, giving images and videos a rich, golden tone that's often associated with warmth, nostalgia, and romance. This color effect can enhance skin tones and make landscapes more vibrant.

- **Longer Shadows**: The angle of the sun creates long shadows, adding dimension and depth to photos and videos. These shadows can emphasize shapes and add layers to compositions, which can be creatively used for dramatic effects in both landscapes and portraits.

- **Enhanced Color Saturation**: Because of the lower light intensity, colors appear more saturated and less washed out than they might under the direct midday sun. This saturation is especially beneficial for nature shots, urban landscapes, and skin tones in portraits, providing a richer, more vivid palette.

Figure 6-1. The golden hour. Image via Wikipedia

Techniques for Shooting During the Golden Hour

- **Backlighting**: Positioning the subject with the sun behind them can create beautiful rim lighting, where light outlines the subject. This technique works well for adding a soft glow around people or objects.

- **Silhouettes:** The warm, directional light can also create dramatic silhouettes if the subject is placed directly in front of the sun, giving an image or video a striking contrast between light and dark areas.

- **Lens Flares:** The lower angle of the sun makes it easier to capture natural lens flares by positioning the camera toward the light source. This adds a dreamy, cinematic effect often sought after in both photography and videography.

Golden hour's unique quality of light is highly sought after by photographers and videographers alike for its ability to create visually compelling, emotive scenes that feel both natural and dramatic.

Use Composition Techniques to Guide the Viewer's Eye

Rule of Thirds: The rule of thirds divides an image into a grid of nine equal parts (Figure 6-2). Placing key elements along these grid lines or at intersections can help create balance and naturally guide the viewer's eye. For example, in this photograph, the photographer cropped the image so the horizon was along the bottom third and the tree was contained along the far-right line. This kind of composition draws the viewer into the scene and creates a more pleasing and compelling scene. Most cellphones have a rule of thirds grid available in the Camera app. Look for it in your settings.

CHAPTER 6   CONTENT CREATION 101: STRATEGIES FOR CAPTIVATING YOUR AUDIENCE

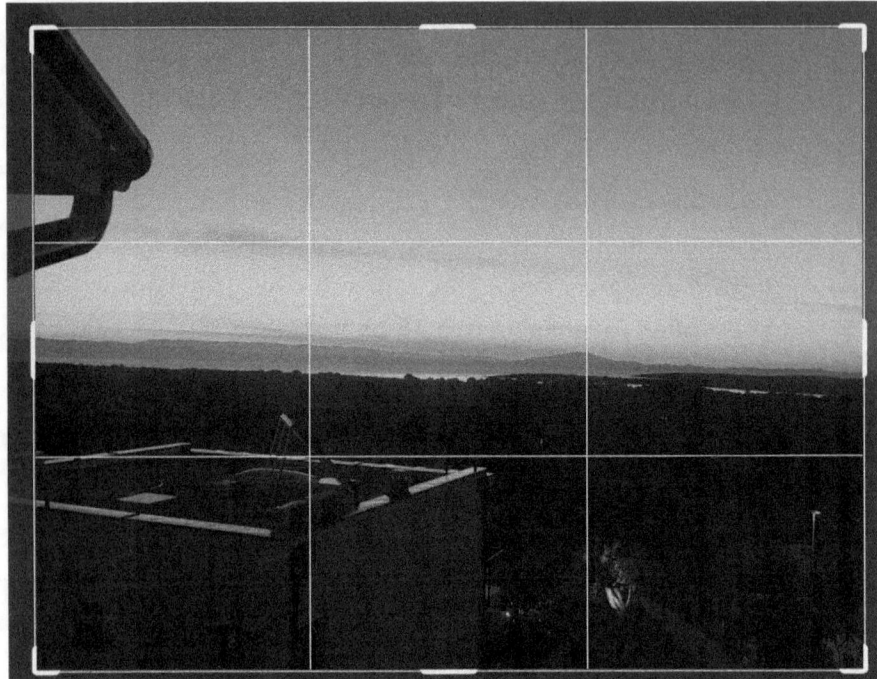

Figure 6-2. *A photo cropped to the rule of thirds. Credit: John Biggs*

> ***Leading Lines and Framing:*** Incorporating leading lines (such as roads, railings, or pathways) can direct the viewer's gaze toward the subject, creating a strong focal point (Figure 6-3). Framing subjects within natural elements, such as windows or doorways, creates depth and draws attention to the main focus of the image.

Figure 6-3. *Leading lines on a cathedral. Credit: John Biggs*

Prioritize Sharp Focus and Use Depth of Field Creatively

In photography, mastering focus and depth of field can transform a simple image into a powerful visual story. Sharp focus directs the viewer's attention to key details, while depth of field allows you to control what remains sharp and what fades into a soft blur, shaping the image's mood and composition. With lenses, these effects are achieved primarily through aperture settings. For instance, using a low f-stop (like f/1.8 or f/2.8) produces a shallow depth of field, which isolates the subject against a smooth, blurred background—perfect for portraits where you want the eyes to captivate. A higher f-stop (such as f/8 or f/11) increases depth of field, bringing more of the scene into focus, making it suitable for landscapes or group shots where more detail is desired. With practice and the right settings, you can creatively use focus and depth of field to elevate your photography.

Focus on the Eyes: Especially in portrait photography, sharp eyes are crucial. Using a single-point autofocus and locking onto the subject's eye creates a captivating, engaging portrait.

Experiment with Aperture for Depth of Field: Playing with aperture settings can significantly impact your image. A low f-stop (e.g., f/1.8 or f/2.8) creates a shallow depth of field, making the subject stand out against a blurred background, ideal for portrait and close-up photography. Conversely, a higher f-stop (e.g., f/8 or f/11) will bring more of the scene into focus, great for landscape and group shots.

Enhance Your Storytelling Through Visual Style

Establishing a consistent aesthetic is essential for photographers looking to build a distinct visual identity. By consistently using a specific color palette or lighting setup, your images become instantly recognizable and memorable, reinforcing your brand. Developing this unique style involves experimenting with different elements that evoke the emotions you want to communicate. Adding backgrounds and props is another powerful tool for enhancing storytelling within your images. Incorporating textured fabrics, natural elements, or urban features can add depth and context, creating a richer visual narrative around your subject. Through thoughtful choices in style and setting, photographers can craft images that not only attract attention but also convey a cohesive message.

Consistent Aesthetic Choices: A clear, consistent style helps build a brand identity. For example, using a particular color palette or lighting setup across your work can make your images instantly recognizable. Photographers are encouraged to experiment and develop a unique style that aligns with the emotions they want to evoke.

Background and Props: Integrating props and textured backgrounds can add interest to photos. Using fabrics, plants, or urban elements enhances storytelling by adding layers of context around your subject.

Utilize Movement in Video for Dynamic Shots

In videography, incorporating controlled camera movements and timing adjustments can bring a dynamic, cinematic quality to your shots. Subtle movements like pans and tilts add depth, and using a gimbal stabilizer for handheld shots helps achieve smooth, polished footage. Slowly moving around the subject also allows you to capture varied angles, making the scene more engaging. Techniques like slow motion add emphasis to specific moments, ideal for fashion or action-focused scenes. Speed ramping, where the footage transitions seamlessly between slow and regular speed, can further highlight key parts of a scene, guiding the viewer's focus and adding dramatic impact.

Camera Movement: Subtle camera movements, like pans or tilts, can create a more cinematic feel in video. For handheld shots, a gimbal stabilizer can ensure smooth, professional-looking footage. Moving around the subject slowly can help capture different angles, adding variety and interest.

Slow Motion and Speed Ramping: Adding slow motion to highlight specific moments can be powerful, especially in fashion or action-focused shoots. Speed ramping, where you smoothly transition between slow and regular speed, can draw attention to key parts of the scene.

Make the Most of Post-production

Editing software is an essential tool for photographers, allowing them to make subtle adjustments that enhance a photo without losing its natural feel. Programs like Adobe Lightroom and Photoshop offer a range of options, and beginners can start with basics like adjusting exposure, contrast, and white balance to refine their images gently. For a cohesive look across multiple photos, presets or filters are helpful in creating consistency, while color grading adds depth by shaping the mood and tone. Experimenting with these tools can help photographers achieve a polished, unified aesthetic that complements their creative vision.

Editing Software: Tools like Adobe Lightroom and Photoshop are valuable for photo editing, focusing on subtle enhancements rather than over-editing. We particularly like Pixelmator Pro for its price

CHAPTER 6   CONTENT CREATION 101: STRATEGIES FOR CAPTIVATING YOUR AUDIENCE

and ease of use. For beginners, starting with basic adjustments—tweaking exposure, contrast, and white balance—helps maintain the natural look of the photo while enhancing it.

Things to Try

Here's a series of steps to help get the most out of a photo in Photoshop, focusing on foundational tools and features to enhance and refine images.

1. Adjust Exposure and Contrast (Figure 6-4)

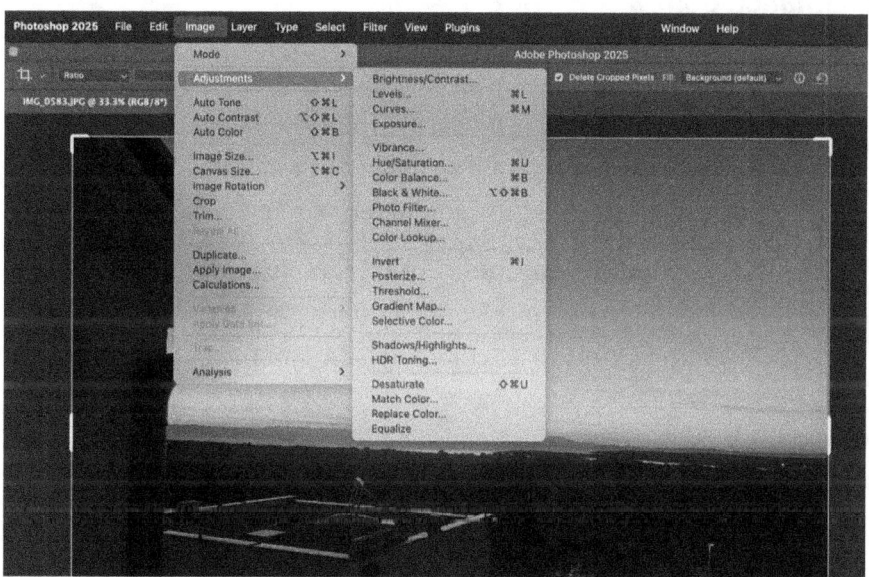

Figure 6-4. The Photoshop Adjustments menu

- **Brightness/Contrast**: Start with adjusting overall brightness and contrast to bring out details. Go to *Image ▶ Adjustments ▶ Brightness/Contrast* and move the sliders to find a balanced look.

103

- **Levels:** For more control, use *Levels* (*Image ➤ Adjustments ➤ Levels*) to adjust the shadows, midtones, and highlights individually.

- **Curves:** If you want even finer control, *Curves* (*Image ➤ Adjustments ➤ Curves*) allows you to brighten or darken specific tonal ranges by adjusting points along a curve.

- **Auto Mode:** You can also simply select auto settings, which will balance the photo using preset algorithms.

2. Enhance Colors

- **Color Balance:** Use *Color Balance* (*Image ➤ Adjustments ➤ Color Balance*) to adjust tones and remove color casts. You can enhance or reduce specific color ranges in shadows, midtones, or highlights.

- **Vibrance and Saturation:** For subtle color adjustments, *Vibrance* (found in *Image ➤ Adjustments ➤ Vibrance*) increases color intensity without oversaturating the photo.

- **Hue/Saturation:** For more direct control, *Hue/Saturation* (Ctrl+U or *Image ➤ Adjustments ➤ Hue/Saturation*) lets you adjust the saturation of individual colors, creating more defined adjustments.

3. Sharpen the Image (Figure 6-5)

Figure 6-5. Use the Filter menu to Sharpen and Stylize your photos

- **Unsharp Mask**: Go to *Filter ➤ Sharpen ➤ Unsharp Mask* and adjust the Amount, Radius, and Threshold. This tool sharpens edges and enhances details without introducing too much noise.

- **High Pass Filter**: For targeted sharpening, duplicate your layer, apply *Filter ➤ Other ➤ High Pass* to the new layer, and set the blend mode to *Overlay* or *Soft Light*. This sharpens edges while leaving flat areas unaffected.

4. Use Layers for Non-destructive Editing (Figure 6-6)

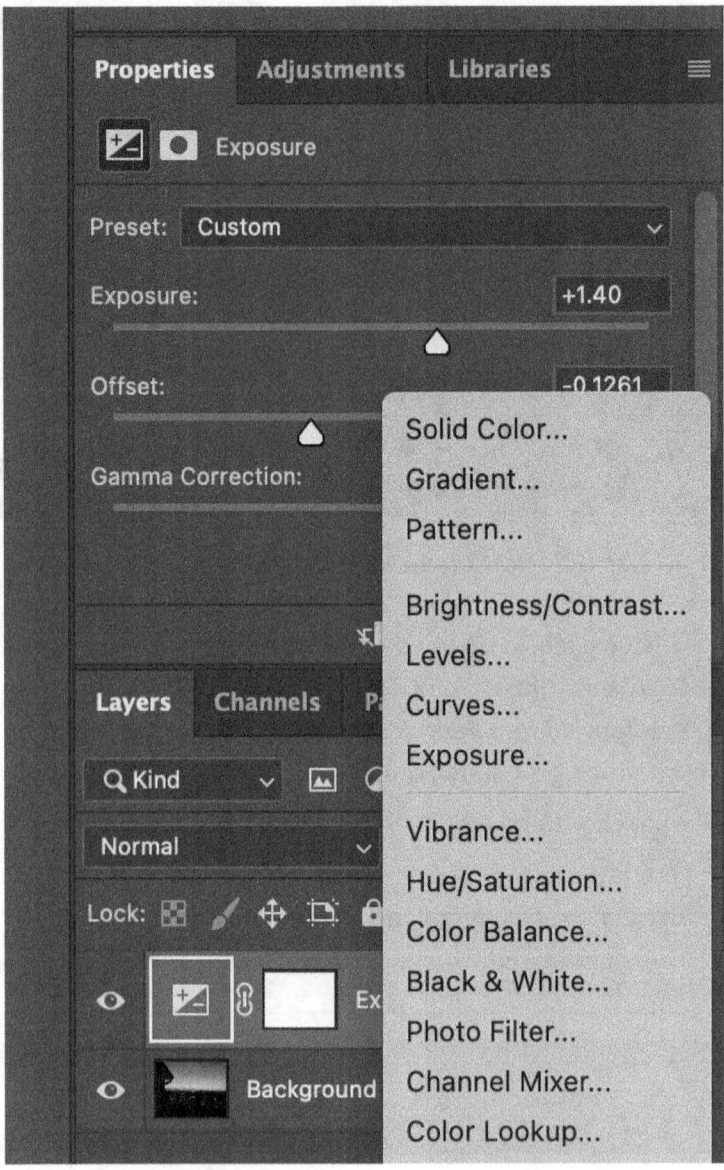

Figure 6-6. Layers at work

CHAPTER 6   CONTENT CREATION 101: STRATEGIES FOR CAPTIVATING YOUR AUDIENCE

- Work with adjustment layers, which can be found in the *Layers panel* under *Create New Fill or Adjustment Layer*. These layers (e.g., Levels, Curves, Hue/Saturation) allow you to make adjustments without directly changing the original image.

5. Retouch with the Healing Brush and Clone Stamp (Figure 6-7)

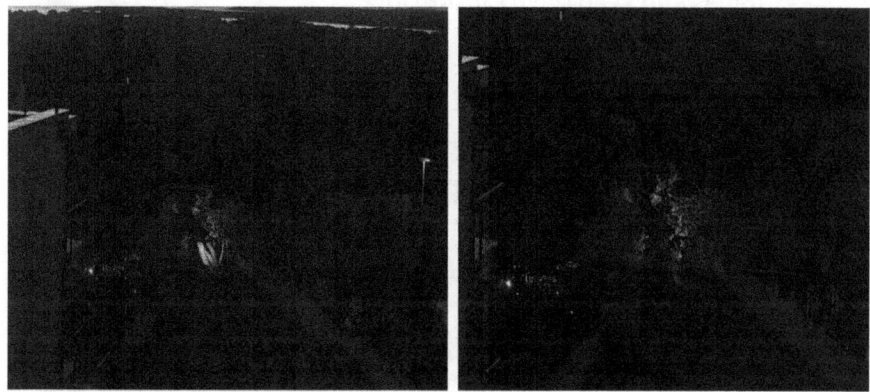

Figure 6-7. *Using the Healing Brush*

- **Spot Healing Brush**: This tool (J on the keyboard or *in the Tools panel*) is great for removing small imperfections. Simply click blemishes, dust, or minor distractions, and Photoshop automatically fills in the area.
- **Clone Stamp**: For more precise retouching, use the Clone Stamp (S on the keyboard). Alt-click to set a source point, and then paint over the areas you want to replace, ideal for more complex touch-ups.

107

6. Apply Dodge and Burn for Highlights and Shadows

- **Dodge Tool**: Use the *Dodge tool* (O on the keyboard) to brighten specific areas, like highlights on a subject's face. Set the Range to *Highlights* or *Midtones* and use a low Exposure (around 10–20%) for subtle adjustments.

- **Burn Tool**: Similarly, use the *Burn tool* to darken areas and add depth. Set the Range to *Shadows* for darker tones, and keep the Exposure low.

7. Work with Selections to Edit Specific Areas

- **Quick Selection Tool**: The Quick Selection tool (W on the keyboard) is useful for selecting parts of the image to edit. Once selected, adjustments like brightness, contrast, and color can be applied specifically to that area.

- **Select and Mask**: If you need a refined selection, use *Select and Mask* (found under *Select* ➤ *Select and Mask*) to smooth and feather edges.

8. Experiment with Color Grading

- **Color Lookup Adjustments**: For quick color grading, use *Color Lookup* adjustment layers (found in the Layers panel). These allow you to apply film-like color tones to your image.

- **Gradient Map**: A Gradient Map (found under *Image* ➤ *Adjustments* ➤ *Gradient Map*) can also create unique looks by mapping colors to tonal ranges in the image.

9. Crop and Straighten for Better Composition (Figure 6-8)

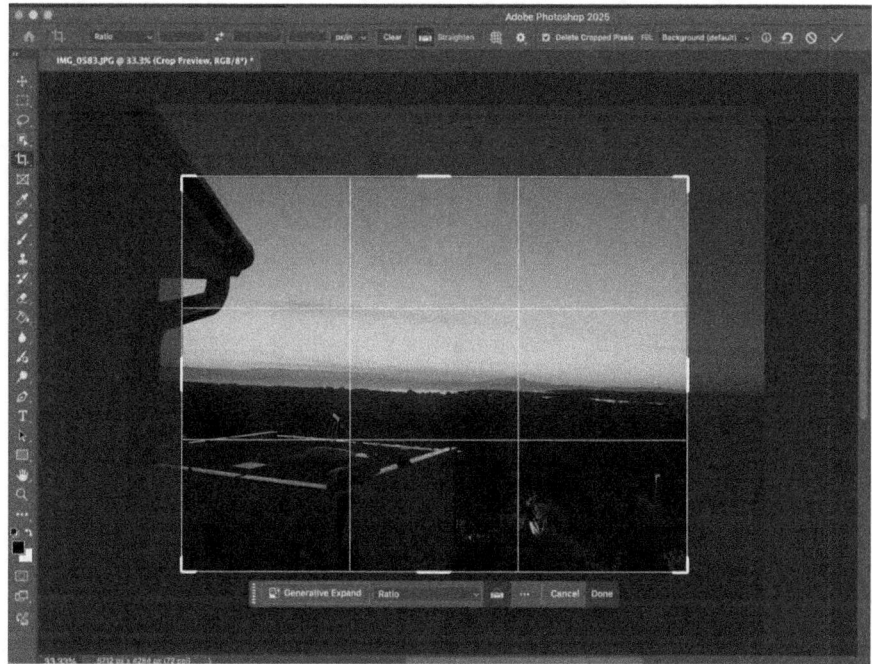

Figure 6-8. Crop and straighten

- **Crop Tool**: Use the Crop tool (C on the keyboard) to reframe the image. Adjust composition by following the rule of thirds or centering key elements.
- **Straighten Tool**: Inside the Crop tool, there's an option to straighten the image if the horizon or main lines are tilted.

Practice, Patience, and Experimentation

In photography, practice and patience are essential to refining your skills and developing your unique style. Trial and error allow photographers to explore different angles, lighting setups, and compositions, adapting each approach to the unique qualities of every scene. Taking multiple shots and evaluating the results helps build a deeper understanding of what works and why, sharpening your technique over time. Continued learning is equally important, as even experienced photographers benefit from staying current with new equipment, trends, and techniques. Through steady practice and a commitment to learning, photographers can evolve their craft and bring more depth and precision to their work.

> **Trial and Error:** Developing skills takes practice. Experiment with different angles, lighting setups, and compositions to find what works best in each unique situation. Taking multiple shots, analyzing them, and learning from each attempt can help refine technique.
>
> **Continued Learning:** Even seasoned professionals continue to learn and adapt. Exploring new equipment, trends, and techniques can keep skills fresh.

Crafting Compelling Social Media Content: A Visual and Copywriting Guide

Attention spans are short. Visual content lets people process quickly what your account's message is. To create compelling social media posts, it's essential to master the art of combining captivating visuals with persuasive copywriting.

First, some basics. In her book, *Capture Your Style*, Aimee Song offers a very simple glossary of terms that we thought might be helpful. We've paraphrased it here.

CHAPTER 6   CONTENT CREATION 101: STRATEGIES FOR CAPTIVATING YOUR AUDIENCE

Social Media Terms

Feed (Figure 6-9)

Figure 6-9. Your feed

Your Instagram profile, where all your photos live. Expect friends, exes, and colleagues to scroll through to catch up on your life since you joined the platform.

111

CHAPTER 6   CONTENT CREATION 101: STRATEGIES FOR CAPTIVATING YOUR AUDIENCE

Post

An individual photo you upload for others to see (or just your followers, if your account is private). Each post contributes to your feed. Posts on a blog are called blog posts, not blogs.

Handle (Figure 6-10)

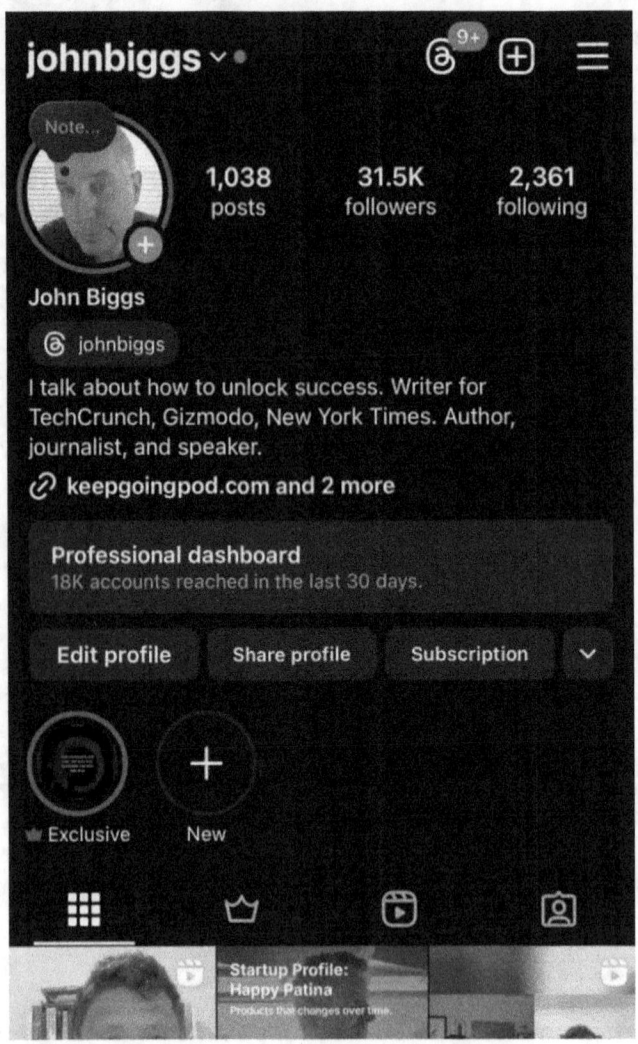

Figure 6-10. Your page with your handle

Your Instagram username, preceded by @, for instance, @johnbiggs.

Follow
Choosing to watch another user's posts so they appear in your home stream. You can also mute and unfollow users.

Stream or River
The collection of posts from accounts you follow, displayed on your main feed.

Story
These are the round circles at the top of some social media sites, notably Instagram. These are temporary images and clips that are designed for single-swipe consumption. You can add posts to your Story, thereby showing them to casual browsers who are usually friends.

Likes
The "double taps" you receive from followers on your photos. You might find yourself refreshing to see how many likes each post collects.

Caption
The text you add to each photo, describing it or adding context.

Hashtag
A single word or phrase without spaces, made searchable by adding a # symbol, for example, #GeniusIdea.

Visuals: The Core of Engagement

First, remember that influencing is mostly a visual medium. People stop scrolling when they see arresting visuals. Taking great photos and sharing them can definitely get you attention, but being extremely careful when it comes to lighting, layout, and design is equally important. Let's talk a bit about how to create great visuals:

- **High-Quality Imagery:** Content should have professional-quality photos or graphics. Blurred or low-resolution images can detract from your message.

Smartphones have genuinely high-tech cameras and are portable. Our recommendation, however, is to learn some basic photography and invest in a tripod and perhaps a steadicam device. There are a number of inexpensive options for influencers. Also, if you are shooting indoors (or even out), invest in some LED lights that offer warm and cold colors of varying intensity. These will help keep you well-lit while maintaining a natural effect.

- **Relevance and Authenticity**: Ensure visuals align with your brand's identity and the content's theme. Authentic, relatable images resonate with audiences. We went through a period where everything was heavily filtered, and it was all about the "aesthetic." That's over. Many influencers are producing content that looks rugged and rough, and artistic efforts are now rewarded. That doesn't mean you should make your work look bad in order to be cool, but a little authenticity goes a long way.

- **Visual Storytelling**: Use visuals to tell a story or evoke emotions. A well-crafted image can convey more than words alone. Every individual post/photo tells a story, but what is the actual goal of the accounts? What would you, the creator, like to showcase? Remember that your followers and fans see your life and, in a sense, covet it. They want to be your friend as you travel, eat, read, and enjoy life.

- **Visual Trends**: Keep up with emerging visual trends like short-form videos, GIFs, and interactive elements to stay relevant. Everything old can be new again, so feel free to mine old trends including stickers, animations, and the like. Also, don't be afraid to try new things as soon as you see them!

CHAPTER 6   CONTENT CREATION 101: STRATEGIES FOR CAPTIVATING YOUR AUDIENCE

The Power of Words

When crafting written content for social media, you have to consider various elements that make your message effective and engaging. First, think about the tone you want to set by asking key questions about your audience. **Who are they, what do they value, and where do they spend their time online?** By understanding these aspects, you can decide on an appropriate way to address them, whether it's professional, casual, humorous, or something else that resonates. What kinds of things would you want to read? And what kinds of things do you think they'd enjoy?

Next, prioritize clarity and conciseness in your writing. Keep your message straightforward and avoid jargon or complicated language that could alienate or confuse your audience. People engage more readily with content that's easy to understand and quickly digestible.

A strong call to action (CTA) is crucial to encourage interaction. Whether you want followers to comment, share, or visit a link, make your CTA direct and appealing. A clear invitation to engage can drive more interactions and boost visibility. You don't always have to have an "ask," but always make sure you're encouraging people to subscribe or like.

Emotional resonance also plays a key role in creating meaningful connections. When you appeal to your audience's emotions—whether through stories, humor, or relatable experiences—you foster a stronger bond and make your content more memorable. People tend to remember content that made them feel something, so don't hesitate to bring a touch of personality or relatability into your posts. Be real and be approachable.

Keyword optimization is another important element. By incorporating relevant keywords naturally within your content, you can enhance its discoverability and improve search rankings. This practice makes it easier for people to find your content when searching for related topics. This is often harder than it needs to be, but you're optimizing for views and traffic, potentially off a major social network; you will need to

115

consider keywords and hashtags. Unfortunately, the rise of AI has made it harder to game SEO algorithms.

Consistency is key for brand recognition and trust. Maintaining a consistent tone and style across all your social media platforms helps to establish a recognizable presence that followers can count on, whether they see your content on Instagram, LinkedIn, or Twitter. You will need to create a voice for yourself. Are you conversational? Cathartic? Funny? Pick one and keep writing in that style.

Lastly, consider breaking the fourth wall as part of your approach to tone. This technique, where you directly address your audience as if speaking to them one-on-one, adds a personal touch that can make followers feel like they're part of the conversation. While this style may not suit every brand, it can create a sense of intimacy and direct connection with your audience, fostering a more engaged and loyal following.

The Influencer Creation Process

Influencers usually follow a structured process for creating content, which includes planning, producing, and promoting. Note: all of these rules are meant to be broken. Feel free to experiment, repeat what works, and avoid what doesn't. Here's a more detailed look at each step.

1. Planning and Ideation

Look around. What are other influencers doing? What haven't you done yet? What trends are blowing up? If you need inspiration, simply scroll a bit to see what influencers are doing to spread their message. Are you a food writer? Film your favorite spot. Marketer? Do something wild in the style of a popular meme. The possibilities are endless.

- **Brainstorming**: Influencers begin by brainstorming ideas that align with their niche, personal brand, and current trends. They may draw inspiration from their own interests, audience feedback, and what's currently popular on social media.

- **Research**: To ensure their ideas are both relevant and unique, influencers research topics and keywords that resonate with their audience. They also examine competitor content to find gaps they can fill or identify areas where they can provide a fresh perspective.

- **Planning**: Once they have a list of content ideas, influencers organize these into a content calendar. This calendar helps them maintain a consistent posting schedule, ensuring their audience knows when to expect new posts and allowing them to plan around special events or seasonal trends.

2. Content Creation

- **Scripting**: For content like videos, podcasts, or tutorials, influencers often prepare scripts or outlines. This structure helps them stay organized, cover key points, and maintain flow throughout the content.

- **Filming or Shooting**: Influencers capture visuals and audio using equipment like cameras, smartphones, tripods, or microphones. Attention to lighting, angles, and sound quality ensures their content is visually appealing and professional.

- **Editing**: Once content is captured, influencers edit it using software like Adobe Premiere Pro, Final Cut Pro, or Canva. Editing includes trimming footage, adding visual effects, adjusting color, and enhancing audio quality. This step refines the final product, ensuring it aligns with their aesthetic and brand standards.

3. Testing and Optimization

- **A/B Testing**: To identify what resonates best, influencers may create different versions of content and test them with their audience. For example, they might try out two captions or different visuals to see which generates more engagement.

- **Analytics**: Influencers rely on analytics tools, such as Instagram Insights or Google Analytics, to track metrics like views, likes, shares, and comments. Analyzing this data helps them understand audience behavior, spot trends, and gauge content performance.

- **Optimization**: Using insights from analytics, influencers refine their content strategy by adjusting posting times, tweaking hashtags, or modifying visuals. Regular optimization improves future content performance by aligning with audience preferences.

- **SEO**: For text-based content or platforms with search algorithms, influencers apply SEO basics to enhance visibility. Learning SEO fundamentals, such as keyword usage and title optimization, can boost reach and increase content engagement.

4. Promotion and Engagement

- **Sharing**: Influencers distribute their content across social media platforms and relevant channels, such as Instagram, TikTok, YouTube, or even blogs. This multi-platform sharing helps maximize reach and engagement.

- **Engagement**: Actively interacting with followers is essential to building a loyal audience. Influencers respond to comments, reply to messages, and acknowledge mentions, creating a sense of community and encouraging continued engagement.

- **Collaboration**: Teaming up with other influencers or brands allows influencers to tap into new audiences and expand their reach. Collaborative content, such as co-hosted videos or joint livestreams, adds creativity and strengthens relationships within their network.

Crafting a Content Calendar: Influencer Strategies

Influencers, the digital age's modern-day celebrities, rely heavily on a well-structured content calendar to maintain a consistent and engaging presence. This strategic tool outlines their posting schedule, topics, and themes.

Here's how you build a content calendar (Figure 6-11):

- **Identify Goals**: Clearly define your influencer goals, whether it's increasing followers, boosting brand partnerships, or driving sales. Aim for KPIs to hit, and strategize how to get there.

- **Audit Existing Content**: Analyze your past performance to identify what resonates with your audience.

- **Plan Themes**: Create a mix of evergreen content (timeless topics) and timely content (trending subjects).

- **Schedule Posts**: Allocate time for different content formats (e.g., videos, photos, blog posts) based on audience preferences and your resources.

- **Be Open to Spontaneity**: Trends are often organic and happen because users are playing with fashion, art, and ideas. This book is meant to give an overview of tools to use and to create a base for understanding the link between social media and influence. It's not meant to be a strict plan—organic social media is powerful, and the organic influence is actually far more valuable overall than everything technical—but having a knowledge of the basics means you can decide what to keep and what to throw away. Some accounts grow by community engagement, some by beauty, and a lot are because someone is obsessed with an idea and wants others to be excited. A strategy can begin by being as simple as aiming to post once a day, organically, on X (formerly known as Twitter) and Facebook. It can be as complex as a production. It depends on the realistic goals set.

CHAPTER 6   CONTENT CREATION 101: STRATEGIES FOR CAPTIVATING YOUR AUDIENCE

INSTA CALENDAR

	S	M	T	W	T	F	S
S	Behind the scenes	What inspires you?	What is your Sunday routine?	Daily tip of the day	Introduce a loved one		
M	Describe your morning routine	One thing you can't live without	Daily snack of the day	Where are you from?	What do you do?		
T	Describe your ideal day	Outfit of the day	Snapshot of blog post	What is your favorite food?	What is your workout routine?		
W	Inspiring quote	Show your work space	Introduce your pets	What is something you love?	The origins of your blog story		
T	What is your healthy regime?	What habits help you in life?	Share a memory	What makes you fired up?	Daily quote of the day		
F	Share a personal story	Why did you want to start a blog?	Niche news	Best moment of the day	Promote blog post		
S	What do you do to relax?	Show off your brand	Talk about what's next	Share your favorite life hack	Fun fact about yourself		

Figure 6-11. A simple content calendar. Credit: Jessa Moore

CHAPTER 6 CONTENT CREATION 101: STRATEGIES FOR CAPTIVATING YOUR AUDIENCE

How Content Performs on Different Platforms: A Quick Overview

Each social media platform has its own unique algorithm, user demographics, and cultural nuances that influence how content performs. Here's a brief breakdown of how content might fare on these popular platforms.

Instagram

The de facto influencer realm, Instagram is a place to share short videos and photos. It works by bringing popular content to the top, constantly refreshing a user's feed and stories to encourage them to scroll more.

Success on Instagram requires a very detailed monetization strategy and a focus on aesthetics. You can easily begin making money by pitching products on your feed, an interesting prospect for gadget, fashion, and make-up bloggers.

- **Quick Hits:** Instagram posts are supposed to make people jealous of your life or inspire them to be like you. Candid, quick content works best.

- **Consistency**: Almost constant posting is required to truly beat the algorithm. That said, highly curated and well-produced content does amazingly well.

TikTok

TikTok is, ostensibly, for kids. This means it rewards content that skews toward pop culture and music. This doesn't mean mature content doesn't appear there; it just means it's hard to get to trend.

One influencer, Matt Burns, posted a number of videos of a robotic mower that he, obviously, called Mowses. Mowses would get stuck in mud, lose power, and get clogged, and Burns' clever commentary and shooting style help him hit millions of views.

- **Short-Form Video**: TikTok's algorithm prioritizes engaging, fast-paced videos.

- **Sounds and Trends**: Viral sounds and trends can significantly boost a video's reach.

- **Hashtags and Captions**: Using relevant hashtags and descriptive captions can help with discoverability.

Facebook

Facebook has become the dumping ground for nearly every type of content, from videos to photos to text posts. Our recommendation is simple: cross-post everything you do to Facebook, just to keep it fresh in Meta's algorithms, thereby potentially giving you slightly better reach.

- **Long-Form Content**: Facebook is more conducive to longer articles, blog posts, and videos.

- **Engagement**: Posts that spark conversations and interactions tend to perform better.

- **Target Audience**: Understanding your target audience's interests and demographics is crucial for success.

X (Formerly Twitter)

Influencers use X as a broadcast medium. If you have a big enough audience, it is possible to monetize your success, but in most cases you will want to use Twitter to send traffic to your other social media sites.

- **Text-Based Content**: Tweets with strong, concise messaging often perform well.

- **Links and Visuals**: Sharing links to relevant articles or engaging visuals can increase engagement.

- **Timeliness**: Trending topics and timely news can drive significant reach.

YouTube

- **Long-Form Videos**: YouTube is ideal for in-depth tutorials, reviews, and vlogs.

- **SEO**: Optimizing videos with relevant keywords and descriptions can improve search rankings.

- **Community**: Building a strong community of subscribers can help with video discovery and retention.

Key Considerations for Content Performance

- **Platform-Specific Best Practices**: Adhere to each platform's guidelines and formatting recommendations. Learn the basic technical aspects first; that will cut down on editing time.

- **Audience Engagement**: Interact with your audience through comments, likes, and shares.

- **Consistency**: Regularly post high-quality content to maintain a consistent presence.

- **Analytics**: Use platform-specific analytics tools to track performance and make data-driven decisions. Metricool has a robust analytics system and is fairly user-friendly. It's often used by creators as they grow.

Remember: While these are general guidelines, the performance of your content can vary depending on factors like your niche, target audience, and the specific content you create. Experimentation and A/B testing can help you determine what works best for your brand on each platform.

Key Takeaways

- Everyone can form their own independent media company and use social media techniques to utilize social media and create a personal brand. Social media is democratic in that everyone has an opportunity to build a brand.

- Editing content can be handled with both platforms and apps. Learning the technical aspects of editing provides versatility and professionalism, which builds trust.

- Understanding the different platforms allows the creator to prioritize which platforms will build the most interest in their chosen niche.

- Take time to research and learn the landscape of both your niche and the platforms. This will help develop a solid base for community engagement.

- While it's not necessary to be on every single platform, the depth of knowledge of strategy and technical expertise is essential to growth in a competitive atmosphere.

- It is more important to be consistent than to be perfect. Creating systems and calendars keeps you accountable and on track. The back end is invisible, but essential.

CHAPTER 7

Growing Your Audience: Techniques for Increasing Followers and Engagement

Growing an audience takes work. Organic is actually the earned media of the social media world—it is worth more than automated. The best community builders run their communities themselves—even if they have a team. They maintain visibility and run the account with a personal touch—often breaking the fourth wall. This technique transfers across all verticals and is the main reason people choose their favorite influencers—the connection. The best of the best use a blend of vulnerability, charm, storytelling, and technology. There are guidelines, but no laws, so to speak. Relationship building is probably the top-of-mind aspect of community building. Social media has a direct connection with the consumer that allows that relationship—it's an important aspect of building the community mindfully.

To build a community mindfully as an influencer, prioritize authentic engagement with your audience by sharing relatable content, actively responding to comments, hosting interactive events, fostering open dialogue, promoting diversity within your community, and being transparent about your values and experiences, all while respecting the boundaries of your followers and prioritizing their well-being over purely promotional content.

Another thing to really bear in mind with social media is that there is a lot of experimentation on what will work for each individual account. Hashtag strategies are a really good case in point—many people swear using only 5–7 is effective, while others want to use 12, which is the old-time strategy, way back when Instagram was new. Often experimentation works as testing and can lead to insights that are actionable and allow you to find insights on your own. Too much automation is also the enemy—social media is a high-touch media project, and intuition often allows insights to be found that are valuable.

Here are key strategies for mindful community building:

Authenticity:

- Share personal stories and experiences to connect on a deeper level.
- Be transparent about challenges and imperfections to build trust.
- Avoid overly curated content and present yourself as a real person.

Active Engagement:

- Respond to comments and messages thoughtfully and promptly.
- Ask questions to spark conversation and encourage feedback.
- Host Q&A sessions or live streams to directly engage with your audience.

CHAPTER 7 GROWING YOUR AUDIENCE: TECHNIQUES FOR INCREASING FOLLOWERS AND ENGAGEMENT

Valuable Content:

- Focus on providing informative, entertaining, or educational content aligned with your niche.
- Share diverse perspectives and highlight underrepresented voices.
- Offer actionable insights and tips relevant to your audience's interests.

Community Building Initiatives:

- Launch challenges or contests to encourage participation and interaction.
- Create a dedicated space for community discussion (e.g., Discord server, Facebook group).
- Collaborate with other influencers in your niche to cross-promote and expand reach.

Mindful Promotion:

- Balance sponsored content with organic posts to maintain credibility.
- Clearly disclose partnerships and avoid misleading claims.
- Prioritize the needs of your community over purely promotional goals.

Diversity and Inclusion:

- Represent a variety of demographics and perspectives in your content.
- Be conscious of language and avoid stereotypes.
- Actively seek out collaborations with diverse creators.

Setting Boundaries:

- Establish healthy boundaries between your personal life and online presence.
- Communicate expectations regarding interactions with your followers.
- Take breaks from social media to maintain mental well-being. iravukku

Growing Your Audience: Techniques for Increasing Followers and Engagement

Social media influencers primarily identify their demographic through a combination of **direct engagement** with their audience and **data analysis** tools.

Here are some specific methods they use.

Direct Engagement

- **Comments and Direct Messages:** Engaging with followers through comments and direct messages allows influencers to directly ask questions about their audience's demographics. This relationship building is vital when interacting with fans, customers, and potential sponsors.
- **Polls and Surveys:** Running polls and surveys on their social media platforms can provide immediate insights into their audience's age, location, interests, and behaviors.

Data Analysis Tools

- **Social Media Analytics Platforms**: Platforms like Hootsuite, Sprout Social, and Buffer provide detailed analytics on an influencer's audience, including demographics like age, gender, location, and interests.

- **Engagement Metrics**: Tracking metrics like likes, comments, shares, and click-through rates can help influencers understand their audience's preferences and behaviors.

- **Follower Analysis**: Analyzing the profiles of followers can provide insights into their demographics, interests, and online behavior.

By combining these methods, social media influencers can gain a deeper understanding of their audience's demographics, which helps them tailor their content and partnerships to better resonate with their followers. Platforms also have their own algorithms and quirks, as well as TOS. Every professional social media manager and content creator is always trying to keep up with the platforms—which change often and with no notice.

Content Creation and Optimization

- **Create High-Quality Content**: Ensure your content is valuable, informative, and visually appealing. Always give more than you receive—generosity pays.

- **Optimize for Search Engines**: Use relevant keywords and meta descriptions to improve your content's visibility.

- **Leverage Visual Content**: Images, videos, and infographics can capture attention and increase engagement. Memes talk.

- **Experiment with Different Formats**: Try various content formats (e.g., blog posts, podcasts, webinars) to see what resonates best. Often a strategy involves several of these. For example, blogs perform well alongside Facebook or Instagram. X performs well alongside LinkedIn. Most creators actually aren't active on all—they choose two or three and refine each channel.

Engagement Strategies

- **Encourage Comments and Conversations**: Respond to comments promptly and engage in meaningful discussions.

- **Run Contests and Giveaways**: Offer incentives to encourage participation and attract new followers.

- **Utilize Polls and Surveys**: Gather insights from your audience to tailor your content and improve engagement. Be aware, though, that there are rules for giveaways. Check the federal rules associated with giveaways to make sure you're not breaking laws by holding illegal lotteries.

- **Create Joint Content**: Create joint content with other influencers like videos or blog posts, to share expertise and attract new followers. By merging your audiences you can create a synergistic effect and improve both of your social media audiences.

- **Collaborate with Other Influencers**: Partner with complementary accounts to reach a wider audience.

Platform-Specific Tactics

- **Instagram**: Utilize Instagram Stories, Reels, and IGTV to increase visibility. Use relevant hashtags and engage with other users.

- **TikTok**: Create short, engaging videos that align with trending sounds and challenges.

- **Twitter**: Use Twitter Lists to organize your followers and engage in relevant conversations.

- **Facebook**: Post regularly, run Facebook Ads, and join relevant groups.

Community Building

- **Create a Strong Community**: Encourage interaction and foster a sense of belonging among your followers.

- **Listen to Your Audience**: Pay attention to their feedback and address their concerns.

- **Build Relationships**: Connect with your followers on a personal level to strengthen your bond.

Hashtag Optimization

- **Research Relevant Hashtags**: Find popular and niche hashtags related to your content.

- **Use a Mix of Hashtags**: Combine popular and less competitive hashtags to increase visibility.

- **Avoid Overusing Hashtags:** Too many hashtags can appear spammy. Identify 3–5 strong cultural hashtags and the platform will be more cooperative than if you use 12.

Paid Advertising

- **Target Your Audience:** Use paid advertising platforms to reach specific demographics.
- **Track Your ROI:** Monitor the effectiveness of your paid ads to optimize your campaigns.

By implementing these strategies and consistently creating valuable content, you can effectively grow your audience and build a loyal fan base.

Drew Barrymore's Influential Community

Drew Barrymore has cultivated a strong and engaged community through her various platforms, including her talk show, social media channels, and business ventures—which include a production company. Here are some key aspects of her influential community:

- **Authenticity and Relatability:** Barrymore's open and honest approach to sharing personal experiences resonates with her audience. She often discusses topics like motherhood, mental health, and personal growth, creating a sense of connection and relatability. She has lived in the spotlight and been open about her experiences in rehab as a teen, as well as her divorce and her time as a "normal" barista and single mom. She also talks about both her joy in life and the struggles to fit in.

CHAPTER 7   GROWING YOUR AUDIENCE: TECHNIQUES FOR INCREASING FOLLOWERS AND ENGAGEMENT

- **Empowerment and Inspiration**: Her journey from child star to successful entrepreneur and advocate for mental health has inspired many. She often uses her platform to promote positive messages and encourage others to overcome challenges.

- **Diverse Demographic**: Barrymore's community spans a wide range of ages, genders, and backgrounds. Her ability to connect with people from different walks of life is a testament to her versatility and relatability. She is the poster child for diversity and makes a point of welcoming everyone onto her show.

- **Strong Online Presence**: Her social media channels, including Instagram and TikTok, have a large and active following. She uses these platforms to share behind-the-scenes glimpses of her life, engage with fans, and promote her projects. She takes on other projects, like Etsy's Chief Gifting Officer, as they align with her brand and personal mission.

- **Business Ventures**: Through her ventures like Flower Films and Flower Beauty, Barrymore has built a loyal customer base who admire her entrepreneurial spirit and the products she endorses. She also partners with other entertainment figures, brands, creators, and influencers that tell stories that further her own.

In essence, Drew Barrymore's community is drawn to her authenticity, relatability, and inspiring message. Her ability to connect with people on a personal level has made her a powerful influencer in the entertainment and lifestyle industries. Another influential community builder in entertainment is Reese Witherspoon.

135

CHAPTER 7 GROWING YOUR AUDIENCE: TECHNIQUES FOR INCREASING FOLLOWERS AND ENGAGEMENT

Reese Witherspoon's social media clout played a crucial role in building Hello Sunshine, her platform. Here's how she used her personal brand to launch and grow her production company:

1. **Building a Community**: Witherspoon's active presence on social media, particularly Instagram and Twitter, allowed her to connect with a large and engaged audience. She used these platforms to share her love of books, discuss her book club selections, and interact with her followers. This created a strong sense of community and helped to establish her as a trusted voice in the entertainment industry.

2. **Promoting Book Club Selections**: Witherspoon used her social media channels to promote the books featured in her book club, "Reese's Book Club." She shared book covers, excerpts, and behind-the-scenes glimpses of her book club meetings. This helped to increase awareness of the books and encourage her followers to read them.

3. **Generating Excitement for Adaptations**: As Witherspoon started to develop adaptations of her book club selections, she used social media to generate excitement and anticipation. She shared casting news, behind-the-scenes footage, and sneak peeks of the projects. This helped to build buzz around the adaptations and attract potential viewers.

4. **Engaging with Fans**: Witherspoon's social media accounts allowed her to engage directly with her fans. She responded to comments, answered

questions, and shared personal anecdotes. This helped to foster a sense of connection and loyalty among her followers.

5. **Leveraging Influencer Partnerships**: Witherspoon collaborated with other influencers and celebrities to promote Hello Sunshine's projects. She appeared on their shows, participated in joint interviews, and shared each other's content. This helped to expand her reach and introduce her projects to new audiences.

So you can say Reese Witherspoon's social media and sense of community was instrumental in building Hello Sunshine. By using her platforms to connect with fans, promote her book club selections, and generate excitement for adaptations, she was able to create a strong foundation for her production company and attract a loyal audience.

Another social media influencer who has achieved influencer stardom is Gary V. He has leveraged both his personality and no-nonsense advice into a brand that speaks to entrepreneurs.

Gary Vaynerchuk, also known as Gary V., has built a massive online community through his consistent and strategic use of social media. Here's a breakdown of how he achieved this.

Early Beginnings on YouTube

- **WineLibraryTV**: Gary V. started his online journey with his YouTube channel, "WineLibraryTV," where he reviewed wines and built a following of wine enthusiasts. This early success laid the foundation for his future endeavors.

CHAPTER 7   GROWING YOUR AUDIENCE: TECHNIQUES FOR INCREASING FOLLOWERS AND ENGAGEMENT

Transition to Social Media

- **Embracing Multiple Platforms**: As social media platforms like Twitter, Instagram, and Facebook gained popularity, Gary V. embraced them to expand his reach and connect with a wider audience.

- **Consistent Content Creation**: He consistently posted engaging content, including videos, articles, and blog posts, across various platforms. This frequent presence kept him top of mind for his followers.

Building a Personal Brand

- **Authenticity and Relatability**: Gary V. is known for his authentic and relatable personality. He shares personal stories, insights, and advice, which resonates with his audience.

- **Value-Driven Content**: His content often focuses on topics like entrepreneurship, business, and personal development. This provides value to his audience and establishes him as a thought leader.

Leveraging Social Media Features

- **Live Streams and Q&A Sessions**: Gary V. frequently conducts live streams and Q&A sessions on social media. This allows him to interact directly with his followers, build stronger connections, and get real-time feedback.

- **Engaging with Followers**: He actively responds to comments, messages, and mentions, fostering a sense of community and making his followers feel valued.

Community Building Initiatives

- **Challenges and Campaigns**: Gary V. often organizes challenges and campaigns to encourage engagement and create a sense of shared purpose among his community.

- **Collaborations with Other Influencers**: He frequently collaborates with other influencers and brands, expanding his reach and introducing his content to new audiences.

Key Takeaways

- **Consistency**: Gary V.'s success can be attributed to his unwavering commitment to creating and sharing content on a regular basis.

- **Authenticity**: His genuine personality and relatable approach have helped him build trust and loyalty among his followers.

- **Engagement**: By actively engaging with his community, he has fostered a strong sense of connection and belonging.

- **Value**: His content provides value to his audience, making him a trusted source of information and inspiration.

CHAPTER 7   GROWING YOUR AUDIENCE: TECHNIQUES FOR INCREASING FOLLOWERS AND ENGAGEMENT

By following these strategies, Gary V. has grown his social media community into a massive and influential force in the online world. He advises far outside small businesses.

Another way to build a community is through aspirational lifestyle—and Ballerina Farm has become immensely successful tapping into the "traditional lifestyle" aspect of homesteading.

Ballerina Farm: A Community Built on Homesteading

Ballerina Farm is a family-run homestead located in Oakley, Utah, known for its YouTube channel showcasing the family's journey towards self-sufficiency. The farm is operated by Hannah and Daniel Neeleman, who left their city lives to pursue a simpler, more sustainable lifestyle.

Building a Community

The Neelemans have built a strong community around their farm through several avenues:

- **YouTube Channel**: Their channel provides a glimpse into their daily lives, sharing their experiences with gardening, animal husbandry, and homesteading. This has attracted a large following who connect with their values and lifestyle.

- **Online Store**: Ballerina Farm offers a variety of products, including farm-fresh meats, baked goods, and other homemade items. This allows them to connect with their community on a more personal level.

- **Social Media**: Through platforms like Instagram and Facebook, the Neelemans engage with their followers, sharing updates, answering questions, and fostering a sense of community.

- **In-Person Events**: They occasionally host events at their farm, inviting visitors to learn about their lifestyle and connect with other like-minded individuals.

Key Values and Goals

- **Self-Sufficiency**: The Neelemans strive to grow their own food, raise their own animals, and produce as much as possible for themselves.

- **Sustainability**: They prioritize environmentally friendly practices, like composting, rainwater harvesting, and natural pest control.

- **Community**: Building a supportive community of like-minded individuals is a central goal for the Neelemans.

By sharing their journey and connecting with others, Ballerina Farm has become a symbol of the homesteading movement and a source of inspiration for many. They have also received a fair amount of criticism for the lack of accessibility, but the glossy content is alluring in its own right.

Ballerina Farm's Social Media Engagement

Ballerina Farm uses social media platforms like Instagram and Facebook to connect with their audience on a more personal level. Here are some ways they engage with their followers:

- **Sharing Daily Updates**: They post regular updates about their farm life, including photos and videos of their animals, garden, and family. This helps followers feel connected to their journey.

- **Responding to Comments**: The Neelemans actively respond to comments and questions from their followers, creating a sense of community and fostering meaningful conversations.

- **Running Contests and Giveaways**: They often run contests and giveaways to encourage engagement and reward their loyal followers.

- **Sharing Behind-the-Scenes Content**: They provide glimpses into their daily routines, challenges, and successes, offering a more authentic and relatable experience.

- **Collaborating with Other Creators**: They sometimes collaborate with other homesteading or farming influencers, expanding their reach and introducing their audience to new content.

By using social media in these ways, Ballerina Farm has created a strong and engaged community around their brand. They are able to share their passion for homesteading, inspire others, and build relationships with their followers.

Key Takeaways

- Strategic vulnerability and connection is what drives the leader of a community. There is an element that is found among movie stars, a quality that makes people want to learn more. Being an influencer has aspects of that. While many influencers display their lives, there is the fact that everything is essentially curated. It is up to the influencer to curate and show what they believe followers want to see. Elements of the personality of the

CHAPTER 7 GROWING YOUR AUDIENCE: TECHNIQUES FOR INCREASING FOLLOWERS AND ENGAGEMENT

influencer are strategically covered, in order to achieve strategic goals in what they believe is their value.

- In the influencer model, collaboration is magic. It's an opportunity to reach out and broaden the audience, and done well, it can bring new followers. Gatekeeping—in which a "secret" product or service is used or in which a community is hidden from view—actually works against engagement. People love to be in on something, and the intimacy of sharing is amplified with collaborations with fellow influencers. The same intimacy can develop brand awareness or relationships, creating a 360-degree lifecycle.

- Time tells. Influencers are not an instant channel. There is no way to grow a channel completely artificially. And an artificial channel doesn't resonate the way authenticity does. While you can buy followers, or buy ads, this just doesn't work, and people are savvy enough to recognize it. An influencer is a trusted source—it's not worth losing credibility for speed.

Leveraging Platforms: Maximizing Your Presence on Social Media Channels

Here's a deep dive into the major social media platforms, including best practices for content optimization, algorithm insights, and platform-specific strategies.

Elon Musk loves Twitter so much as a marketing tool that he actually bought Twitter, so he could turn X into his social media Shangri-La, a place where people could meet and talk about important subjects, like business, politics, science, and technology—without fear of being censored. X soon took on the brash persona of the new owner, leaving users wondering whether or not their voices would be heard—and leaving brands and

CHAPTER 7   GROWING YOUR AUDIENCE: TECHNIQUES FOR INCREASING FOLLOWERS AND ENGAGEMENT

influencers in a hot debate about the role social media plays in society and culture. It also led to debates over personal branding and the appropriate boundaries of social media and the larger impact of influence. This is actually a really interesting space, and influencers in general should learn both the climate and the context of the social media platforms—because leveraging insights in a holistic manner is actually what separates the truly influential from the lucky. Social media is also a very good way to stay up to date on news and pop culture—although there is a reason we now have to teach media literacy. You have great news producers producing content, as well as a lot of "opinion" and "alternative facts."

Every social media platform has its own unique personality and usage. This means the users do as well. We all know the stereotypes—your parents use Facebook, the Instagram girls pout at the camera, the YouTubers love their games and bros, and X (formerly known as Twitter) is Elon's baby. LinkedIn is where your resume goes and where you go to brag about your job—but ...where do YOU go? Once you know the landscape, you can play where you want.

Facebook's audience has a diverse demographic, spanning all age groups. Facebook is where you go to share engaging posts, videos, and interactive content. Use Facebook Live for real-time engagement. The algorithms prioritize content from friends and family, but also consider engagement, relevance, and recency, as well as likes.

Instagram's audience is primarily a younger demographic, focused on visuals. Instagram is where you share high-quality images and videos, use relevant hashtags, and engage with the community through Stories and Reels. The algorithms prioritize content that is visually appealing, engaging, and relevant to the user's interests.

X's (formerly known as Twitter) audience has a diverse demographic, with a focus on news, updates, politics, B2B, and discussions. X is where you share concise, informative tweets, use relevant hashtags, and participate in trending conversations. The algorithms prioritize tweets that are relevant to the user's interests, engaging, and timely.

CHAPTER 7   GROWING YOUR AUDIENCE: TECHNIQUES FOR INCREASING FOLLOWERS AND ENGAGEMENT

LinkedIn's audience is primarily a professional audience, seeking networking opportunities and industry insights. The content share's industry news and thought leadership pieces and engages in professional discussions. Algorithms prioritize content that is relevant to the user's professional interests, engaging, and shared by influential people.

TikTok's audience is primarily a younger demographic, focused on short-form video content. Content is creative, engaging videos that follow trends and challenges. Algorithms prioritize content that is viewed, shared, and liked by users.

Content Optimization and Algorithm Insights

Know Your Audience: Understand your target audience's interests, preferences, and behaviors.

Create High-Quality Content: Invest in visually appealing and informative content that resonates with your audience.

Optimize for Search: Use relevant keywords and hashtags to improve discoverability.

Engage with Your Audience: Respond to comments, messages, and mentions to foster a community.

Analyze Your Performance: Track metrics like engagement, reach, and conversions to measure your success.

CHAPTER 7   GROWING YOUR AUDIENCE: TECHNIQUES FOR INCREASING FOLLOWERS AND ENGAGEMENT

Platform-Specific Strategies

- **Facebook**: Experiment with different post formats, use Facebook Ads for targeted reach, and leverage Facebook Groups for community building.
- **Instagram**: Utilize Instagram Stories and Reels for behind-the-scenes content and quick engagement.
- **Twitter**: Use Twitter Lists to organize followers and engage with specific communities.
- **LinkedIn**: Build a strong professional profile, join relevant groups, and participate in industry discussions.
- **TikTok**: Stay up to date with the latest trends and challenges, and collaborate with other creators.

By understanding the unique characteristics of each platform and implementing effective strategies, you can maximize your presence on social media and achieve your marketing goals.

The Cultural Landscape of Social Media Platforms

Social media platforms have become integral parts of our cultural landscape, shaping how we communicate, consume information, and interact with others. Here's a breakdown of their influence on various aspects of culture:

1. Communication and Social Interaction

- **Evolution of Language**: Social media has led to the emergence of new slang, acronyms, and communication styles.

- **Shifting Social Norms**: Platforms have influenced our expectations for social interactions, privacy, and online behavior.

- **Virtual Communities**: People can connect with like-minded individuals from around the world, forming tight-knit online communities.

2. News and Information Consumption

- **Algorithmic News Feeds**: Platforms curate content based on individual preferences, potentially leading to filter bubbles and echo chambers.

- **Fake News and Misinformation**: The rapid spread of information on social media can contribute to the dissemination of false or misleading content.

- **Citizen Journalism**: Platforms have empowered individuals to report news and events directly, challenging traditional media outlets.

3. Entertainment and Pop Culture

- **Viral Trends**: Social media has played a significant role in launching viral trends, memes, and challenges.

- **Celebrity Culture:** Platforms have transformed how celebrities interact with fans and shaped the rise of influencers.

- **Streaming Services:** Social media platforms have been instrumental in promoting streaming services and content discovery.

4. Politics and Social Movements

- **Political Engagement:** Platforms have provided a space for political discussions, organizing, and mobilization.

- **Social Movements:** Social media has been a catalyst for social movements, like the Arab Spring and Black Lives Matter.

- **Political Polarization:** The algorithms of some platforms can contribute to political polarization and echo chambers.

5. Ecommerce and Consumer Culture

- **Influencer Marketing:** Social media influencers have become powerful marketing tools for brands.

- **Online Shopping:** Platforms have transformed the way we shop, making it easier to discover and purchase products.

- **Consumer Trends:** Social media can shape consumer trends and preferences.

In conclusion, social media platforms have had a profound impact on our cultural landscape. Understanding their influence can help us navigate these platforms more effectively and critically evaluate the information we encounter.

A Deeper Dive into Social Media's Cultural Impact

Communication and Social Interaction

- **Evolution of Language**: Social media has accelerated the evolution of language, with the emergence of new slang, acronyms, and emojis. Platforms like TikTok have popularized new phrases and dance trends that quickly spread across the globe.

- **Shifting Social Norms**: Social media has influenced our expectations for social interactions, privacy, and online behavior. For example, the rise of social media has led to a decline in face-to-face interactions and a shift toward virtual relationships.

- **Virtual Communities**: People can connect with like-minded individuals from around the world, forming tight-knit online communities. These communities can provide support, information, and a sense of belonging.

News and Information Consumption

- **Algorithmic News Feeds**: Platforms like Facebook and Twitter use algorithms to curate content based on individual preferences. This can lead to filter bubbles, where users are exposed only to information that aligns with their existing beliefs.

- **Fake News and Misinformation**: The rapid spread of information on social media can contribute to the dissemination of false or misleading content. This can have serious consequences, like influencing elections or fueling social unrest.

- **Citizen Journalism**: Platforms have empowered individuals to report news and events directly, challenging traditional media outlets. This can lead to a more diverse and inclusive news landscape, but it can also raise concerns about the accuracy and reliability of information.

Entertainment and Pop Culture

- **Viral Trends**: Social media has played a significant role in launching viral trends, memes, and challenges. Platforms like TikTok have been particularly effective at identifying and promoting emerging trends.

- **Celebrity Culture**: Platforms have transformed how celebrities interact with fans and shaped the rise of influencers. Social media has made it easier for celebrities to connect with their fans and build personal brands.

- **Streaming Services:** Social media platforms have been instrumental in promoting streaming services and content discovery. Platforms like Instagram and TikTok are often used by creators to promote their content on streaming platforms.

Politics and Social Movements

- **Political Engagement:** Platforms have provided a space for political discussions, organizing, and mobilization. Social media has been used to raise awareness about political issues, mobilize voters, and organize protests.

- **Social Movements:** Social media has been a catalyst for social movements, like the Arab Spring and Black Lives Matter. Platforms have allowed activists to connect with each other, coordinate actions, and amplify their message.

- **Political Polarization:** The algorithms of some platforms can contribute to political polarization and echo chambers. By recommending content that aligns with users' existing beliefs, these algorithms can reinforce biases and make it difficult for people to engage with diverse perspectives.

CHAPTER 7   GROWING YOUR AUDIENCE: TECHNIQUES FOR INCREASING FOLLOWERS AND ENGAGEMENT

Ecommerce and Consumer Culture

- **Influencer Marketing**: Social media influencers have become powerful marketing tools for brands. Brands often collaborate with influencers to promote their products and reach a wider audience.

- **Online Shopping**: Platforms have transformed the way we shop, making it easier to discover and purchase products. Social media platforms often feature shopping features that allow users to browse and buy products directly from the app.

- **Consumer Trends**: Social media can shape consumer trends and preferences. Platforms like TikTok have played a significant role in popularizing new products and trends.

By understanding the cultural impact of social media, we can better navigate these platforms and critically evaluate the information we encounter.

Becoming an Influencer: Tips for the Ordinary Person

While celebrities have a built-in advantage due to their fame, ordinary people can also build a strong online presence and become influential figures. Here are some tips.

1. Niche Down and Find Your Voice

- **Identify Your Passion**: What are you truly interested in? This could be anything from cooking to gaming or technology.

- **Find Your Unique Angle**: How can you offer a fresh perspective or unique take on your niche?
- **Develop Your Voice**: Your personality and style should shine through in your content.

2. Create High-Quality Content Consistently

- **Plan Your Content**: Create a content calendar to ensure a regular posting schedule.
- **Invest in Quality**: Use good equipment (camera, microphone) and editing software to improve the production value of your content.
- **Be Consistent**: Stick to a consistent posting schedule to keep your audience engaged.

3. Engage with Your Audience

- **Respond to Comments and Messages**: Show your audience that you value their feedback.
- **Ask Questions**: Encourage your audience to participate in discussions.
- **Collaborate with Others**: Partner with other influencers in your niche to reach a wider audience.

4. Utilize Different Platforms

- **Experiment with Different Platforms**: Determine which platforms best suit your content and audience (e.g., Instagram, TikTok, YouTube, Twitter).

- **Cross-Promote**: Share your content across different platforms to maximize reach.

- **Understand Platform-Specific Best Practices**: Tailor your content to the specific requirements and audience of each platform.

5. Build Relationships

- **Network with Other Influencers**: Connect with people in your niche to build relationships and support each other.

- **Collaborate with Brands**: Partner with brands that align with your values and audience.

- **Attend Industry Events**: Connect with other influencers and industry professionals at conferences and meetups.

6. Be Patient and Persistent

- **Building an Audience Takes Time**: Don't get discouraged if you don't see results immediately.

- **Stay Persistent**: Keep creating content and engaging with your audience, even if it feels like you're not making progress.

CHAPTER 7 GROWING YOUR AUDIENCE: TECHNIQUES FOR INCREASING FOLLOWERS AND ENGAGEMENT

- **Learn from Your Mistakes**: Analyze your performance and make adjustments as needed.

Remember, becoming an influencer is a journey, not a destination. Focus on building a genuine connection with your audience and creating valuable content, and you'll be well on your way to success.

Kate Casey, of *Reality Life with Kate Casey*, a daily podcast on pop culture, is a master at capitalizing on news stories that capture the public's interest and has built a large community on both Facebook and other social platforms that remains as active and entertaining as the actual podcast—completely organically and with no team. She does the work herself and has become an influencer in her own right—we are offered glimpses into her own life, as well as interesting characters she runs across. You might even call her the real Housewife of Orange County. Her topics include a mix of true crime, Bravo, Scandoval, and her upbringing in the East. We see glimpses of her husband and children, adding to the sense we are allowed into her life. Her topics also include a mix of trends and evergreen—with a lot of deep dives—and she scoops a lot of reality, so she has become a trusted source in entertainment. By scoring interviews with hot media properties, scouting new and interesting features, and keeping an eye on the pulse of her community, she manages to build a fresh podcast daily tailored to her cross-managed community, which is hugely popular and grows daily.

Another strategy that utilizes strong social media is *The Joe Rogan Experience*, which is widely emulated—Joe Rogan has his own personal page, a page for community called The Joe Rogan Experience, a YouTube channel for the streaming of the podcast, and the actual podcast. By showcasing the clips and interacting as a community, he has built a strong community and excitement and often collaborates with like-minded guests—who often use his strategy and invite him on theirs, forming a community within the community. These chains of influence within media are actually their own platform and can be very effective. Unlike Kate Casey, however, he has a team, but these are strategies that can be done solo or with smaller teams.

CHAPTER 7   GROWING YOUR AUDIENCE: TECHNIQUES FOR INCREASING FOLLOWERS AND ENGAGEMENT

The other aspect of social media and becoming a creator that probably is overlooked and really hasn't been talked about is also probably the most challenging—in order to be rewarded by the algorithms, a creator has to be very dedicated to consistency. Constant posting is really necessary for growth, and it actually is not just the way to learn—it makes up for a lot of sins in content and polish, which is learned. It's very difficult to post on every platform every day—this is an enormous undertaking—which is why many social media managers use schedulers professionally. Fatigue for content ideas is a real thing—and while social media is dynamic, the need for consistency is possibly the most important aspect of posting. Most of the influencers you see actually prioritized posting regularly over nearly everything else, except value of information. It's better to post than be perfect. Another thing to bear in mind is that we have nearly constant shifts in algorithms now, and constant shifts in audience, so diversifying your content across platforms is a really good idea, instead of focusing on one. It's honestly not enough to focus heavily on one platform now. There is no magic. It just is some consistency and attention to the daily analytics—these give a story and can tell you what is needing focus. There are also content creators to follow for social media and communities where tips and tricks are shared—groups exist for nearly every interest on Facebook and are often more engaged than pages.

The last thing to cover is etiquette—every community has its own rules and social mores, and people online are people offline as well. When you are trying to build a base for yourself as an influencer, it's important to be authentic—but also to approach people as if you are dealing with them as people in real life. People remember how they are treated, and the attitude online can be unclicked in a moment. The sole history you have is your last exchange. People are looking for connection, not arguments. If you are likable, great—controversial can work too—but enough arguments for no reason and no one will want to consume anything you have to say. Most influencers end up having to moderate fairly heavily, seen or unseen, as well.

CHAPTER 7   GROWING YOUR AUDIENCE: TECHNIQUES FOR INCREASING FOLLOWERS AND ENGAGEMENT

Expanding Your Reach and Building a Loyal Fan Base

To grow your social media audience and foster a dedicated following, consider these strategies.

Use storytelling to create your accounts and engage interest. You can

- **Use High-Quality Visuals**: Use eye-catching images and videos.

- **Write Engaging Captions**: Write concise, informative, and captivating captions.

- **Use Storytelling**: Use storytelling techniques to connect with your audience on an emotional level. Here are some storytelling techniques you can use in your content:

- **Use a strong opening**. Grab your reader's attention with a compelling hook, such as a surprising fact, a thought-provoking question, or a vivid anecdote.

- **Create relatable characters**. Your audience should be able to empathize with your characters, whether they're real people or fictional ones. Give them distinct personalities, goals, and challenges.

- **Build tension and conflict**. A good story needs conflict to keep the reader engaged. This could be a character struggling to overcome a challenge, a company facing a difficult decision, or a product trying to solve a problem.

- **Use vivid language.** Paint a picture with your words by using descriptive language, strong verbs, and sensory details.

- **Show—don't tell.** Instead of simply stating facts, use examples, anecdotes, and dialogue to illustrate your points.

- **Use a clear structure.** Your story should have a beginning, middle, and end. Each part should flow logically and build on the previous one.

- **End with a call to action.** Tell your reader what you want them to do next, whether it's visiting your website, signing up for your newsletter, or buying your product.

A Comprehensive Hashtag Strategy for Social Media

Hashtags are powerful tools to increase your content's visibility and reach on social media. Here's a breakdown of best practices for each major platform.

Instagram

- **Relevant Hashtags:** Use hashtags directly related to your content. For example, if you're posting a photo of a sunset, use #sunset, #beach, #nature, etc.

- **Branded Hashtags:** Create a unique branded hashtag to encourage user-generated content.

- **Trending Hashtags**: Use trending hashtags to reach a wider audience, but make sure they're relevant to your content.

- **Hashtag Clusters**: Group your hashtags into clusters of three to five to improve readability.

Twitter

- **Real-Time Hashtags**: Use hashtags related to current events or trending topics to join the conversation.

- **Campaign Hashtags**: Create specific hashtags for marketing campaigns or product launches.

- **Community Hashtags**: Participate in online communities by using relevant hashtags.

TikTok

- **Trending Sounds and Effects**: Use popular sounds and effects to make your videos more discoverable.

- **Challenge Hashtags**: Participate in trending challenges to gain exposure.

- **Niche Hashtags**: Use specific niche hashtags to reach a targeted audience.

Facebook

- **Page-Specific Hashtags**: Create a branded hashtag for your page and encourage users to use it.
- **Event Hashtags**: Use a unique hashtag for events to track conversations and engagement.
- **Group Hashtags**: Use relevant hashtags in Facebook groups to increase visibility.

LinkedIn

- **Industry-Specific Hashtags**: Use hashtags related to your industry or profession.
- **Company Hashtags**: Promote your company's brand and culture with a branded hashtag.
- **Campaign Hashtags**: Use hashtags to track the success of your LinkedIn marketing campaigns.

General Hashtag Tips

- **Do Keyword Research**: Use tools like Hashtagify.me to find relevant and popular hashtags.
- **Quality Over Quantity**: Focus on quality content over using too many hashtags. Algorithms change constantly, so keep up with trends, and limit them to three or four each post, but target well.

- **Be Consistent**: Use the same hashtags consistently to build brand recognition.

- **Track Performance**: Use analytics tools to monitor the performance of your hashtags

- **Adapt and Evolve**: Stay up to date with the latest hashtag trends and adjust your strategy accordingly.

- **Consistent Posting Schedule**: Maintain a regular posting schedule to keep your audience engaged.

Leverage Relevant Hashtags

- **Research Relevant Hashtags**: Use tools like Hashtagify.me to find popular and niche hashtags.

- **Use a Mix of Hashtags**: Combine popular and specific hashtags to reach a wider audience.

- **Avoid Overusing Hashtags**: Too many hashtags can look spammy.

Collaborate with Other Creators

- **Partner with Complementary Accounts**: Collaborate with other creators in your niche to cross-promote each other's content.

- **Host Joint Giveaways or Challenges**: Encourage your audiences to interact and engage with each other.

Utilize Social Media Features

- **Instagram Stories and Reels**: Create short, engaging videos to reach a wider audience.
- **Live Videos**: Host live Q&A sessions or tutorials to connect with your audience in real time.
- **Polls and Quizzes**: Encourage audience participation and gather insights.

Run Contests and Giveaways

- **Incentivize Participation**: Offer attractive prizes to encourage engagement.
- **Set Clear Rules and Guidelines**: Ensure a smooth and fair contest process.
- **Promote Your Contest**: Use paid advertising or influencer partnerships to reach a wider audience. Just be aware of laws and restrictions, as you do contests.

Analyze Your Performance

- **Track Key Metrics**: Monitor your follower growth, engagement rate, and website traffic.
- **Use Analytics Tools**: Utilize tools like Google Analytics and social media insights to gain valuable insights.
- **Adjust Your Strategy**: Make data-driven decisions to optimize your content and engagement.

CHAPTER 7   GROWING YOUR AUDIENCE: TECHNIQUES FOR INCREASING FOLLOWERS AND ENGAGEMENT

By implementing these strategies, you can effectively grow your audience, build a loyal following, and achieve your social media goals.

Key Takeaways

- When an actor learns a script, they learn the whole script, not just their part. We all have our roles to play, and understanding the domain is important—it's important for ethics, legal, and strategy. Putting a new account on a channel with no audience overlap will kill a brand or influencer. The channels are also a moving target right now—we have scandals and legislation going on—and understanding the actual platforms will give you the agility needed to make strategic decisions for where you need to go, so to speak. Social media is so saturated; you don't want to go where it's a community desert.

- Data about you community, and where you want to find your community, is gold. There are myriad ways to research and myriad tools, and research will only help your creative goals.

- A social media expert has to handle behavior, niches, technology, creative visuals, and copy. It is not one thing, although most are strongest in a few things. The more you know of the culture, the better your work will be.

CHAPTER 8

Surviving the Influencer Life

"Influencer" is a cringe word to many. It's also a word that conjures up glamor, fun, and money. Think of an influencer, and you will probably immediately think of a woman who looks a lot like Kim Kardashian, wearing some it bag, showing you a new outfit, while lining her lips. But the fact is we have a different kind of influencer we follow daily, depending on who we are—whether it's a local mom, a lawyer we look to for advice, a restaurant we want to look at for inspiration, you name it, there's someone we are looking at. And the people we are looking at are highly aware. We are in one giant fishbowl, with fame at scale. The attention economy is real, it makes money, it feeds egos, and people do actually build both their lives and businesses around it. So how do we know who to follow? How do we weed through the noise—besides our extremely helpful algorithms?

A lot of the safety of consuming content on social media—for kids and for adults—is the need to parse information, to not get overly involved, to not get taken advantage of, comes down to a few things. We are human. We are not really meant to be consuming huge swaths of content, and there is so much misleading information and agendas. It's especially important to be aware of the algorithms, the agendas, time spent, impact, and safeties—especially for children. "Touch grass" is a meme for a reason. There's also a surprisingly self-aware backlash of mental health awareness among the youngest natives of the digital social users—this is almost instinctive,

CHAPTER 8 SURVIVING THE INFLUENCER LIFE

because there is a lot to be very suspicious of online. Look at elections, look at consumerism, look at bullying, look at the cultural fractions. But the awareness of the ills of social media and digital media is the same basis for the plan for healthy use of social media. And there definitely are addictive aspects—social is built to be addictive. Add in lifestyle needs for brand managers, social media professionals, and influencers—you really need to have best practices and a plan. Awareness is the building block—both of risk and self-awareness. Good habits also protect your business and relationships—which is the actual secret sauce of longevity in a short-lived business and which will allow your business to grow over time. Evolution is always the key with any innovation-based business model—and influencer work is no different. Strategy is a big aspect of influencing, and part of strategy is understanding your role in the relationships between brands, brand managers, and other stakeholders in the industry. Research is important, and so is stamina. Resilience is built through rejection, and this is an industry that is very aspirational, much like entertainment. The actual number of influencers who pull in a living income, much less the big bucks, is actually a very small percentage. Social media is a very smoke and mirrors machine, where people edit content highly, no matter how much authenticity is their mission. The follower count is a metric that follows the creator everywhere, and bullying can become a daily habit. Perspective is truly the key to survival—a mission is always bigger than numbers. It has to be. The most successful creators who reach an audience want to build awareness for a pet project or nonprofit or disability or a true passion—they want to help people, they want to connect. Consumers can smell a money grab a mile away. Controversy is always a big seller, but the creator has to live with the negativity that is a constant companion. It's a trade-off. It's very telling, by the way, that most executives in tech, including social media, seriousoly limit their children's social media and screen time. The age limit for social media is 14, and even then, there are a lot of tech executives who don't allow their kids to use social media, who are severely monitored.

CHAPTER 8   SURVIVING THE INFLUENCER LIFE

Social media managers and influencers often have demanding schedules, but many prioritize self-care to maintain their well-being. Here are some common strategies they use.

Structured Routines

They often create structured daily routines to ensure they allocate time for self-care, including exercise, meditation, and relaxation.

Here's an example of a daily time schedule for a social media manager.

Sample Daily Schedule

8:00–9:00 a.m.: Breakfast

- **Outline daily tasks.**

9:00–10:00 a.m.: Social Media Monitoring

- Check notifications and messages.
- Review analytics from previous posts.
- Identify trends and relevant news.

10:00 a.m.–12:00 p.m.: Content Creation

- Draft new posts (text, images, videos).
- Schedule posts using a content management tool.
- Edit graphics or collaborate with designers.

12:00–1:00 p.m.: Lunch Break

- Disconnect from screens.
- Engage in a relaxing activity (reading, walking).

1:00–2:00 p.m.: Engagement

- Respond to comments and messages.
- Interact with followers and other accounts.
- Participate in relevant conversations.

2:00–3:00 p.m.: Strategy and Planning

- Review and analyze ongoing campaigns.
- Brainstorm ideas for future content.
- Plan upcoming promotions or collaborations.

3:00–4:00 p.m.: Research

- Stay updated on industry trends and competitor activity.
- Gather inspiration from other creators and brands.

4:00–5:00 p.m.: Wrap-Up Tasks

- Finalize any outstanding posts.
- Prepare reports on engagement and performance metrics.
- Plan the next day's tasks.

5:00–6:00 p.m.: Professional Development

- Take an online course or read articles about social media trends.
- Network with other professionals.

6:00 p.m.: End of Workday

- Log off and engage in personal activities or relaxation.

Tips for Flexibility

- Adjust the schedule based on specific projects or campaigns.
- Allow for spontaneous tasks, as social media can be unpredictable.
- Incorporate breaks throughout the day to maintain focus and energy.

This schedule can serve as a framework, but it's important for social media managers to tailor it to their own needs and work style. The important aspect is the understanding that any unstructured environment as large as social media needs to be heavily managed. Productivity apps and tools are great, but the important aspect is that the individual pays attention to their individual needs. Also, needs change, so personal audits are an ongoing priority.

Time Blocking

Many use time blocking techniques to designate specific hours for work, content creation, and personal time, helping them stay organized and avoid burnout.

Example Time Blocking Schedule

8:00–8:30 a.m.: Morning Routine

- Breakfast and coffee
- Quick review of the day's tasks

8:30–9:00 a.m.: Email and Notifications

- Respond to urgent emails.
- Check social media notifications.

9:00–10:30 a.m.: Content Creation

- Write captions and create graphics for upcoming posts.
- Film or edit video content.

10:30–11:00 a.m.: Break

- Short walk or stretch.
- Hydrate and refresh.

11:00 a.m.–12:00 p.m.: Scheduling Posts

- Use a content management tool to schedule posts for the week.
- Ensure optimal posting times.

12:00–1:00 p.m.: Lunch Break

- Step away from work.
- Enjoy a relaxing activity (reading, listening to music).

1:00–2:00 p.m.: Engagement

- Respond to comments and DMs.
- Engage with followers and related accounts.

2:00–3:00 p.m.: Strategy Session

- Review analytics from previous posts.
- Plan upcoming campaigns and brainstorm ideas.

3:00–4:00 p.m.: Research

- Explore industry trends
- Check competitor social media activities.

4:00–4:30 p.m.: Wrap-Up Tasks

- Finalize any pending tasks for the day.
- Prepare a to-do list for tomorrow.

4:30–5:00 p.m.: Professional Development

- Read articles or take an online course related to social media marketing.

5:00 p.m.: End of Workday

- Log off and unwind.

Key Tips for Effective Time Blocking

- Use a digital calendar or planner to visualize your blocks.
- Be flexible—adjust blocks as needed based on priorities.
- Limit distractions during focused work blocks to enhance productivity.

This approach helps to maintain focus and structure throughout the day, making it easier to manage multiple tasks effectively.

Digital Detox

Regular breaks from social media can help recharge their mental health. Some schedule "off" days or set app limits.

CHAPTER 8   SURVIVING THE INFLUENCER LIFE

A digital detox involves taking a break from digital devices and social media to recharge mentally and emotionally. Here's an example of how someone might implement a digital detox over a weekend.

Weekend Digital Detox Plan

Preparation (Friday Evening):

- **Set Boundaries**: Inform friends and family that you'll be offline for the weekend.
- **Unsubscribe**: Remove distracting apps from your phone and turn off notifications.
- **Plan Activities**: Organize offline activities you'd like to do, such as hiking, reading, or cooking.

Saturday:
Morning

- **Wake Up Without Screens**: Start your day without checking your phone or any devices.
- **Morning Routine**: Enjoy breakfast, meditate, or do yoga.

Mid-morning

- **Engage in Nature**: Go for a hike or a walk in a park. Focus on your surroundings and enjoy the fresh air.

Afternoon

- **Creative Pursuits**: Spend time painting, journaling, or engaging in a hobby you love. Disconnect from digital distractions and immerse yourself in creativity.

Evening

- **Socialize**: Have dinner with friends or family without phones at the table. Enjoy conversation and connection without digital interruptions.

Sunday:
Morning

- **Read a Book**: Spend time reading a physical book instead of browsing online.
- **Cook a Healthy Meal**: Prepare a new recipe without any digital distractions.

Afternoon

- **Physical Activity**: Engage in a sport, take a class, or practice yoga. Enjoy being active and present.

Evening

- **Reflect and Journal**: Write about your experiences during the detox. Consider how you felt being offline and what you learned.

Post-detox:

- **Gradual Re-entry**: When returning to digital life, limit screen time and set specific times for checking social media.
- **Establish Boundaries**: Create a plan for maintaining a healthier relationship with technology, such as regular digital detox days or screen-free evenings.

This plan allows for a break from the digital world, promoting mindfulness and a stronger connection to real-life experiences. The important aspect is to have sensory input other than digital.

Mindfulness Practices

Incorporating mindfulness practices like yoga or meditation helps them manage stress and stay grounded.

Physical Activity

Many prioritize physical health by incorporating workouts, whether at the gym, at home, or outdoors, to boost energy and mood.

Yoga three times a week or walking a half hour every day is a good way to destress and offset stress. It also keeps you off screens.

Healthy Boundaries

Setting boundaries around work hours and availability helps them separate personal life from professional obligations. No is a full sentence.

Setting boundaries as a social media manager is essential for maintaining a healthy work–life balance and ensuring your professional success. Here are some key strategies to consider:

Define Your Availability:

- **Set Office Hours:** Communicate your working hours to clients and colleagues. This helps manage expectations and prevents after-hours interruptions.

- **Limit Response Time:** Establish a reasonable response time for emails, messages, and calls. This allows you to prioritize tasks and avoid feeling constantly on call.

Establish Communication Channels:

- **Choose Preferred Platforms:** Determine which channels you'll use for professional communication (e.g., email, project management tools). This helps keep conversations organized and avoids distractions from personal accounts.

- **Set Expectations Early and Often. Rinse and Repeat:** Clearly communicate your preferred communication methods to clients and team members. This ensures everyone is on the same page and reduces unnecessary back-and-forth.

Prioritize Tasks and Delegate:

- **Create a Schedule:** Plan your workweek and allocate specific time blocks for different tasks. This helps you stay focused and avoid feeling overwhelmed.

- **Delegate When Possible:** If you have a team, delegate tasks that can be handled by others. This frees up your time for more strategic work and reduces your workload.

Learn to Say No:

- **Evaluate Requests:** Assess the impact of each request on your workload and priorities. If a task doesn't align with your goals or exceeds your capacity, politely decline.

- **Offer Alternatives:** If you can't take on a new project, suggest alternative solutions or refer the client to someone else. This helps maintain positive relationships while protecting your time.

Take Breaks and Disconnect:

- **Schedule Breaks:** Incorporate short breaks throughout your workday to rest and recharge. This helps improve focus and productivity.

- **Set Boundaries with Technology:** Turn off notifications during off-hours and designate specific times for checking emails and social media. This helps you disconnect from work and enjoy personal time.

Continuous Evaluation and Adjustment:

- **Reflect on Your Boundaries:** Regularly assess your boundaries and identify areas where you may need to make adjustments.

- **Communicate Changes:** If you need to modify your boundaries, inform your clients and team members in advance. This ensures everyone is aware of your expectations.

By implementing these strategies, you can establish healthy boundaries as a social media manager, improve your work–life balance, and achieve greater professional success. Remember, setting boundaries is not selfish; it's essential for your well-being and productivity.

Support Systems

Building a network of friends, family, and fellow creators for support can help them cope with the pressures of their roles. Everyone needs people who can understand their work pressures, and assist them when they're overwhelmed, sad, or angry. Find people you trust. Maybe they're family members, close friends, or other influencers. These people will be your port in the storm.

Self-Reflection

Regular self-reflection through journaling or therapy allows them to process their experiences and maintain emotional health.

By being intentional about their self-care, they can sustain their productivity and creativity in a fast-paced environment.

The other survival tactic is to treat influencer work exactly like what it is—a business. As an influencer, you own a media business, and knowing best practices, culture, and relationships are key. You never know who's in the elevator with you. And manners go a very long way—many, many influencers crash and burn because they are not well-rounded and don't really understand the nuances of relationships.

Key Takeaways

- The culture of digital media is unrelenting, and it's easy to get so involved in "the followers" that you can lose your perspective of balance—mental health and stress management is important. Working with social media is a creative act, but it's fast-paced and can offer very low reward, especially if your expectations are not managed. In the beginning, there is a very small audience, but as you grow, the audience will have opinions. It's common for bullying to be in the comments, and the focus can often be on appearance or audience expectations, not reality.

- Self-care in the digital world isn't just lip service; it's a necessity. We live in a hyper-focused, lightning-fast world, and social media has its own individual risks to mental health. Take care of your own wellness.

- A routine is not necessarily set in stone, and everyone has different responsibilities, but these sample routines can provide guidance. A routine that is set is good for brain health and can add in accountability both for tasks and offline.

- In general, time spent on social media should have a limit and not be endless doom scrolling.

CHAPTER 9

Monetization Methods: Turning Influence into Income

Social Media and Your Wallet

Social media is the link between entertainment and brands—much like TV was in the early days. The direct line brands have to consumers is very valuable, and the data collected and used by social media platforms themselves are huge. Brands are always looking for fresh faces, as well as new communities to be introduced to. Influencers are the stars of branding—although, to be clear, not every Influencer converts to sales, which is actually the number one thing brands look for. If your community engages with you as an expert, that's money in the bank.

Influencers monetize their online presence in several ways, leveraging their audience, content, and personal brand. Here are some of the most common methods.

CHAPTER 9   MONETIZATION METHODS: TURNING INFLUENCE INTO INCOME

Sponsored Content

Influencers partner with brands to promote products or services in exchange for payment. This can take many forms:

- **Posts**: Sponsored Instagram photos, TikToks, YouTube videos, etc.
- **Stories/Live Streams**: Influencers integrate product mentions into live sessions or stories.
- **Blog Posts/Articles**: Longer-form written content with product recommendations.

Affiliate Marketing

Influencers promote products using affiliate links. They earn a commission on any sales generated through those links. This is a performance-based model, meaning they only earn money if their followers make a purchase. Popular platforms for this include

- Amazon Associates
- RewardStyle (LTK)
- ShareASale
- Rakuten

Product Collaborations/Brand Ambassadorships

Some influencers partner with brands for long-term collaborations or become brand ambassadors. These relationships often involve

- Co-branded products (e.g., a makeup line with a beauty influencer)

- Exclusive deals or product launches
- Ongoing sponsorship agreements where the influencer consistently promotes the brand

Selling Digital Products or Services

Influencers can create and sell their own digital offerings, such as

- **Ebooks, Courses, and Webinars**: Influencers share their expertise on a particular topic, like fitness, fashion, marketing, etc.
- **Membership/Subscription**: Offering exclusive content on platforms like Patreon or OnlyFans.
- **Templates/Presets**: Selling photography presets, business templates, or other digital tools.

Merchandise Sales

Many influencers develop their own branded merchandise, such as clothing, accessories, or other products. This is particularly popular in lifestyle, fashion, and entertainment niches. Some use platforms like Teespring or Shopify to manage sales.

Crowdfunding or Donations

Platforms like **Patreon**, **Ko-fi**, or **Buy Me a Coffee** allow influencers to get direct support from their followers. Fans can donate money, subscribe to premium content, or support their favorite creators with one-time or recurring payments.

CHAPTER 9   MONETIZATION METHODS: TURNING INFLUENCE INTO INCOME

Ad Revenue (YouTube, TikTok, etc.)

Influencers with significant followings on platforms like YouTube, TikTok, or Facebook can earn money through ad revenue. These platforms place ads in their videos, and the influencers receive a portion of the ad income:

- **YouTube Partner Program**: Earns revenue through ad views, super chats, channel memberships, etc.
- **TikTok Creator Fund**: Pays influencers based on video views and engagement

Paid Appearances/Speaking Engagements

Some influencers monetize their status by appearing at events, speaking at conferences, or participating in podcasts and webinars. These opportunities often come with a speaking fee or appearance fee.

Licensing Content

Influencers can license their content (photos, videos, etc.) to companies or media outlets for a fee. This often happens when a company wants to use an influencer's content in their marketing materials.

Selling Physical Products

Besides merchandise, some influencers sell physical products directly to their followers, either through partnerships or their own brands, for example:

- **Beauty products** like skincare or cosmetics
- **Fitness equipment** or apparel
- **Tech gadgets or accessories**

Consulting/Coaching

Influencers who have established authority in a particular niche (e.g., business, fitness, fashion) often offer consulting or coaching services, either one-on-one or in group settings.

Licensing or Selling Intellectual Property

As influencers grow their brand, they may also monetize their intellectual property (IP). For example, a popular influencer might sell their brand name or content rights to a larger company or license it out for use in different media.

Summary

The key to monetizing as an influencer is diversifying income streams. Most successful influencers use a combination of the methods above to create a sustainable business model. They also need to maintain a strong and engaged audience, as that is the foundation for all of these revenue-generating activities.

How Do Sponsors Judge You?

Influencers can be classified based on their **audience size**, **reach**, **engagement**, and **niche**. Compensation models vary based on these classifications, as well as the influencer's level of influence, the type of partnership, and the type of platform they use.

Here's an overview of common classifications of influencers and how compensation typically works for each.

CHAPTER 9   MONETIZATION METHODS: TURNING INFLUENCE INTO INCOME

1. Classification of Influencers
By Audience Size (Followers)

- **Nano-influencers:**
  - **Audience Size**: 1,000–10,000 followers.
  - **Characteristics**: Highly engaged, niche communities, personal relationships with followers.
  - **Compensation**: Typically receive free products, small fees, or affiliate commissions. Some may also work for exposure, depending on their niche and brand fit.
- **Micro-influencers:**
  - **Audience Size**: 10,000–100,000 followers.
  - **Characteristics**: Strong, niche communities; higher engagement rates compared with larger influencers.
  - **Compensation**: Compensation often includes a mix of free products, small payments for posts, or affiliate marketing commissions. Brands may offer a fixed fee for posts or sponsorship deals, often ranging from $100 to $2,000 per post, depending on the niche.
- **Mid-tier Influencers:**
  - **Audience Size**: 100,000 to 1 million followers.
  - **Characteristics**: Broader reach, but still niche-specific, with a good balance between influence and engagement.

CHAPTER 9   MONETIZATION METHODS: TURNING INFLUENCE INTO INCOME

- **Compensation**: Can earn substantial fees for sponsored content, ranging from $2,000 to $15,000 per post. Also can earn affiliate commissions, payment for appearances, or ongoing brand ambassadorship deals.
- **Macro-influencers:**
  - **Audience Size**: 1–10 million followers.
  - **Characteristics**: Large, diverse followings; often have partnerships with global brands.
  - **Compensation**: These influencers can command high fees per post—ranging from $10,000 to $50,000 or more. They are often compensated through both direct payments and commissions on sales from affiliate links or sponsored campaigns.
- **Mega-influencers (Celebrities):**
  - **Audience Size**: More than 10 million followers.
  - **Characteristics**: Global reach, broad audience, celebrity status, or massive social media followings.
  - **Compensation**: Typically receive very high fees, ranging from $100,000 to millions of dollars per campaign. They may also negotiate a percentage of revenue generated from sales or long-term brand ambassadorships.

By Niche

- **Lifestyle Influencers**: Cover a wide range of topics, including fashion, beauty, travel, fitness, and personal growth.

CHAPTER 9   MONETIZATION METHODS: TURNING INFLUENCE INTO INCOME

- **Niche Influencers**: These influencers focus on specific, often more specialized areas (e.g., veganism, technology, gaming, or finance).

- **Celebrity Influencers**: Recognized public figures like actors, athletes, musicians, etc., who use their platform to endorse products and services.

- **Industry Experts**: These are influencers known for their expertise (e.g., financial experts, nutritionists, tech reviewers, etc.).

2. Compensation Models for Influencers

A. Flat Rate (Fixed Fee)

- **What It Is**: A brand pays the influencer a fixed amount for a single post, video, or series of content.

- **How It's Used**: Common for micro- to macro-influencers. Payment is typically agreed upon in advance and is based on the influencer's audience size, engagement, and the complexity of the content.

- **Example**: A mid-tier influencer with 300,000 followers may charge $5,000 for a sponsored post on Instagram.

B. Cost per Engagement (CPE)

- **What It Is**: Influencers are paid based on the level of engagement (likes, comments, shares, clicks) their posts generate.

CHAPTER 9   MONETIZATION METHODS: TURNING INFLUENCE INTO INCOME

- **How It's Used**: This can be used in both small and large campaigns. It's often used in influencer marketing platforms or for influencers with niche, highly engaged audiences.

- **Example**: An influencer could receive $0.50 per click or $5 per comment/engagement on a post.

C. Affiliate Marketing

- **What It Is**: Influencers promote products using unique affiliate links or codes and earn a commission for sales generated through those links.

- **How It's Used**: This model is popular among micro- and mid-tier influencers, as they can earn money from conversions. It's also used as a supplementary income for larger influencers.

- **Example**: An influencer promotes a clothing brand's affiliate link and earns 10% of each sale made through that link.

D. Performance-Based Compensation

- **What It Is**: Payment based on specific performance metrics, such as sales, app downloads, or lead generation.

- **How It's Used**: Often used in affiliate marketing or when influencers are part of a larger digital marketing campaign.

- **Example**: An influencer could earn $5 for every new customer who signs up or makes a purchase through their promo code.

E. Product Gifting

- **What It Is**: In exchange for promoting a product or service, influencers receive free products or services, rather than direct payment.

- **How It's Used**: Especially common with nano- and micro-influencers. This can also be part of a larger campaign where influencers receive products for exposure.

- **Example**: A beauty influencer receives a set of skincare products worth $100 in exchange for posting a review on Instagram.

F. Long-Term Brand Ambassadorship

- **What It Is**: Influencers enter long-term partnerships with brands, committing to consistently promote the brand's products over a period of months or even years.

- **How It's Used**: Popular among mid-tier, macro-, and mega-influencers who have established a strong brand presence.

- **Example**: A fitness influencer could be hired as a brand ambassador for a sportswear company, receiving a monthly retainer and earning a percentage of sales linked to their promotion.

G. Revenue Share or Commission-Based Deals

- **What It Is**: Influencers earn a percentage of the revenue generated through their promotion or product launch.

- **How It's Used**: Often used when influencers collaborate with a brand on a co-branded product or launch.

- **Example**: An influencer may design a limited-edition clothing line and earn 20% of the revenue from sales.

H. Paid Appearances/Speaking Engagements

- **What It Is**: Influencers are paid to attend events, give talks, or participate in webinars and podcasts.

- **How It's Used**: Often for influencers with significant authority or expertise in a niche. It may also include influencer participation in media campaigns, live Q&As, or other public events.

- **Example**: An influencer with a large following in the tech space might be paid $10,000 to speak at a conference or to moderate a panel.

I. Exclusive or Premium Content Subscriptions

- **What It Is**: Influencers earn money by offering exclusive content behind a paywall, often through platforms like Patreon, OnlyFans, or Substack.

- **How It's Used**: This is common among creators who provide niche, highly engaged content and can build a loyal fan base willing to pay for more intimate, exclusive content.

- **Example**: An influencer might offer behind-the-scenes access, personal advice, or early access to content for paid subscribers.

3. Factors Influencing Compensation

- **Audience Engagement**: High engagement rates (likes, comments, shares, etc.) can lead to higher compensation, even if the follower count is lower.

- **Platform**: Certain platforms tend to offer higher payouts than others (e.g., YouTube videos tend to have a higher payout than Instagram posts due to ad revenue models).

- **Industry/Niche**: Influencers in competitive, high-value niches (like finance, health, luxury, or tech) can often command higher fees compared with influencers in more general categories.

- **Content Quality and Production Value**: Influencers who invest in professional-looking content, such as high-quality video production, will often receive higher compensation.

- **Campaign Type**: One-time posts might pay less than long-term brand ambassadorships or co-branded product launches.

CHAPTER 9   MONETIZATION METHODS: TURNING INFLUENCE INTO INCOME

Summary

Influencers are compensated in various ways depending on their follower count, niche, and engagement levels. The compensation structure can range from free products or affiliate commissions to significant payments for sponsored posts, long-term partnerships, or exclusive content. Understanding the influencer's audience, platform, and relationship with followers plays a crucial role in determining the appropriate compensation model for each partnership.

Finding Your Niche

Influencers are also typically classified into different **tiers** based on the size of their following, engagement rate, and overall influence. Each tier has its own compensation model, which varies depending on the influencer's audience size, platform, and the type of campaign or partnership. Below is an overview of the **different tiers of influencers** and the **typical compensation** for each.

1. Nano-influencers

Audience Size

1,000–10,000 followers

Characteristics

- Typically have small, but highly engaged and loyal audiences
- Often serve niche markets with very specific interests (e.g., local businesses, personal brands, niche hobbies)
- Known for having close, personal relationships with their followers

Compensation

- **Product Gifting**: Many nano-influencers start with free products in exchange for posts.
- **Small Payments**: Typically, payment ranges from $50 to $500 per post, depending on the campaign, brand, and influencer's engagement rate.
- **Affiliate Commissions**: Often paid on a commission basis for sales generated via unique affiliate links or promo codes (typically 5-10% per sale).

Monetization Strategy

- Many nano-influencers monetize through affiliate marketing, brand collaborations, and paid campaigns, but some may focus primarily on organic content and community engagement.

2. Micro-influencers

Audience Size

10,000–100,000 followers

Characteristics

- Strong engagement rates (higher than macro- or celebrity influencers).
- Focus on niche topics such as fitness, beauty, travel, food, or specific lifestyle areas.

- Followers tend to be highly engaged and trust the influencer's opinions.

Compensation

- **Product Gifting**: Common in the early stages or with smaller brands.
- **Sponsored Posts**: Payment for posts generally ranges from **$100 to $2,500** per post, depending on the platform (Instagram, TikTok, YouTube) and the influencer's engagement.
- **Affiliate Marketing**: Micro-influencers often earn 5–10% commission from products sold via affiliate links or promo codes.
- **Event Appearances**: Some micro-influencers are paid to attend brand events, webinars, or product launches (ranging from $300 to $5,000).

Monetization Strategy

- Focus on sponsored content, affiliate partnerships, and collaborations with smaller-to-medium-sized brands

3. Mid-tier Influencers

Audience Size

100,000 to 1 million followers

CHAPTER 9   MONETIZATION METHODS: TURNING INFLUENCE INTO INCOME

Characteristics

- Larger followings that still maintain good engagement rates
- Often work with a mix of lifestyle brands, entertainment, or specialized companies
- Can span multiple platforms, often creating content across Instagram, YouTube, TikTok, and blogs

Compensation

- **Sponsored Content**: Payment ranges from **$2,000 to $10,000** per post (depending on the platform and specific campaign).
- **Affiliate Marketing**: Mid-tier influencers often use affiliate marketing as a supplementary income stream, earning 5–10% commission per sale.
- **Long-Term Partnerships**: Many mid-tier influencers secure longer-term brand ambassadorships or recurring campaigns with brands, earning monthly retainers or exclusive deals.
- **Event Hosting/Speaking**: They can be paid anywhere from $5,000 to $20,000 for hosting events or speaking engagements.

Monetization Strategy

- A mix of sponsored content, brand ambassadorships, affiliate commissions, and long-term deals with brands

CHAPTER 9   MONETIZATION METHODS: TURNING INFLUENCE INTO INCOME

4. Macro-influencers

Audience Size

1–10 million followers

Characteristics

- Large, diverse audiences across multiple platforms.
- Influencers at this level have more mainstream recognition but still maintain a degree of niche specialization (e.g., fashion, lifestyle, fitness, travel).
- Engagement is still important, though less personal than with smaller influencers.

Compensation

- **Sponsored Posts**: Macro-influencers charge **$10,000 to $50,000** or more per post, depending on the platform, type of content, and brand alignment.
- **Long-Term Collaborations/Brand Ambassadorships**: These influencers are often signed for multi-month or multi-year brand deals, with payment ranging from **$50,000 to $500,000** or more per year.
- **Affiliate Marketing**: Though commissions are lower due to the size of their audience, they can still earn significant money through affiliate links. Commissions may range from **2 to 5%**, but they have higher volume.
- **Event Appearances**: They can be paid **$10,000 to $100,000** for public appearances, speaking engagements, or hosting events.

Monetization Strategy

- Sponsored content, brand partnerships, affiliate marketing, and exclusive collaborations with global brands

5. Mega-influencers (Celebrities)

Audience Size

More than 10 million followers

Characteristics

- Often celebrities, actors, athletes, musicians, or other high-profile public figures.

- Have broad appeal, spanning multiple industries and often worldwide reach.

- Their engagement can vary widely, as they have massive audiences, but the level of personal interaction tends to decrease.

Compensation

- **Sponsored Content**: Mega-influencers earn **$100,000 to $1,000,000** or more per post, depending on the platform and brand. For example, a major Instagram or TikTok star could command over $1,000,000 for a single sponsored post.

CHAPTER 9   MONETIZATION METHODS: TURNING INFLUENCE INTO INCOME

- **Long-Term Brand Partnerships**: These influencers often enter high-value contracts with brands, including signing multi-year brand ambassadorships worth **millions of dollars**.

- **Affiliate Marketing**: Due to the sheer volume of their audience, mega-influencers can earn substantial commissions through affiliate sales, even with a relatively low percentage. Commissions may range from **1 to 5%**, but the volume leads to significant earnings.

- **Exclusive Campaigns**: Mega-influencers often work with global brands on exclusive campaigns or co-branded product lines, which can be worth tens of millions of dollars.

- **Paid Appearances/Speaking**: They can earn **$100,000 to several million dollars** for public appearances, hosting gigs, or attending high-profile events.

Monetization Strategy

- Sponsored content, large-scale brand deals, global ambassadorships, exclusive product lines, affiliate marketing, public speaking, and media appearances

CHAPTER 9   MONETIZATION METHODS: TURNING INFLUENCE INTO INCOME

Summary of Compensation by Influencer Tier

Influencer Tier	Audience Size	Sponsored Content (per Post)	Affiliate/ Commission	Other Income Sources
Nano-influencers	1,000–10,000 followers	$50–500	5–10% per sale	Product gifting, free samples, small-scale campaigns
Micro-influencers	10,000–100,000 followers	$100–2,500	5–10% per sale	Sponsored posts, affiliate marketing, event appearances
Mid-tier influencers	100,000 to 1 million followers	$2,000–10,000	5–10% per sale	Sponsored content, long-term partnerships, event hosting
Macro-influencers	1–10 million followers	$10,000–50,000	2–5% per sale	Brand ambassadorships, public speaking, event hosting
Mega-influencers	More than 10 million followers	$100,000–1,000,000+	1–5% per sale	Global brand partnerships, co-branded product lines, high-profile appearances

As influencers rise through the tiers from nano to mega, their **compensation increases dramatically**. Nano- and micro-influencers often start with product gifting and smaller payments, while macro- and mega-influencers can command substantial fees for sponsored content and brand partnerships. Each influencer tier has its own monetization methods, but the larger the influencer's following, the more they can charge for posts, campaigns, and collaborations.

CHAPTER 9   MONETIZATION METHODS: TURNING INFLUENCE INTO INCOME

Building Engagement, Reaping the Benefits

A real-life example of an influencer discussing the monetization of their social media accounts is **Kristin Johns**, a popular lifestyle and fashion influencer. Kristin has a YouTube channel, a blog, and a highly engaged Instagram following. She has openly talked about the various ways she monetizes her social media presence, offering insights into the different streams of income she leverages.

Example: Kristin Johns on Monetizing Social Media

Kristin Johns has shared several times in her videos and blog posts how she generates revenue through her social media platforms. Here's a breakdown of the key methods she uses.

1. Brand Sponsorships and Collaborations

Kristin often collaborates with brands that align with her lifestyle and interests. She works with companies in the fashion, beauty, and home decor industries. In one of her videos, she explained that brand collaborations are one of her primary sources of income. These sponsorships typically involve her creating content (like Instagram posts, YouTube videos, or blog features) that showcases the brand's products or services.

For example, she might post a sponsored Instagram photo wearing an outfit from a clothing brand, with a caption about how much she loves the pieces. In return, she gets paid a flat fee, and sometimes, the brand offers additional compensation if the campaign performs well.

CHAPTER 9   MONETIZATION METHODS: TURNING INFLUENCE INTO INCOME

Kristin's Tip   "I always try to choose brands that I truly believe in and use in my daily life. Authenticity is key, and that's what keeps my audience engaged."

2. Affiliate Marketing

Kristin is also a big proponent of affiliate marketing. She shares affiliate links in her Instagram stories, YouTube descriptions, and blog posts. This means that when her followers purchase products through her unique links, she earns a commission.

In her Instagram stories, Kristin might show off a new skincare product or an outfit she's wearing and then include a swipe-up link (or a link in her bio) that takes followers to the product page. If someone buys the product using her link, she gets a percentage of the sale.

Kristin's Tip   "Affiliate marketing is a great way to monetize when you don't want to sell your own products. But it's important to recommend products that truly fit with your brand and your audience's interests."

3. Ad Revenue from YouTube

Kristin also earns money from ad revenue on her YouTube channel. In a vlog or a tutorial video, YouTube places ads, and she gets paid based on how many people watch or interact with those ads. YouTube's Partner Program allows content creators like Kristin to monetize videos through ads, and the amount she earns depends on the number of views, the demographics of her viewers, and the type of ads displayed.

Kristin's Tip "Ad revenue on YouTube isn't as high as brand deals or affiliate sales, but it's consistent, especially if you have a lot of content and a loyal audience."

4. Selling Digital Products or Services

Kristin has also created and sold her own products, like digital guides, ebooks, and online courses. For example, she might create a downloadable ebook on styling tips or a guide for managing a lifestyle blog. She markets these products through her social media platforms and makes passive income every time someone buys.

Kristin's Tip "Selling your own digital products is a great way to create a more passive income stream, especially if you have a niche audience that's interested in learning from you."

5. Sponsored YouTube Videos

Kristin works with brands to create long-form, sponsored content on her YouTube channel. These are often product reviews, tutorials, or "day-in-the-life"-style videos, where she integrates the brand or product naturally into her content. In these instances, she might negotiate a higher fee because she's creating more extensive content (a full video vs. a short Instagram post).

Kristin's Tip "Sponsored videos take more time and effort, but they also pay better than shorter sponsored posts. Brands are willing to pay more for a dedicated video because it's seen by your audience for a longer period."

6. Exclusive Content on Patreon or Other Platforms

Kristin also offers exclusive content to her most dedicated followers through a subscription service like Patreon. For a monthly fee, followers can access behind-the-scenes content, personal updates, and special discounts. This is another way she diversifies her income beyond traditional sponsored content and affiliate marketing.

Kristin's Tip   "Patreon is a great way to build a community and offer extra value to your most loyal fans. It's all about creating a sense of exclusivity."

Summary of Kristin's Monetization Strategy

- **Brand Sponsorships**: Sponsored Instagram posts, YouTube videos, and blog features
- **Affiliate Marketing**: Links to products with commissions for sales
- **Ad Revenue**: Income from ads on YouTube.
- **Digital Products**: Selling ebooks, guides, and online courses
- **Patreon**: Offering exclusive content for subscribers

Kristin's Advice for Aspiring Influencers

Kristin often shares practical advice for those looking to monetize their own social media accounts:

- **Stay Authentic:** "Be true to yourself and only promote things that align with your values. Your audience will appreciate that and trust your recommendations."

- **Diversify Your Income:** "Don't rely on just one revenue stream. It's important to have multiple ways of making money so that you can remain financially stable."

- **Engagement Is Key:** "Focus on building a strong community. It's not just about the number of followers you have, but how engaged they are with your content."

- Kristin Johns provides an excellent example of how influencers can monetize their social media by leveraging a variety of strategies: brand deals, affiliate marketing, ad revenue, digital product sales, and more. She emphasizes the importance of authenticity, diversification, and community engagement as key components to a successful influencer business.

Key Takeaways

- Influencers make money. That is part of the fascination with the role. Fame itself does not translate to dollars, but marketing strategy does. Educating yourself on best practices, as well as strategies and techniques, allows a business to grow legs. Just like actors are products, so are influencers—it's a business. Treat it like one.

CHAPTER 9   MONETIZATION METHODS: TURNING INFLUENCE INTO INCOME

- Authenticity is easy in the beginning, but as opportunities arise, it becomes easier to give in to lip service. Authenticity is what actually drives most creators, and the audience is more important than the creator.

- Learn engagement techniques. This is probably the most important aspect of personal branding.

CHAPTER 10

The Importance of Authenticity: Maintaining Trust with Your Audience

In the world of endless marketing, where followers can quickly spot inauthenticity, staying true to who you are is not just a nice-to-have—it's essential. Authenticity is what builds trust, keeps your audience engaged, and ultimately makes your influence valuable. Today's audiences are smart. They can tell when something feels off or when an influencer is simply pushing a product for the sake of a paycheck. If you want to keep your followers loyal and maintain credibility, you have to be real with them.

Let's dive into why authenticity matters so much and how you can make sure you stay true to yourself while navigating the demands of brand partnerships.

CHAPTER 10   THE IMPORTANCE OF AUTHENTICITY: MAINTAINING TRUST WITH YOUR AUDIENCE

Why Authenticity Matters

1. Trust Is Everything

In the age of social media, people don't just want to hear about products—they want to hear from real people. When your followers trust you, they're more likely to engage with your content, buy from the brands you endorse, and support you long-term. But if they sense that you're only saying things because you're being paid, that trust evaporates fast.

2. Building Long-Term Relationships

The key to staying relevant as an influencer is long-term connection, not just quick gains. Authenticity allows you to create lasting relationships with your audience. People will continue to follow you because they believe in what you stand for, not because of a one-off post or flashy ad. This, in turn, strengthens your overall influence, because your audience feels genuinely connected to you.

3. Your Reputation Is Your Brand

When you're authentic, people see you as credible. Your followers believe in you because your content matches your values. When you promote something, they trust that it's because you truly believe in it, not just because it's a paid partnership. The moment you start promoting things that don't align with your personal brand, your credibility takes a hit—and that can be hard to rebuild.

4. Loyalty Over Numbers

It's easy to get distracted by follower counts or likes, but genuine engagement is what matters most. When you're authentic, your audience will feel more connected to you. They'll engage with your posts, comment on your stories, and share your content with others. And that's how you build a loyal following that sticks around, even as trends and algorithms change.

How to Stay Authentic While Working with Brands

1. Know What You Stand For

Before you can be authentic, you need to know what you believe in. What are your core values? What topics or causes matter most to you? Whether it's sustainability, mental health, fitness, or personal growth, your audience follows you for a reason. Make sure the content you create and the brands you partner with reflect those values.

2. Be Transparent

The audience today values honesty. If you're working with a brand, let your followers know. Always disclose when something is a paid partnership or sponsored content. Being up-front about your relationships with brands doesn't diminish your influence—it builds trust. Your followers will appreciate the honesty, and they'll respect you for it.

3. Only Promote What You Truly Use

This one is simple: if you wouldn't use a product in your everyday life, don't promote it. Your followers can tell when you're just pushing a product for the paycheck, and they won't appreciate it. Endorse products you believe in, things that align with your lifestyle. When you do this, your endorsement feels natural, and your audience will be more likely to trust your recommendations.

4. Engage Meaningfully with Your Audience

Being authentic doesn't stop at your posts—it's about how you engage with your followers. Respond to comments, answer messages, and show that you're a real person behind the screen. When followers feel like they're part of a conversation, they're more likely to trust you and stay engaged. Authenticity is built on connection, not just content.

5. Stick to Your Style and Voice

Consistency is key when it comes to authenticity. If your followers come to expect a certain tone or style from you, don't change that just to fit a brand's campaign. Whether you're posting a sponsored product or sharing a personal story, it should feel like something they would expect from you. Authenticity comes from being true to your voice, not trying to fit a mold.

6. Don't Overwhelm with Promotions

It's tempting to jump at every opportunity that comes your way, especially when the payout is good. But flooding your feed with sponsored posts can turn your audience off. Find a balance between organic, non-promotional content and sponsored content. Too much selling can make your followers feel like they're just being marketed to, and that's not authentic.

7. Be Honest About Your Journey

No one expects you to be perfect. In fact, your imperfections are part of what make you relatable. Don't shy away from sharing your personal struggles, challenges, or growth. People connect with real stories, and when you share your authentic self—both the successes and the setbacks—it builds a stronger bond with your audience.

8. Choose Partnerships That Fit

When a brand reaches out to you, take a moment to think about whether their product or message fits with what your audience expects from you. If it feels out of place or doesn't align with your values, it's okay to pass. Authenticity isn't about saying yes to every deal—it's about saying yes to the ones that fit your personal brand.

The Big Picture: Why Authenticity Is Crucial for Your Personal Brand

At the end of the day, authenticity is the backbone of a strong personal brand. It's not about selling your followers on every product—it's about building a relationship with them based on trust. When you stay true to who you are, you attract followers who believe in you, not just what you promote. They'll stick with you through thick and thin because they trust you, and that's what keeps you relevant in the long run.

In the noisy, crowded world of influencer marketing, it's easy to get lost in the race for numbers or the next big brand deal. But in the end, your authenticity will always be your strongest asset. When you stay true to yourself and build genuine, honest relationships with your followers, you're creating something that's far more valuable than just a paycheck—you're creating a lasting, meaningful connection that will support your career for years to come.

Remaining authentic as an influencer is key to building trust and maintaining long-term relationships with your audience. It's about staying true to your values, voice, and personal brand, even as opportunities for sponsored content and partnerships arise.

Here are some practical strategies to help you remain authentic while navigating the influencer landscape.

1. Know Your Values and Stick to Them

Before you even start collaborating with brands or posting content, take some time to define what you stand for. Whether it's sustainability, mental health, fitness, fashion, or something else, make sure your content and partnerships align with these values. Authenticity comes from consistency in what you promote and how you present yourself.

- **Tip**: Write down your core beliefs and values as a guide. Use this as a compass when deciding what content to create and which brands to partner with.

2. Be Transparent About Sponsored Content

Honesty is a huge part of authenticity. Your audience can spot when you're hiding a promotion or being vague about paid partnerships. Being up-front about sponsored content not only helps maintain trust but also shows that you respect your audience's intelligence.

- **Tip**: Always disclose when something is a paid partnership (e.g., "This post is sponsored by …"). Transparency is key, and most social media platforms have specific rules for this, so make sure you're following them.

3. Promote What You Truly Believe In

One of the best ways to maintain authenticity is to only promote products or services that you genuinely use or believe in. If a brand offers you a deal, ask yourself: "Would I use this in my own life? Would I recommend it to my friends or family?" If the answer is no, then it's probably not a good fit.

- **Tip**: Be selective with partnerships. Don't feel pressured to say yes to everything that comes your way. Your followers will respect you more for staying true to what you believe in.

4. Engage with Your Audience Genuinely

Authenticity isn't just about what you post; it's also about how you engage with your followers. Respond to comments, answer questions, and show that you're a real person behind the screen. Don't just use your followers as numbers—use them as a community to build genuine connections.

- **Tip**: Set aside time each day or week to engage with your followers, whether that's responding to DMs, liking their comments, or participating in meaningful conversations.

5. Avoid Over-promotion

While sponsored content is a source of income, constantly promoting products can make your feed feel like one big ad. This can turn off followers who feel like they're being sold to rather than engaged with.

- **Tip**: Maintain a balance between promotional content and personal content. Share your day-to day life, behind-the-scenes moments, and opinions that resonate with your audience, not just brand deals.

6. Share Your Personal Journey

One of the most authentic things you can do is to be real about your own experiences, struggles, and growth. People follow you not just for your style or expertise but because they relate to you on a personal level. By sharing personal stories—whether they're successes or challenges—you create a deeper connection with your followers.

- **Tip:** Don't be afraid to show vulnerability. Share your ups and downs, whether it's dealing with mental health, career changes, or personal growth. Authenticity thrives in transparency.

7. Stay Consistent in Your Message

Consistency is crucial to maintaining authenticity. Your audience follows you because they resonate with the message you put out, whether it's your fashion sense, wellness tips, or motivational posts. If you suddenly shift your messaging or promote things that feel out of character, you risk losing that connection.

- **Tip:** Stay true to your voice. If you're known for promoting self-care and wellness, don't suddenly pivot to a purely commercial tone unless it feels authentic to your brand and audience.

8. Set Boundaries with Brands

Sometimes, brands may approach you with campaigns or ideas that don't quite fit with your style or values. It's important to have the confidence to say no if a partnership doesn't align with your personal brand, even if the financial offer is tempting.

- **Tip:** Politely decline partnerships that don't resonate with your audience or personal values. Remember, it's better to turn down a deal than to risk damaging your relationship with your followers.

9. Maintain a Clear Brand Identity

Authenticity means staying true to your personal brand, and that brand should be something you clearly define and evolve over time. Whether you're known for a specific niche or have a broader appeal, always make sure your content aligns with who you are and what your audience expects.

- **Tip**: Define your personal brand's mission. Is it about empowering others, sharing knowledge, or showcasing a specific lifestyle? Keeping this in mind will help guide your content creation and brand collaborations.

10. Be Patient and Take Your Time

Building an authentic presence doesn't happen overnight. It takes time to build trust, develop your voice, and curate content that feels true to you. Don't rush the process or feel pressured to be everything to everyone. Stay patient, stay consistent, and focus on long-term growth rather than short-term success.

- **Tip**: Take your time to develop relationships with your followers. Growth doesn't happen instantly, but when you remain authentic, your audience will grow with you in a meaningful way.

11. Don't Be Afraid to Evolve

Being authentic doesn't mean staying static. It's about being true to who you are *now*—and if you evolve, that's okay. Whether it's a change in your personal interests, style, or messaging, it's natural to grow, and your followers will appreciate your honesty as you navigate those changes.

- **Tip**: Let your audience in on your journey. If you're trying new things, whether it's a new hobby, business venture, or lifestyle shift, share it with them. Growth is a part of authenticity, and showing it can deepen your connection with your community.

By following these strategies, you can maintain your authenticity while growing as an influencer. The key is to always keep your audience's trust and relationship at the forefront of your decisions. When you're true to yourself, your audience will reward you with loyalty, engagement, and long-term support.

A Spotlight on Authenticity

Three cases of authenticity leveraged in different ways are Emma Chamberlain, Zoe Sugg, and Alexandria Ocasio-Cortez. These are very different women, who use social media messaging to their advantage.

1. Emma Chamberlain: The Queen of Relatable, Unpolished Content

Known For: *Realness, humor, and imperfection*

Emma Chamberlain became a YouTube sensation thanks to her authentic, off-the-cuff style. Unlike many influencers who meticulously curate their content, Emma's charm lies in her unpolished, raw approach. She embraces imperfections, whether it's quirky editing, self-deprecating humor, or showing the behind-the-scenes mess of her life.

How She Leverages Authenticity

Emma's authenticity shines through in her videos and social media, where she often discusses her mental health, body image, and struggles with fame.

By openly sharing her challenges and the less-glamorous side of influencer life, she connects deeply with her audience. Her willingness to be vulnerable made her a relatable figure for young people who felt disconnected from the more polished, traditional influencers.

Emma also built her brand around being "real" in an often manufactured space. She's not afraid to show her true personality, even if it means not always fitting the typical influencer mold. This has resonated with millions of followers who value genuineness over perfection. Her partnership with brands like Louis Vuitton, despite her casual, down-to-earth style, proves that authenticity doesn't need to mean "low-budget" or "unpolished"—it can also translate into high-end collaborations when done right.

Key Takeaways

- Embrace your imperfections.
- Don't be afraid to show your true, vulnerable side.
- Relatability can be more powerful than perfection when building a loyal audience.

2. Zoe Sugg (Zoella): The Power of Consistency and Self-Branding

Known For: *Beauty, lifestyle, and positivity*

Zoe Sugg, better known as Zoella, initially gained fame through her beauty and lifestyle YouTube channel. Over time, she turned her personal brand into a full-blown business empire, including books, beauty products, and home goods. What sets Zoella apart is her ability to stay authentic while expanding her brand.

CHAPTER 10 THE IMPORTANCE OF AUTHENTICITY: MAINTAINING TRUST WITH YOUR AUDIENCE

How She Leverages Authenticity

Zoe's authenticity has been key to her long-standing success. Even as she built a multi-million-dollar brand, she maintained a consistent, relatable presence on her YouTube channel and Instagram. Zoe is known for her wholesome, positive persona, and she's made her content not just about beauty tips, but about self-care, mental health, and living a balanced life. She has always positioned herself as someone who champions body positivity and self-acceptance, which resonates with her predominantly young female audience.

Zoe also built a personal connection with her followers by sharing her life beyond just the influencer persona. She's been open about her relationships, her struggles with anxiety, and even her experience with pregnancy and motherhood. This transparency about her real-life challenges has helped humanize her and set her apart from influencers who might lean heavily into aspirational content.

Key Takeaways

- Consistency in your message and content builds trust over time.
- Sharing your personal experiences and struggles deepens your connection with followers.
- Authenticity doesn't mean sharing everything—Zoe knows how to maintain boundaries while still being relatable.

3. Alexandria Ocasio-Cortez (AOC): Authenticity in Politics and Activism

Known For: *Progressive politics, advocacy, and unfiltered communication*

While not a traditional "influencer," Alexandria Ocasio-Cortez (AOC) has effectively leveraged social media and her platform to build a personal brand rooted in authenticity and activism. AOC's ability to communicate directly with her followers and express her beliefs unambiguously has made her a powerful force in both politics and social media.

How She Leverages Authenticity

AOC's authenticity lies in her direct, unfiltered communication with her followers. She regularly engages with her audience on platforms like Instagram and Twitter, where she shares everything from behind-the-scenes glimpses into her life as a congresswoman to her unvarnished thoughts on policy, activism, and social justice. Her "Instagram lives" and stories often feel like conversations with a friend rather than scripted political speeches.

One of the ways AOC has built her authenticity is by staying true to her roots. She openly discusses her working-class background, her experience growing up in the Bronx, and the challenges she faced as a young woman in politics. She isn't afraid to challenge the status quo and call out issues like income inequality, climate change, and racial injustice. Her authenticity resonates with millions of followers who see her as a genuine voice for change, not a politician who is just playing the game.

Moreover, AOC uses her platform to advocate for causes she believes in and responds to her audience in real time. This two-way communication strengthens her credibility, as people feel that they are part of the conversation. She often shares her thoughts directly, even when it's controversial, which builds an image of someone who is unwaveringly true to their principles.

CHAPTER 10   THE IMPORTANCE OF AUTHENTICITY: MAINTAINING TRUST WITH YOUR AUDIENCE

Key Takeaways

- Authenticity can extend beyond influencer culture into areas like politics and activism.
- Open, unfiltered communication can create strong, direct connections with your audience.
- Staying true to your roots and beliefs, even in the face of opposition, helps build a powerful personal brand.

Final Thoughts

These influencers show how authenticity can be leveraged in various ways to build a personal brand. Whether it's by embracing imperfections (Emma Chamberlain), staying consistent and relatable (Zoella), or advocating for values and communicating directly with followers (AOC), each of these influencers has created a strong, authentic connection with their audiences. Their authenticity isn't just about being "real"—it's about showing up as their true selves, even when it's challenging, and building a brand that resonates with others because it reflects who they truly are.

Key Takeaways

- Authenticity is a quality of transparency and vulnerability, as well as personality. It is what separates the creator from the masses—we see a lot of inauthenticity in the digital space, and while it is tolerated, it is not aspirational. And being an influencer is an aspirational role. Creators come onto social media with personal goals—whether it is to educate, inspire,

CHAPTER 10   THE IMPORTANCE OF AUTHENTICITY: MAINTAINING TRUST WITH YOUR AUDIENCE

or shine a light on a chosen issue. The relationship between a creator and their community is the single aspect of influencing that cannot be faked. AI, for example, is a huge buzzword, but we just don't have the same reaction to a created identity that we do to a real human character. It's important to gain trust and to understand the fragility of the relationship with the community. It can be destroyed by bad behavior or unacceptable behavior to the audience.

- Consistency is also important for community—not just for growth, but to bond with the creator. People follow people who are consistent in posting, as well as outlook.

CHAPTER 11

Handling Challenges: Dealing with Criticism, Burnout, and Changes in Algorithms

Influencer Exhaustion

Being an influencer can be incredibly rewarding, but it's also filled with challenges. From dealing with criticism to managing burnout and adapting to constant changes in social media algorithms, it's important to have strategies to handle these hurdles.

Here's how to navigate these common challenges.

CHAPTER 11   HANDLING CHALLENGES: DEALING WITH CRITICISM, BURNOUT, AND CHANGES IN ALGORITHMS

Dealing with Criticism

Criticism is inevitable when you're putting yourself out there for an audience. Whether it's negative comments on your posts or harsh feedback from followers, it's important to stay grounded.

Here are some tips for managing criticism:

- **Don't Take It Personally**: Most negative comments are a reflection of the commenter's own feelings, not of your worth. It's easy to get discouraged, but remember that everyone faces criticism, especially public figures.

- **Separate Constructive Criticism from Trolling**: Constructive feedback can help you grow, while trolling is just meant to bring you down. Learn to tell the difference and focus on what's useful.

- **Respond Calmly (or Not at All)**: Sometimes, it's best to ignore unhelpful comments. If you do choose to respond, try to keep it respectful and professional.

- **Take Breaks from the Comments**: Constantly reading feedback can wear you down. Give yourself time away from your phone or computer to recharge mentally.

Managing Burnout

Burnout is a real risk in the influencer industry because there's often pressure to constantly create and stay relevant. Here are some strategies to prevent or cope with burnout:

- **Set Boundaries**: It's easy to get caught up in the hustle of creating content 24/7, but it's essential to set limits. Make time for other aspects of your life, whether it's spending time with family, taking up hobbies, or simply resting.

CHAPTER 11 HANDLING CHALLENGES: DEALING WITH CRITICISM, BURNOUT, AND CHANGES IN ALGORITHMS

- **Focus on Quality, Not Quantity**: You don't have to post all the time to stay relevant. Create meaningful content that resonates with your audience rather than feeling pressured to churn out posts.

- **Ask for Support**: Whether it's a manager, a fellow influencer, or a close friend, don't be afraid to ask for help when you need it. Sharing the workload or just talking about your feelings can help lighten the load.

- **Take Time Off When Needed**: If you're feeling overwhelmed, it's okay to step away from social media for a bit. A few days of rest can do wonders for your mental health and help you return with a fresh perspective.

Adapting to Algorithm Changes

Social media platforms are always tweaking their algorithms, which can impact how your content is seen by your audience. While it's frustrating to feel like you have no control over these changes, there are ways to stay adaptable:

- **Stay Informed**: Keep up with any changes to the platforms you use. Many social media sites provide updates about new features or changes in their algorithms. Understanding how these updates affect content visibility can help you adjust your strategy.

- **Diversify Your Platforms**: Relying on just one platform can be risky. If one algorithm changes and it impacts your reach, being active on multiple platforms can help ensure that you're not left behind.

- **Engage with Your Audience**: The algorithms tend to prioritize content that generates engagement. Respond to comments, ask questions, and encourage interaction in your posts to boost engagement.

- **Experiment and Adapt**: If something stops working, don't be afraid to try new approaches. Experiment with different types of content, posting schedules, and formats to see what resonates with your audience under the new algorithm.

Learning about social media algorithms can seem tricky, but there are plenty of ways to stay informed and adapt to changes. Here's how you can get a better understanding of how algorithms work on platforms like Instagram, TikTok, YouTube, and others.

1. Follow Official Social Media Blogs and Resources

Most social media platforms regularly update their users about changes in algorithms, new features, and best practices. Here are some great places to look for this information:

- **Facebook and Instagram Blog**: These platforms (which are owned by Meta) have a blog where they post updates on algorithm changes, new tools, and tips for content creators.

- **Twitter Blog**: Twitter also shares updates, especially on new features or changes that impact visibility and engagement.

- **TikTok Creator Portal**: TikTok offers its own set of resources for creators, including insights on how their content is ranked and suggestions for success.

- **YouTube Creators Blog**: YouTube frequently posts about algorithm updates, changes to monetization, and tips for improving your channel's performance.

2. Experiment with Your Content

A practical way to learn about algorithms is to experiment with different types of content and posting strategies to see what works best. Track how your posts perform over time and adjust based on what you notice. Some things to try include

- **Posting at Different Times**: See when your audience is most active and which times seem to give your content better reach.

- **Varying Your Content Format**: Test out videos, carousels, stories, and live streams to see which formats get the most engagement.

- **Adjusting Your Captions and Hashtags**: Experiment with different combinations to understand what resonates with your audience and boosts visibility.

3. Engage with Other Creators and Communities

Networking with other influencers and creators is a great way to share insights about what's working and what's not. Many influencers openly discuss the latest changes they've noticed in algorithms, and you can learn a lot from their experiences.

- **Join Facebook Groups, Reddit Threads, and Other Creator Forums**: There are many communities where creators exchange tips, discuss algorithm changes, and share what's working for them.

- **Follow Experts in Social Media Marketing**: Influencers, marketers, and agencies often analyze and break down algorithm changes in detail. People like Neil Patel, Social Media Examiner, or Hootsuite regularly post updates and articles on algorithm trends.

4. Use Analytics Tools

Most social media platforms provide built-in analytics that can give you insights into how your content is performing. By paying attention to key metrics like engagement rates, impressions, reach, and audience demographics, you can better understand what factors the platform's algorithm is prioritizing.

- **Instagram Insights, TikTok Analytics, YouTube Studio**: These native tools give you a sense of how your content is performing and help you tweak your strategy.

- **Third-Party Tools**: Platforms like Buffer, Sprout Social, or Later also offer more in-depth analytics and recommendations based on how well your content is doing.

5. Stay Updated with News and Research

Social media algorithms are always evolving, and some websites and newsletters track these changes in real time. Subscribing to industry news sources or following tech journalists can help you stay on top of the latest updates.

- **Tech Blogs and News Websites**: Websites like TechCrunch, Wired, and The Verge often write about changes in algorithms or trends in the social media industry.

CHAPTER 11   HANDLING CHALLENGES: DEALING WITH CRITICISM, BURNOUT, AND CHANGES IN ALGORITHMS

- **Marketing Newsletters**: There are several newsletters dedicated to digital marketing and social media trends, such as the *Social Media Examiner* newsletter or *Later's Social Media Trends*.

6. Learn from Online Courses or Tutorials

If you want a more structured approach, there are many online courses and tutorials that focus on social media algorithms and how they impact your strategy.

- **Udemy, Coursera, or Skillshare**: These platforms offer courses on social media marketing that include modules on algorithms and strategies to work with them.

- **YouTube Tutorials**: Many creators post free tutorials on YouTube about understanding social media algorithms and optimizing your content.

7. Observe Industry Experts and Case Studies

Watching how major brands and influencers adapt to algorithm changes can be eye-opening. Many big names in the industry will share their tips, and analyzing case studies can reveal what works and why.

- **Case Studies on Platforms like HubSpot or Hootsuite**: These sites often share successful examples of brands and influencers who have adapted well to algorithm changes.

- **Follow Social Media Strategists on Twitter or LinkedIn**: These professionals regularly comment on shifts in social media behavior and offer their insights.

CHAPTER 11 HANDLING CHALLENGES: DEALING WITH CRITICISM, BURNOUT, AND CHANGES IN ALGORITHMS

How to Handle Critics

Handling a crisis or dealing with trolling on social media can be stressful, but there are effective strategies you can use to manage these situations with professionalism and protect your mental well-being. Here are some strategies to deal with a social media crisis or trolling.

1. Stay Calm and Don't Respond Immediately

The first and most important step when dealing with a crisis or trolling is to stay calm. Responding in the heat of the moment can escalate the situation or make things worse. Take a step back, breathe, and give yourself time to think before replying, if at all.

- **Pause Before Reacting**: Whether it's a negative comment, a troll, or a crisis situation, don't rush to react. Take a break to collect your thoughts and assess the situation from a neutral standpoint.
- **Step Away from Your Phone**: Give yourself a few hours (or even a day) to gain emotional distance from the situation before you decide how to respond.

2. Don't Engage with Trolls

Trolls thrive on attention, and responding to them often leads to more conflict. If someone is deliberately trying to provoke you or disrupt your peace, it's best to ignore them. Here's what you can do:

- **Ignore or Block**: If someone is consistently trolling or being offensive, you can block or mute them. This prevents them from getting more attention, which is often their goal.

- **Delete Harmful Comments**: If a comment crosses a line (e.g., hate speech, bullying, or harassment), delete it. Many platforms also allow you to report abusive comments to the platform moderators.

- **Don't Fuel the Fire**: Engaging with trolls usually leads to more negativity and drama. It's often better to let the comment go and not give them what they want: a reaction.

3. Address the Crisis Professionally

If you're facing a more serious crisis (like a backlash to a post, a controversial statement, or a misunderstanding), it's important to address it with transparency and professionalism. Here's how:

- **Acknowledge the Issue**: If you've made a mistake or caused unintended harm, owning up to it can go a long way. A simple, honest acknowledgment can help defuse tension. For example: "I understand that my recent post upset some of you, and I sincerely apologize for that. It was never my intention."

- **Take Responsibility If Necessary**: If the crisis involves something you did or said, take accountability. Don't deflect blame onto others, and avoid making excuses. Show that you understand why people are upset and that you care about their concerns.

- **Offer a Solution or Plan for Change**: If applicable, explain how you plan to address the issue moving forward. For example, if your content unintentionally offended people, you could commit to educating yourself or changing your approach.

4. Use "The Power of the Delete Button"

In some cases, if the situation is escalating and you feel that continuing the conversation will not lead to a productive outcome, it's okay to delete comments or posts. This can be particularly useful when

- **Comments Are Getting Toxic**: If the comments on a post or thread are turning into an argument, with people attacking each other or you, it might be helpful to delete or hide comments to stop the negativity from spreading.

- **You're Being Harassed**: When the comments cross a line into harassment or threats, don't hesitate to delete and block the individuals involved. Many platforms now allow you to automatically filter out offensive language or comments.

5. Use Humor (When Appropriate)

Sometimes, responding with humor can defuse a tense situation, but this should be used carefully. Humor works best when the situation is lighthearted, and you're responding to playful teasing rather than serious trolling or harassment.

- **Be Careful with Humor**: Humor can backfire if it seems dismissive or out of touch with the feelings of others. It's important to assess whether humor will ease the situation or make things worse.

6. Take the High Road

If the crisis or trolling is personal or directed at your character, it's important to take the high road and remain professional. Responding with kindness, empathy, and maturity often silences negativity.

- **Don't Retaliate**: Even if you feel hurt or upset, responding with hostility or aggression will escalate the situation. Instead, stay kind and respectful in your responses, showing that you're the bigger person.

- **Deflect Negativity**: If someone is trying to drag you into a negative conversation, politely deflect. You can say something like "I prefer not to engage in negativity. I'm focused on positivity and moving forward." Use this super-carefully, though, because tone deafness can cause a crisis itself.

7. Engage with Your Supportive Community

When dealing with a crisis, don't forget about the people who support you. Your loyal followers can help counter negativity by defending you, sharing positive comments, or offering words of encouragement.

- **Show Appreciation for Supporters**: Thank your followers for their support, and let them know you appreciate them. Their kindness can help shift the focus away from the crisis and back toward your positive impact.

- **Don't Ask for a "Mob Mentality"**: While it's okay to appreciate support, don't encourage followers to attack or shame others. This can escalate the situation and lead to further issues.

8. Take Care of Your Mental Health

Social media crises and trolling can be emotionally draining. It's important to take care of yourself during tough times.

- **Limit Your Social Media Use**: If you're feeling overwhelmed, it's okay to step away from social media for a while. Taking a break can help you regain perspective and recharge mentally.

- **Talk to Someone**: If you're feeling affected by a crisis or trolling, confide in a friend, family member, or professional who can offer support.

- **Practice Self-Care**: Focus on activities that relax and recharge you, whether that's exercising, meditating, journaling, or spending time with loved ones.

9. Learn from the Experience

Once the crisis or trolling has passed, reflect on the situation to learn from it. Ask yourself:

- **What triggered the crisis or trolling?**
- **How did I handle it, and what could I have done differently?**
- **What steps can I take to prevent a similar issue in the future?**

Learning from difficult situations will help you become more resilient and better prepared if something similar happens again.

Handling a crisis or dealing with trolling on social media requires patience, professionalism, and emotional intelligence. By staying calm, addressing issues directly and respectfully, and taking care of yourself, you can navigate these challenges more effectively. Remember, your mental health is just as important as your social media presence—take breaks when you need them, and don't be afraid to lean on your support system.

Dealing With Online Hate

Dealing with hate online is incredibly difficult, and it's something that many people, especially those in the public eye, have to confront at some point. Whether it's hateful comments, cyberbullying, or targeted harassment, the key is to protect your mental health while handling the situation professionally. Here are some strategies to help you deal with hate online.

1. Don't Take It Personally

It's important to remind yourself that hate online often says more about the person leaving the comment than it does about you. People who spread hate typically do so because of their own insecurities or frustrations.

- **Detach Emotionally**: Try to separate yourself from the negativity. Hate is usually rooted in the other person's issues, not yours.

- **Remember Your Worth**: Focus on your positive qualities and your purpose, and don't let one hateful comment shake your confidence.

2. Don't Engage with Hate

One of the best ways to deal with online hate is to **not engage** with it. Trolls and haters thrive on getting a reaction, and responding often makes the situation worse.

- **Avoid Arguing or Defending Yourself**: Engaging with hate often leads to more hate and escalates the situation. It's usually a waste of energy to try to change someone's mind, especially when they're being disrespectful or malicious.

- **Ignore the Hate**: If the comment doesn't require a response, ignore it. Often, leaving a comment or message unanswered can make the person realize they aren't getting the reaction they wanted.

3. Block or Mute Haters

On most social media platforms, you have control over who interacts with you. Don't hesitate to **block** or **mute** people who are spreading hate or negativity. This can be an immediate way to protect yourself from further exposure to harmful content.

- **Block the Person**: If someone is repeatedly hateful or harassing you, blocking them can stop their comments from appearing on your page and prevent them from contacting you.

- **Mute Them**: If you don't want to go as far as blocking, muting allows you to stop seeing a person's posts or comments without them knowing. It can also be a way to avoid unnecessary conflict.

4. Delete Hateful Comments

If someone leaves a hateful or abusive comment on your posts, it's okay to delete it. This shows that you're not tolerating negativity and helps maintain the integrity of your space online.

- **Maintain Your Boundaries**: Social media is your platform, and you get to decide what kind of content or behavior is allowed.

- **Create a Safe Space**: Deleting hateful comments can help ensure that your followers see a more supportive and positive environment, which can ultimately reduce the overall toxicity.

5. Report Abusive Behavior

Most social media platforms have built-in features for reporting abuse, harassment, or hateful comments. If someone is engaging in behavior that violates the platform's terms of service (e.g., hate speech, bullying, threats), report them to the platform.

- **Use Reporting Tools**: Platforms like Instagram, Twitter, and Facebook allow you to report comments or accounts that are violating their guidelines.

- **Escalate If Necessary**: If the hate involves serious threats of violence or harassment, don't hesitate to report it to local authorities, especially if you feel unsafe.

6. Take a Step Back

Dealing with hate online can be emotionally draining, and it's essential to protect your mental well-being. If the situation is overwhelming, take a break from social media to regain your peace of mind.

- **Take a Social Media Detox**: Disconnecting from social media for a day, week, or longer can help you regain a sense of balance and focus on self-care.

- **Reflect and Recharge:** Use the time away to focus on activities that make you feel grounded, such as spending time with friends or engaging in hobbies.

7. Focus on the Positive

Hate is often loud and attention-grabbing, but it's important to focus on the positive support you receive. For every hateful comment, there are likely many more people who support and appreciate you.

- **Engage with Positive Feedback:** Spend time reading the supportive comments or messages from your followers. It's easy to get bogged down by negativity, but remember that most people are kind and appreciative.

- **Thank Your Supporters:** Show gratitude to those who stand by you. Engaging with supportive people can remind you why you do what you do and encourage a sense of community.

8. Respond Thoughtfully (When Necessary)

In some cases, responding to hate with grace and maturity can actually help defuse the situation, especially if the hate is based on a misunderstanding or misinformation.

- **Address the Issue Calmly:** If you feel that responding is necessary, do so in a calm and non-defensive manner. Acknowledge the criticism without escalating the conflict.

- **Correct Misinformation**: If the hate stems from a misunderstanding or misrepresentation of facts, you can politely correct the information without attacking the person who posted it.

9. Set Boundaries

Set clear boundaries with your online presence. Be mindful of how much of yourself you share and what you are willing to tolerate from others.

- **Limit Personal Information**: Avoid sharing sensitive personal details that can make you vulnerable to online attacks.

- **Create Clear Content Guidelines**: If you manage a public platform or community, make it clear that hate speech, harassment, or abusive behavior will not be tolerated. This sets the tone for how others will interact with you.

10. Consider Professional Help

If online hate is affecting your mental health or leading to anxiety, depression, or feelings of isolation, consider seeking professional support.

- **Talk to a Therapist**: A therapist or counselor can help you work through the emotional impact of online hate and provide strategies for coping with stress and negativity.

- **Join Support Groups**: Connecting with others who have faced similar online hate can help you feel less isolated and provide practical advice for handling online harassment.

11. Educate and Advocate

In some situations, hate may be based on ignorance or misinformation. If you're comfortable doing so, you can use your platform to educate and raise awareness about the issues at hand.

- **Advocate for Kindness and Empathy:** Share messages of positivity and inclusivity to create a more supportive online environment.

- **Challenge Harmful Ideas:** If you feel it's appropriate, you can use your voice to challenge hate and educate others, particularly when it comes to issues like racism, sexism, or other forms of discrimination.

12. Keep Perspective

Remember that online hate, while hurtful, is usually temporary. People often forget about things quickly, and the loud voices of hatred will eventually fade.

- **Focus on Long-Term Goals:** Remember why you're online in the first place and keep your eye on the bigger picture. Online hate is a temporary setback, and it won't define your entire journey.

- **Protect Your Peace:** Ultimately, your peace and well-being are what matter most. Don't let the negativity of others drown out the positivity you're creating.

Conclusion

Handling hate online is challenging, but it's possible to navigate it with resilience and grace. By remaining calm, setting boundaries, and focusing on your mental well-being, you can protect yourself from the negativity. Remember, online hate is often more about the person delivering it than it is about you. Stay grounded, focus on your supporters, and take care of yourself. You don't have to let hate take up space in your life.

Case Study: Chrissy Teigen's Response to Past Tweets and Cyberbullying Controversy

The Crisis

In May 2020, Chrissy Teigen faced a significant backlash after past tweets resurfaced in which she had harshly criticized other public figures, including a now-infamous incident where she had made cruel comments toward then-teenager Courtney Stodden. The comments, made years earlier, were seen as mean-spirited and inappropriate, particularly because Stodden was only 16 at the time.

At the same time, Teigen was also called out for her role in cyberbullying. In 2021, Stodden publicly accused Teigen of sending private messages encouraging them to take their own life, which further fueled the controversy. Chrissy faced significant online hate, with people accusing her of hypocrisy and cruelty, especially since she had built her public persona around being an advocate for kindness and empowerment.

CHAPTER 11 HANDLING CHALLENGES: DEALING WITH CRITICISM, BURNOUT, AND CHANGES IN ALGORITHMS

Chrissy Teigen's Response: How She Handled the Crisis

1. **Public Acknowledgment and Apology**

    - **Immediate Admission**: Teigen did not shy away from the situation. Rather than deflecting or minimizing the impact of her past actions, she publicly acknowledged the harm she had caused. She issued a heartfelt apology through a statement on social media, expressing deep regret for her previous behavior.

    - **Sincere and Personal**: In her apology, Chrissy didn't make excuses. She fully admitted that her past comments were "cruel" and apologized specifically to Courtney Stodden for her actions. Her apology was personal and detailed, with no attempts to downplay the gravity of the situation.

2. **Quote from Teigen's Apology:**

    "Not a day, not a single day has gone by where I haven't felt the crushing weight of regret for the things I've said in the past … I am so sorry for being a troll. I am so sorry I let you down."

3. **Public Accountability**

    - **Direct Engagement with the Affected Party**: After the public apology, Chrissy Teigen took the initiative to reach out to Courtney Stodden directly. In a private conversation, she expressed her remorse in person and offered a sincere apology.

CHAPTER 11   HANDLING CHALLENGES: DEALING WITH CRITICISM, BURNOUT, AND CHANGES IN ALGORITHMS

While Stodden initially expressed skepticism about her apology, Teigen's willingness to engage personally was seen as a step toward mending the relationship.

- **Taking Responsibility**: Teigen didn't shift blame onto anyone else. She owned up to her actions, saying, "I was a troll, I was mean, I was unkind." She also acknowledged the privilege that had allowed her to escape accountability for her behavior until now, showing self-awareness about the power dynamics at play.

4. **Reflection and Public Education**

- **Educating Her Audience**: Chrissy Teigen used her platform not just to apologize but to educate others about the impact of online trolling and bullying. In interviews and social media posts, she shared her reflection on how social media can be a toxic space and how easy it is to get caught up in the culture of cruelty that often pervades it.

- **Commitment to Change:** Teigen emphasized that she was committed to doing better moving forward. She spoke about taking time to educate herself, and even though she had previously been an advocate for social justice, she admitted that her actions didn't align with those values at the time.

241

CHAPTER 11   HANDLING CHALLENGES: DEALING WITH CRITICISM, BURNOUT, AND CHANGES IN ALGORITHMS

5. **Long-Term Actions**

    - **Stepping Back from Public Life**: Chrissy Teigen took a temporary step back from social media in the aftermath of the controversy. She acknowledged that she needed time to reflect on her actions and focus on personal growth. Her absence from the public eye was seen as an example of stepping back to reflect rather than doubling down or continuing to defend herself.

    - **Rebuilding Trust**: Teigen also focused on rebuilding her reputation by continuing her advocacy for mental health awareness, supporting charitable causes, and staying open about her growth. She continued to share her vulnerability with her audience, showing that she was actively learning from her mistakes.

6. **Engaging in Positive Online Spaces**

    - **Reaffirming Values**: When Teigen returned to social media, she made a conscious effort to focus on positivity and kindness. Her posts were more reflective, self-aware, and supportive of her community. She made it clear that she was focusing on creating a healthier relationship with her audience.

CHAPTER 11   HANDLING CHALLENGES: DEALING WITH CRITICISM, BURNOUT, AND CHANGES IN ALGORITHMS

Key Strategies That Contributed to Her Successful Crisis Management

1. **Transparency and Vulnerability:** Teigen's willingness to openly admit her mistakes and show vulnerability helped rebuild trust with her audience. In a world where influencers often deflect blame or issue vague apologies, her sincerity stood out.

2. **Acknowledging the Harm:** Rather than making it about herself, Teigen focused on the impact of her words on others, particularly Courtney Stodden. She took full responsibility for her actions and made it clear that she understood the gravity of the situation.

3. **Private and Public Apologies:** By reaching out privately to Stodden, Teigen showed that her apology wasn't just a public relations move. This added a layer of authenticity to her response. Public acknowledgment combined with private reconciliation can go a long way in defusing crises.

4. **Education and Growth:** Instead of just apologizing and moving on, Teigen demonstrated a commitment to personal growth and learning. Her willingness to engage in self-reflection and educate both herself and her followers about online harm was an important step in showing accountability.

5. **Taking Responsibility and Stepping Back:** By stepping away from the public eye for a while, Teigen allowed space for the controversy to settle down. It also allowed her to focus on her personal growth and prioritize her mental health.

CHAPTER 11 HANDLING CHALLENGES: DEALING WITH CRITICISM, BURNOUT, AND CHANGES IN ALGORITHMS

Outcome and Public Perception

Chrissy Teigen's handling of the situation wasn't without controversy, and some people remained critical, believing that her apology wasn't enough. However, the general consensus was that her response was one of genuine remorse and growth. Over time, she was able to rebuild her reputation and restore much of the goodwill she had with her audience.

Her crisis management was widely praised for its transparency, vulnerability, and commitment to doing better. The controversy also sparked broader conversations about cyberbullying, accountability in the digital age, and the responsibility influencers have for their past actions.

Conclusion

Chrissy Teigen's public crisis was a moment that could have severely damaged her career, but her honest and thoughtful approach to acknowledging and learning from her mistakes set a positive example for how influencers can handle controversy. By taking full responsibility, apologizing sincerely, and committing to positive change, she demonstrated that it's possible to come back from a public crisis with integrity and growth.

Key Takeaways

- Handling challenges is a key part of being an influencer, as the role often comes with criticism, burnout, and the constant evolution of social media algorithms. Dealing with criticism requires staying grounded and maintaining perspective. It's important not to take negative comments personally, as they often reflect the

CHAPTER 11 HANDLING CHALLENGES: DEALING WITH CRITICISM, BURNOUT, AND CHANGES IN ALGORITHMS

critic's own issues rather than your worth. Separating constructive feedback from trolling can help you focus on what is useful. Responding calmly or choosing not to engage at all can prevent unnecessary conflict, and taking breaks from reading comments can protect your mental well-being.

- Burnout is another significant risk in this field due to the pressure to constantly create and remain relevant. Setting boundaries between your work and personal life is essential to avoid overworking. Focus on quality over quantity by creating meaningful content rather than feeling pressured to post constantly. Seek support from managers, peers, or friends to lighten your workload and share your feelings. Taking time off when overwhelmed can help you recharge and return with a fresh perspective.

- Adapting to algorithm changes is an ongoing challenge for influencers, as platforms frequently update their systems. Staying informed by following official platform blogs and industry experts can help you adjust your strategies effectively. Diversifying your presence across multiple platforms reduces the risk of overreliance on a single one. Engaging with your audience and experimenting with different types of content and posting strategies can improve visibility and relevance despite algorithm changes. These approaches collectively help influencers navigate the challenges of their profession with resilience and adaptability.

CHAPTER 12

Looking Ahead: Trends and Opportunities in the Influencer Industry

The influencer marketing landscape is constantly evolving, driven by changes in technology, consumer behavior, and new platforms. As we look ahead to the next few years, several trends are shaping the future of the industry. Here's a deep dive into these emerging trends and the opportunities they present for influencers and brands alike.

The Rise of New Platforms and Digital Spaces

TikTok and Short-Form Video Domination

TikTok has quickly become the leading platform for influencers, and its format of short, creative videos is rapidly being embraced by other platforms. Instagram Reels, YouTube Shorts, and even Facebook have introduced similar features in response to TikTok's success.

- **Opportunity**: Influencers who adapt to short-form video content are likely to see substantial growth. These formats encourage creativity, engagement, and virality, offering opportunities for influencers to reach new audiences.

- **Trend**: The "snackable" content trend is likely to continue, with more emphasis on quick, entertaining, and easily digestible videos. Brands will increasingly work with influencers to produce this kind of content that aligns with consumer demand for speed and instant gratification.

New Platforms and Communities

While TikTok is the current front-runner, other platforms are also emerging. Platforms like **Clubhouse** (audio-based social networking), **BeReal** (emphasizing authenticity), and **Substack** (focused on newsletters and community building) are examples of platforms that were growing in popularity. These platforms cater to niche audiences, and as they grow, new influencer opportunities will emerge. While these may not be the juggernauts of the future, they serve as examples of platforms that exist outside the big ones—and new ones are being built every day.

- **Opportunity**: Influencers who are early adopters of emerging platforms can establish themselves as pioneers, attracting loyal followers and potential brand deals in these spaces. BeReal, for example, taps into a desire for authenticity, presenting an opportunity for influencers to showcase their unfiltered selves.

- **Trend**: As new platforms rise, influencers will need to diversify their presence and adapt to different formats and audiences. The "creator economy" will continue to expand across multiple platforms.

Evolving Consumer Behaviors
Authenticity and Relatability

In an era where audiences are becoming more skeptical of overly polished content, **authenticity** continues to be a driving force in influencer marketing. Consumers increasingly prefer influencers who feel "real" and relatable, rather than those who appear to be perfect or highly curated.

- **Opportunity**: Influencers who embrace vulnerability, share their personal journeys, and present a more "real" side of themselves will likely attract more engagement and loyalty. The audience is craving genuine connections, and this is particularly true for younger generations like Gen Z.

- **Trend**: Expect more influencers to embrace unfiltered content, such as behind-the-scenes footage, "day-in-the-life" stories, and content that shares both successes and failures.

Purpose-Driven Influence

Consumers, especially Millennials and Gen Z, are increasingly driven by values and social issues. Influencers who use their platforms for advocacy—whether it's about mental health, sustainability, diversity, or social justice—are seeing greater engagement.

- **Opportunity**: Brands are keen to partner with influencers who align with their own values. Influencers with a clear personal mission or cause can attract brand partnerships that go beyond traditional product placements, such as those focused on social good, sustainability, or advocacy.

- **Trend**: The rise of purpose-driven influencers will continue, with brands seeking to collaborate with creators who can genuinely speak to social, environmental, and cultural issues in an authentic and meaningful way.

The Growth of the Creator Economy

Monetization Beyond Sponsorships

While brand partnerships are still the primary revenue source for many influencers, we're seeing an explosion in alternative monetization options. Platforms like **Patreon**, **Substack**, and **OnlyFans** allow influencers to build direct revenue streams through memberships, subscriptions, and content sales.

- **Opportunity**: Influencers can create diversified income streams by offering exclusive content to paid subscribers, providing coaching or workshops, selling merchandise, or even launching their own product lines. This reduces reliance on brand deals and offers more financial independence.

- **Trend**: Expect the rise of **creator-owned businesses**, where influencers take a more entrepreneurial approach. This includes launching personal brands, creating digital products (like ebooks or courses), and offering paid content or fan clubs.

Virtual and Augmented Reality (AR/VR) Experiences

The metaverse and the rise of virtual experiences are beginning to intersect with influencer marketing. As AR and VR technologies continue to advance, brands and influencers are experimenting with immersive experiences, like virtual fashion shows, interactive product launches, and branded virtual worlds.

- **Opportunity**: Influencers with a tech-savvy or creative edge could capitalize on the metaverse and AR/VR opportunities by hosting virtual events or creating interactive content that bridges the gap between digital and real-world experiences.

- **Trend**: Expect AR filters and VR experiences to become a common part of influencer content, especially in industries like fashion, gaming, and entertainment. Brands will partner with influencers to create virtual experiences that engage customers in new and innovative ways.

CHAPTER 12   LOOKING AHEAD: TRENDS AND OPPORTUNITIES IN THE INFLUENCER INDUSTRY

Shifting Marketing Budgets and Brand Expectations

Increased Investment in Micro- and Nano-influencers

While top-tier influencers still garner a lot of attention, many brands are shifting marketing budgets toward **micro-** (10,000–100,000 followers) and **nano-** (under 10,000 followers) influencers. These influencers often boast higher engagement rates and have more niche, loyal audiences.

- **Opportunity**: If you're a micro- or nano-influencer, you're in a strong position to attract brands looking for highly engaged, hyper-targeted audiences. Brands are recognizing the value of community over sheer numbers.

- **Trend**: Expect more brands to partner with smaller influencers who can deliver personalized, authentic content that resonates with specific demographics. Micro-influencers may find themselves with more collaboration opportunities than ever before.

Long-Term Partnerships Over One-Off Campaigns

Brands are increasingly looking for **long-term relationships** with influencers, rather than focusing on one-off campaigns. This trend is driven by the desire to foster stronger, more authentic connections between influencers and their audiences.

CHAPTER 12   LOOKING AHEAD: TRENDS AND OPPORTUNITIES IN THE INFLUENCER INDUSTRY

- **Opportunity**: Influencers who can build lasting partnerships with brands—based on shared values and consistent messaging—will benefit from more stable income streams. Long-term collaborations create the possibility for deeper storytelling, recurring brand ambassadorships, and greater influence.

- **Trend**: The influencer-brand relationship will move toward partnerships built on trust and shared values, rather than just transactional campaigns.

The Impact of Artificial Intelligence and Data Analytics

AI-Powered Content Creation and Personalization

AI tools are becoming more sophisticated in helping influencers create personalized content at scale. These tools can help with everything from content recommendations based on audience preferences to generating captions and editing photos.

- **Opportunity**: Influencers can use AI to create more efficient, personalized, and engaging content that resonates with their audiences. By leveraging data and analytics, influencers can deliver highly targeted messages, resulting in increased engagement and conversions.

- **Trend**: Expect AI to play a major role in content optimization, campaign management, and audience analysis, allowing influencers to make data-driven decisions that enhance their brand partnerships.

CHAPTER 12   LOOKING AHEAD: TRENDS AND OPPORTUNITIES IN THE INFLUENCER INDUSTRY

Influencer Marketing Platforms and Data Tracking

The growth of influencer marketing has led to the development of more sophisticated influencer marketing platforms (e.g., **Grapevine**, **Upfluence**, **Influencity**) that help brands find the right creators, track campaign performance, and measure ROI.

- **Opportunity**: Influencers can leverage these platforms to connect with brands more easily, track their campaign performance, and fine-tune their strategies. The ability to demonstrate ROI with clear analytics will become increasingly important for influencers looking to attract long-term brand deals.

- **Trend**: Data-driven marketing will continue to grow, with influencers and brands using analytics to refine their approaches and ensure campaigns are delivering real, measurable results.

Preparing for the Future

The future of influencer marketing is dynamic and full of potential. Influencers who adapt to new platforms, embrace authenticity, and capitalize on the evolving monetization opportunities will thrive in the coming years. As the digital landscape evolves, there will be more opportunities for influencers to build meaningful, sustainable careers and for brands to forge deeper, more authentic connections with their audiences.

Staying informed about these trends, being flexible in your approach, and continuously evolving your strategies will be key to success in the influencer industry's future.

CHAPTER 12   LOOKING AHEAD: TRENDS AND OPPORTUNITIES IN THE INFLUENCER INDUSTRY

The future of influencer marketing is poised to be shaped by several key trends and technological advancements. As the digital landscape evolves, influencer marketing will continue to grow, but it will also become more sophisticated, diversified, and integrated with emerging platforms and technologies. Below are the major directions we can expect influencer marketing to take in the coming years.

1. Increased Focus on Authenticity and Niche Communities

Consumers are becoming more discerning and skeptical of traditional advertising methods, which has led to a growing demand for **authenticity** in influencer marketing. Instead of relying on celebrities with millions of followers, brands will focus more on working with **micro-** and **nano-influencers** who have smaller but highly engaged and loyal followings. These influencers are seen as more relatable and trustworthy, which drives higher engagement rates.

- **Niche Influencers**: The rise of niche communities means influencers who cater to specific interests (e.g., sustainable living, pet care, DIY beauty, mental health) will become more valuable to brands targeting specialized markets.

- **Authentic Content**: There will be an increasing emphasis on content that feels organic and authentic, as audiences demand transparency and vulnerability from influencers, particularly those in the Gen Z and Millennial demographics.

2. Shift Toward Long-Term Partnerships Over One-Off Campaigns

Brands are beginning to recognize the value of **long-term relationships** with influencers rather than short-term, one-off campaigns. Long-term partnerships help brands build trust and consistency, while influencers benefit from stable revenue streams and deeper relationships with their audiences.

- **Brand Ambassadors**: Influencers will move toward being **brand ambassadors**, representing brands over extended periods, integrating them naturally into their everyday content and long-term storytelling.
- **Consistent Messaging**: Brands will increasingly rely on influencers who can consistently communicate their brand's values and products, helping to maintain a coherent and authentic narrative across multiple touchpoints.

3. Emergence of Virtual Influencers and AI Integration

The rise of **virtual influencers** (digital avatars created using artificial intelligence or CGI) and AI-driven content creation tools will revolutionize influencer marketing. These virtual influencers are becoming popular because they offer a degree of control that human influencers can't—no sleep, no mistakes, and the ability to be perfectly on-brand at all times.

- **AI-Generated Content**: Influencers will increasingly use AI-powered tools to streamline content creation. These tools can help influencers optimize content for specific audiences, predict trends, and automate aspects of content production (e.g., generating captions, editing images, analyzing engagement).

- **Virtual Influencers and Brand Control**: Virtual influencers, like **Lil Miquela** or **Shudu**, will continue to rise in popularity, allowing brands to control the messaging and appearance of their spokespersons without the unpredictability that comes with human influencers.

4. Integration of the Metaverse and Augmented Reality (AR)

The **metaverse**—a collective virtual shared space composed of interconnected virtual worlds—will present new opportunities for influencer marketing. Virtual and **augmented reality (AR)** experiences will enable influencers to create interactive, immersive content that blends the digital and physical worlds.

- **Virtual Events and Experiences**: Influencers will host **virtual events** in the metaverse, such as product launches, fashion shows, and concerts, where followers can engage with brands in a more immersive way.

- **AR-Driven Shopping**: Augmented reality will allow influencers to create interactive shopping experiences, where followers can see how products look in their homes, on their skin, or in real life before making a purchase.

5. Greater Integration of Ecommerce and Social Commerce

Social media platforms are already enabling **ecommerce** integration (e.g., Instagram Shopping, TikTok's in-app checkout), and this trend will only grow. Influencers will become more closely aligned with ecommerce strategies, using their content as a direct sales funnel for products and services.

- **Shoppable Content**: Influencers will seamlessly integrate **shoppable posts** and live-streamed shopping experiences into their content, allowing followers to purchase products directly through social platforms without leaving the app.

- **Social Commerce**: The **social commerce** market is expected to grow rapidly, with influencers driving sales through their recommendations, whether through direct product placement, affiliate links, or live commerce (e.g., TikTok live shopping).

6. Data-Driven and Performance-Based Campaigns

With the rise of sophisticated analytics tools, influencer marketing will become more data-driven. Brands will use detailed metrics to track the **ROI** (return on investment) of their influencer partnerships, enabling them to make more informed decisions.

- **Advanced Analytics**: Brands will increasingly rely on **data analytics** to evaluate the performance of influencer campaigns. This includes tracking engagement rates, sales conversions, audience sentiment, and other KPIs.

- **Performance-Based Compensation**: Influencers may be compensated based on **performance metrics** (e.g., sales conversions, clicks, leads generated) rather than flat fees. This will lead to more **affiliate-style** compensation structures.

7. Rise of Purpose-Driven Influencer Marketing

Consumers, particularly younger generations, are increasingly aligning their purchasing decisions with their **values**. This has led to the rise of **purpose-driven influencers** who focus on promoting social, environmental, or ethical causes.

- **Sustainability and Social Good**: Influencers who advocate for issues like **climate change**, **sustainability**, and **social justice** will continue to gain traction. Brands will increasingly partner with influencers who reflect their own values, fostering deeper connections with purpose-driven audiences.
- **Ethical and Transparent Marketing**: Brands will seek to align with influencers who practice **ethical marketing** and are transparent about their sponsored content, product choices, and collaborations with causes.

8. Personalized and Interactive Content

The future of influencer marketing will be more about **personalization** and **direct interaction** between influencers and their audiences. This will be driven by the evolution of AI, machine learning, and social platforms that allow influencers to create hyper-targeted content.

- **Personalized Experiences**: Influencers will use AI tools to craft personalized content for their followers, providing specific recommendations based on individual preferences or behaviors.

- **Increased Interactivity**: Followers will engage with influencers in more **interactive ways**, including live Q&As, interactive polls, virtual meetups, and personalized shout-outs. Platforms will continue to evolve to enable direct, real-time engagement.

9. Expansion of Influencer Marketing into New Industries

While influencer marketing started with beauty, fashion, and lifestyle, it is increasingly spreading into more diverse industries such as **healthcare**, **finance**, **education**, and **B2B marketing**.

- **Niche Sectors**: Influencers will become trusted voices in sectors like **personal finance**, **fitness**, **mental health**, and **business**. Companies in these industries will recognize the power of influencers to build trust and communicate complex topics in a relatable way.

- **B2B Influencers**: Business-to-business (B2B) influencers will become more common, where industry experts, thought leaders, and consultants influence decision-makers in corporate sectors.

CHAPTER 12   LOOKING AHEAD: TRENDS AND OPPORTUNITIES IN THE INFLUENCER INDUSTRY

A More Integrated, Immersive, and Data-Driven Future

The future of influencer marketing is set to be **multidimensional** and **technology-driven**, with influencers leveraging new platforms, virtual experiences, and advanced analytics to create more **personalized**, **authentic**, and **engaging** content. As influencer marketing continues to mature, it will become more seamlessly integrated with ecommerce, augmented reality, and the metaverse, enabling influencers to connect with their audiences in entirely new ways.

For brands, the focus will be on forging **long-term partnerships** with influencers who align with their values and have deep, authentic relationships with niche communities. For influencers, it will mean becoming more than just content creators—**entrepreneurs**, **advocates**, and **experiential leaders** who shape the future of online culture, commerce, and creativity.

Building trust between **brands**, **influencers**, and **audiences** is critical in the influencer marketing ecosystem. Trust is a key factor in determining the success of influencer campaigns, as audiences tend to gravitate toward influencers and brands they perceive as authentic, transparent, and aligned with their values. In the future, trust will continue to evolve as the industry incorporates new technologies, platforms, and shifts in consumer behavior. Here's how trust will be built and maintained in the future.

1. Authenticity and Transparency in Content

Consumers, particularly Millennials and Gen Z, are increasingly distrustful of overt advertising and fake personas. For trust to develop, influencers must be transparent in how they present products and brands to their audiences. This includes clear disclosures about paid partnerships and sponsored content.

- **Authenticity in Content**: Influencers who share their genuine opinions about products and services—both positive and negative—will foster stronger connections with their audience. Audiences will trust influencers who showcase the **real person** behind the content, rather than just polished, commercialized representations.

- **Transparent Brand Relationships**: Future influencers will be expected to clearly disclose their partnerships with brands, not just by using hashtags like **#ad** or **#sponsored**, but by being open about their involvement in the creation of campaigns, product testing, and the relationship with the brand itself.

- **Behind-the-Scenes Access**: Audiences will increasingly demand access to the process behind the product endorsements. Influencers will build trust by showing how products are tested, how brands align with their personal values, and how they make decisions about the brands they work with.

2. Building Long-Term Relationships Rather Than One-Off Campaigns

Brands and influencers who focus on **long-term partnerships** rather than one-off campaigns are more likely to build lasting trust with both audiences and each other.

- **Consistency**: When influencers consistently work with the same brands over time, it builds credibility. Audiences begin to see these influencers as brand

CHAPTER 12   LOOKING AHEAD: TRENDS AND OPPORTUNITIES IN THE INFLUENCER INDUSTRY

ambassadors rather than paid promoters, which strengthens the relationship between the influencer and their followers.

- **Shared Values**: Brands and influencers who align on values such as sustainability, inclusivity, or social responsibility will be more likely to earn trust. Audiences are becoming increasingly conscious of the ethical practices of the brands they support, and influencers who share those values will resonate more deeply with their followers.

- **Increased Transparency in Campaign Goals**: For long-term partnerships, brands will need to be transparent not only about the products but also about their broader goals—whether they are focused on environmental impact, diversity, or giving back to communities. Influencers will need to be transparent about their involvement in these larger narratives.

3. Audience Involvement and Interaction

The future of influencer marketing will see more **interactive** and **participatory** content, where audiences feel directly involved in the creation and promotion process.

- **Two-Way Conversations**: Influencers will continue to engage with their audiences through live chats, Q&A sessions, polls, and comments. This real-time interaction helps humanize influencers and fosters a sense of community. When influencers actively listen to their audience's opinions and feedback, trust increases because the relationship feels more personal and reciprocal.

- **Crowdsourced Content**: Brands may invite followers to participate in content creation, whether it's voting on product designs, submitting content, or helping to test new ideas. This level of involvement creates a stronger connection between influencers, brands, and the audience, as people feel like they are part of the process, not just passive consumers.

- **User-Generated Content (UGC)**: In the future, influencer campaigns will often incorporate UGC, where audiences share their own experiences with the products. Influencers can amplify this content by reposting and engaging with it. When audiences see their own content being acknowledged by their favorite influencers, it strengthens the feeling of trust and community.

4. Leveraging Technology and Data for Personalization

AI, data analytics, and machine learning will continue to play a significant role in personalizing the influencer experience for audiences. The more an influencer can tailor content to their audience's preferences, the more trusted they will become.

- **Personalized Content**: Influencers will increasingly use **AI-driven tools** to create content that is tailored to individual audience segments. By delivering more relevant and personalized content, influencers will show they understand their audience's needs and preferences, which strengthens trust.

- **Predictive Analytics**: Data analytics will allow influencers to understand what content resonates most with their audience, allowing them to refine their messaging and deliver even more targeted, valuable experiences. This level of insight helps ensure that influencer campaigns feel authentic and not forced.

- **Tracking and Feedback**: As AI becomes more sophisticated, influencers can track how their content performs in real time and adjust their strategies accordingly. Audiences will trust influencers who are able to **adapt** based on feedback, rather than repeating the same approach over and over.

5. Sustainability and Social Responsibility

Trust is increasingly built on **shared values**, and brands and influencers that prioritize **sustainability**, **ethics**, and **social responsibility** will win the loyalty of future audiences.

- **Purpose-Driven Campaigns**: Influencers who partner with brands that are committed to sustainability, environmental causes, or social justice issues will resonate more strongly with today's socially conscious consumers. For instance, influencers who promote eco-friendly brands or initiatives that align with their values are seen as more trustworthy.

- **Ethical Practices**: Transparency about product sourcing, labor practices, and environmental impact is becoming non-negotiable for both brands and influencers. Audiences are increasingly holding brands and influencers accountable for their actions. The ability to demonstrate genuine commitment to ethical practices will be critical to maintaining trust.

- **Cause Marketing**: As influencers continue to use their platforms to advocate for causes they care about, audiences will increasingly expect this to be part of the overall brand story. Influencers who successfully use their platforms to raise awareness and drive social change will build trust by showing they care about more than just making a sale.

6. Trust via User-Generated and Peer Reviews

Audiences will increasingly rely on the experiences of their peers and fellow consumers to gauge the authenticity of an influencer's recommendations.

- **Peer Reviews and Testimonials**: In the future, platforms will integrate more sophisticated mechanisms for user-generated reviews, where customers can leave feedback about their experience with products. Influencers will amplify these reviews by engaging with their community about their thoughts, which in turn helps build trust in the product or service.

CHAPTER 12   LOOKING AHEAD: TRENDS AND OPPORTUNITIES IN THE INFLUENCER INDUSTRY

- **Crowdsource Endorsements**: Brands and influencers might rely more heavily on **crowdsourced testimonials** and **real-world usage** stories to validate the products being marketed. When an influencer's followers can share their positive experiences with the product in real time, it adds another layer of authenticity and trustworthiness.

7. Authentic Storytelling and Content That Adds Value

Rather than focusing solely on selling products, influencers will increasingly prioritize **storytelling** and content that adds value to their audience's lives.

- **Value-Driven Content**: Influencers who provide practical advice, education, or inspiration (e.g., wellness tips, financial advice, or DIY tutorials) will strengthen their credibility. Their audiences will trust them more if they see the influencer's content as enriching their lives, not just promoting products.

- **Narrative-Based Campaigns**: Influencers who tell stories—whether about personal struggles, success stories, or brand journeys—will continue to build trust with their audience. When a product is tied to a **genuine narrative**, it becomes more relatable and memorable, establishing an emotional connection.

8. Privacy and Data Protection

As data privacy concerns grow, both brands and influencers will need to demonstrate a **strong commitment to protecting user information**. Consumers are becoming more conscious of how their data is being used, and trust will increasingly be built on transparency regarding data collection and usage.

- **Data Transparency**: Influencers and brands who are open about how they collect, store, and use customer data will be trusted more. This could include everything from respecting user privacy in online surveys to being transparent about using consumer data for targeted ads.

- **Security Practices**: Brands and influencers who take measures to ensure **data security** will build trust by reassuring their audience that their personal information is protected. This is particularly important as social media platforms gather more data about consumers' behavior.

The Future of Trust in Influencer Marketing

In the future, trust between brands, influencers, and audiences will be built on authenticity, transparency, and shared values. Influencers will be expected to align with their audience's beliefs and show real, human sides through authentic storytelling and consistent engagement. Data, technology, and ethical practices will help strengthen this relationship, with a growing emphasis on sustainability, social responsibility, and transparency.

The influencers who thrive in this evolving landscape will be those who can create meaningful, value-driven content, prioritize real relationships over transactions, and align with the values that resonate most deeply with their audience. This focus on **genuine connection**, **ethical behavior**, and **personalization** will be the cornerstone of trust in the influencer marketing space moving forward.

The future of consumer behavior in relation to **influencer marketing** will be shaped by a variety of technological, social, and cultural shifts. As consumers grow more sophisticated and their expectations evolve, influencer marketing will need to adapt to these changes. Below are some key ways that consumer behavior is likely to change in the future as a result of influencer marketing.

1. Increased Demand for Authenticity and Transparency

Consumers are becoming more discerning, and the rise of **social consciousness**—especially among Millennials and Gen Z—means they expect brands and influencers to be more **authentic** and **transparent**.

- **Expectation of Genuine Engagement**: Audiences will expect influencers to be more real and vulnerable, sharing both the positive and negative aspects of their lives and products. They'll favor influencers who engage in **honest storytelling** and demonstrate that they truly believe in the brands they promote.

- **Authentic Endorsements**: Consumers will demand transparency around sponsored content, preferring influencers who disclose partnerships clearly and who only promote products they genuinely use or support. Influencers who engage in **authentic product reviews** (whether positive or negative) will build stronger trust with their audiences.

- **Reluctance Toward Overly Commercial Content**: Consumers will increasingly tune out **overly polished, commercialized advertising** and prefer content that feels organic, like behind-the-scenes glimpses or unboxing videos that highlight a more human and relatable side.

2. More Direct Interaction with Brands and Products

Consumers will expect more **interactive** and **immersive** brand experiences facilitated by influencers, especially as new technologies like augmented reality (AR), virtual reality (VR), and the metaverse take hold.

- **Personalized Recommendations:** Through AI and machine learning, influencers will be able to offer **highly personalized product recommendations**, tailored to the specific preferences and past behaviors of their followers. Consumers will appreciate this level of personalization, as it provides them with more relevant suggestions and experiences.

- **Real-Time Feedback and Interaction:** Consumers will expect to interact with influencers and brands in real time via live streams, Q&As, and direct messages. As influencer marketing becomes more dynamic, consumers will want to feel like they have a direct line to the influencers they follow—whether through **live shopping events**, **virtual try-ons**, or **real-time product reviews**.

- **Augmented Reality and Virtual Shopping**: With AR technologies, consumers may use filters to try on clothes or makeup virtually through an influencer's content. They'll increasingly expect these experiences to be integrated directly into their social platforms, making shopping more interactive and seamless.

3. More Active Participation in Campaigns

The future of consumer behavior in influencer marketing will see **greater participation** from audiences in the campaigns themselves, transforming consumers from passive watchers to active contributors.

- **Crowdsourced Content**: Influencers will invite their followers to co-create content, such as **user-generated videos**, polls, or voting on product designs. Consumers will become more involved in shaping the brand narrative by sharing their own experiences, which increases emotional investment in both the product and the influencer.

- **Influencer-Fan Co-creation**: Consumers might become collaborators in the product creation process, whether it's helping design limited-edition items or suggesting features for a new product. This co-creation fosters a sense of ownership and deeper brand loyalty.

- **Crowd-Influenced Purchasing**: Consumers will increasingly look to their peers' recommendations and crowdsourced reviews. Social proof from an influencer's audience (like user-generated content or feedback) will be just as important as traditional influencer endorsements. This leads to greater authenticity and a shift toward **peer-driven influence**.

4. Shift Toward Ethical and Purpose-Driven Purchasing

Consumers will continue to prioritize **ethics** and **values-driven consumption**, particularly as younger generations demand more from the brands they support.

- **Purpose-Driven Consumption**: Influencers will align with brands that share their personal values, such as sustainability, social justice, or ethical labor practices. Consumers will gravitate toward brands and influencers that advocate for meaningful causes, and they'll increasingly make purchasing decisions based on a brand's **corporate social responsibility** (CSR) efforts.

- **Sustainability and Eco-friendly Choices**: As environmental concerns grow, consumers will seek out brands that offer **sustainable, eco-friendly products**. Influencers who promote brands with transparent supply chains, sustainable sourcing, and eco-conscious production practices will earn the trust and loyalty of these values-driven consumers.

- **Trust in Social Impact**: Consumers will seek influencers who advocate for real, tangible change, not just performative actions. If an influencer or brand promises to donate a portion of their profits to charity, consumers will expect proof of these efforts. **Impact-driven influencers** will gain traction as consumers demand accountability.

5. Influencer-Driven Ecommerce (Social Commerce)

The future of consumer behavior will include a **seamless integration** between social media, influencer content, and ecommerce. Consumers will expect to be able to purchase directly from influencers' posts, with minimal friction.

- **Social Commerce**: As platforms like Instagram, TikTok, and YouTube further integrate shopping features, consumers will increasingly expect to shop directly through influencer posts and live streams. Influencers will leverage features like **shoppable posts**, **swipe-up links**, or **in-app checkout** to make the shopping experience more seamless.

- **Live Shopping and Virtual Try-Ons**: Influencers will host **live shopping events**, where they demonstrate products in real time, interact with viewers, and offer exclusive discounts. Consumers will enjoy the interactivity and immediacy of this format, especially if they can engage directly with the influencer and ask questions about the products.

- **Instant Purchase Decision**: With the increasing ease of purchasing directly through social media platforms, consumers will make more **impulsive buying decisions** based on the influence of a trusted creator, particularly in live or video formats. Brands will need to optimize for **impulse buys** and **limited-time offers** to cater to this behavior.

6. Increased Demand for Privacy and Data Control

As concerns over privacy and data security continue to rise, consumers will expect influencers and brands to be more **transparent** about how they collect and use personal data.

- **Data Transparency**: Influencers and brands will be expected to disclose how consumer data is being collected and used for personalization, marketing, and targeting purposes. Consumers will gravitate toward brands that prioritize **data privacy** and ensure that their information is secure.

- **Opt-In/Opt-Out Control**: Consumers will want more control over how their data is used for personalized recommendations. Brands and influencers will need to give followers the ability to opt in or out of certain data-sharing practices, ensuring that their marketing practices remain respectful of privacy.

7. Preference for Virtual and Digital Influencers

The rise of **virtual influencers** (like **Lil Miquela** or **Shudu**) will change how consumers perceive and interact with influencers.

- **Virtual Influencers as Role Models**: As virtual influencers become more sophisticated, some consumers may come to view them as role models in the same way they view human influencers today. These digital personalities will appeal to those who seek highly controlled, curated experiences that traditional influencers cannot provide.

- **Consumer Acceptance of AI**: AI-generated influencers, with their flawless personas and perfectly managed branding, will become more commonplace. These virtual influencers will work with brands in a similar way human influencers do but will likely offer more consistency and less controversy, catering to a different kind of consumer that values **idealized perfection** over authenticity.

8. Hyper-personalization and Predictive Shopping

The future of influencer marketing will involve more **data-driven insights** to provide hyper-personalized recommendations that predict what a consumer will want before they even realize it.

- **Predictive Analytics**: Using AI and big data, brands and influencers will analyze consumer behavior patterns to predict and recommend products that are likely to appeal to individual consumers. Consumers will expect influencers to know them well enough to provide product suggestions tailored specifically to their needs, tastes, and buying habits.

- **Real-Time Customization**: As consumers become accustomed to personalized experiences, they'll expect influencers to adapt their content in real time based on audience preferences, seasonal trends, or shifting interests. The ability to provide **tailored recommendations** during live streams or interactive content will be a major selling point.

CHAPTER 12   LOOKING AHEAD: TRENDS AND OPPORTUNITIES IN THE INFLUENCER INDUSTRY

The Evolution of Consumer Behavior with Influencer Marketing

The future of consumer behavior in influencer marketing will be marked by **greater interactivity**, **ethical consumption**, and **personalized experiences**. Consumers will seek **authenticity** and **transparency** from influencers, and their purchasing decisions will be increasingly driven by social causes, sustainability, and personalization. As technological advancements—like AI, AR, and the metaverse—transform the landscape, consumers will demand more **seamless** and **interactive** shopping experiences directly integrated into the influencer content they follow.

Ultimately, the brands and influencers who succeed will be those who can **forge authentic, values-driven relationships** with their audiences, **embrace new technologies**, and **deliver highly personalized, ethical experiences** that meet the evolving expectations of future consumers.

Key Takeaways

- The influencer industry continues to evolve, shaped by technological advancements, changing consumer preferences, and the emergence of new platforms. Looking ahead, several trends and opportunities stand out for influencers and brands. The rise of short-form video platforms like TikTok, Instagram Reels, and YouTube Shorts highlights the demand for creative, snackable content. These formats are engaging and viral, offering influencers opportunities to expand their reach. Additionally, emerging platforms like Clubhouse and BeReal provide niches for influencers to establish themselves early and cater to specific audiences, emphasizing authenticity and unfiltered content.

CHAPTER 12   LOOKING AHEAD: TRENDS AND OPPORTUNITIES IN THE INFLUENCER INDUSTRY

- Consumer behavior is also shifting, with authenticity and purpose-driven content taking center stage. Audiences are gravitating toward influencers who are relatable and transparent, favoring behind-the-scenes glimpses and content that reflects genuine values. Influencers advocating for social causes, such as sustainability or mental health, are particularly well-positioned to engage with younger, socially conscious demographics.

- Monetization strategies for influencers are diversifying beyond traditional sponsorships. Platforms like Patreon, Substack, and OnlyFans enable influencers to build direct revenue streams through subscriptions and exclusive content.

- Smaller influencers, particularly micro- and nano-influencers, are gaining prominence as brands shift their focus toward highly engaged, niche audiences. These influencers often build deeper connections with their followers, making them valuable partners for brands seeking authentic engagement.

- The influencer industry is heading toward a future defined by authenticity, innovation, and collaboration. Influencers who embrace new platforms, adapt to evolving consumer expectations, and diversify their monetization strategies will thrive. For brands, aligning with influencers who genuinely reflect their values and fostering long-term partnerships will be key to building meaningful connections with audiences.

CHAPTER 13

The Future of Influence: Predictions and Insights into the Next Era of Influencer Marketing

The Evolution of Influence

Influencer marketing has evolved rapidly over the past decade, growing from a niche marketing tactic to a multi-billion-dollar industry. As we look toward the future, several key trends and technological advancements will reshape how brands, influencers, and consumers interact. Below, we'll explore some key predictions and insights about where influencer marketing is headed.

CHAPTER 13   THE FUTURE OF INFLUENCE: PREDICTIONS AND INSIGHTS INTO THE NEXT ERA OF INFLUENCER MARKETING

1. The Rise of AI-Driven Influencer Marketing

Artificial intelligence (AI) will play a pivotal role in transforming influencer marketing. Already, AI tools are being used for tasks such as identifying suitable influencers, automating content generation, and analyzing campaign performance.

- **Predictive Analytics**: AI will help brands forecast the success of influencer campaigns based on historical data, audience behavior, and social media trends. This will enable more accurate budgeting and more effective campaign strategies.

- **Personalized Content**: AI tools can help create highly personalized and engaging content at scale. For instance, using deep learning and data analytics, brands could tailor influencer content to specific audience segments, increasing engagement rates.

- **Influencer Selection Algorithms**: AI will continue to improve at predicting the ideal influencer for a brand based on a combination of factors, such as engagement rates, audience demographics, content style, and even personal values, making influencer selection more efficient.

2. Increased Focus on Micro- and Nano-influencers

While influencer marketing has largely been dominated by macro- and celebrity influencers, we are seeing a shift toward **micro- and nano-influencers**—individuals with smaller, more targeted followings (ranging from 1,000 to 100,000 followers).

- **Authenticity and Trust**: Micro- and nano-influencers often have a more intimate and authentic connection with their followers, which leads to higher engagement rates and more trust. Brands will increasingly prioritize these influencers because their recommendations feel more genuine and less commercialized.

- **Cost-Effectiveness**: Smaller influencers are often more affordable than their macro counterparts, which allows brands to reach niche markets in a more cost-effective manner.

- **Community Engagement**: Nano-influencers, in particular, are highly embedded in tight-knit online communities, making them valuable for niche marketing efforts.

3. The Integration of Virtual Influencers and Digital Avatars

The use of **virtual influencers**—computer-generated characters with social media profiles—will become more prevalent in the future of influencer marketing. These AI-powered personalities can be programmed to act in specific ways and maintain perfect brand alignment.

- **Brand Control**: Virtual influencers provide brands with complete control over their image and messaging. This removes risks like scandals or inconsistent brand representation.

- **New Experiences and Storytelling**: Virtual influencers allow for immersive and creative marketing campaigns that blur the line between reality and fiction, especially in AR/VR environments.

- **Diversity and Representation**: Digital avatars can be created to reflect diverse identities, allowing brands to reach a broader and more inclusive audience.

4. Expansion into New Platforms and Technologies

As platforms like TikTok, Instagram, and YouTube continue to dominate the influencer landscape, we can expect to see new platforms and technologies emerge that will offer new opportunities for influencer collaborations.

- **Social Commerce**: Social commerce (shopping directly through social platforms) will continue to grow, with influencers playing a key role in driving sales through shoppable posts, live streams, and interactive content. Expect to see platforms like Instagram, TikTok, and even Pinterest double down on this trend, integrating more seamless buying experiences directly within influencer content.

- **Metaverse and AR/VR**: As the metaverse becomes more mainstream, influencers will begin operating in virtual worlds, hosting events, promoting products, and engaging with audiences in immersive environments. Augmented reality (AR) technology will also enhance influencer marketing by allowing consumers to interact with products and brands in new, interactive ways through their devices.

- **Short-Form Video and Livestreaming**: The popularity of short-form video will continue to surge, with influencers producing highly shareable, viral content. Livestreaming will also become an increasingly powerful way for influencers to engage audiences in real time, from Q&As to product launches and even virtual shopping experiences.

5. The Convergence of Influencer Marketing with Consumer Activism

As consumer behavior shifts, more brands and influencers are being expected to take stands on social, political, and environmental issues.

- **Purpose-Driven Influence**: In the future, we expect to see a greater emphasis on influencers who align with social causes and sustainability. Consumers, particularly Gen Z, are gravitating toward brands and influencers who are vocal about issues such as climate change, diversity, mental health, and inclusivity.

- **Authenticity and Accountability**: Brands will need to ensure that influencers they work with are genuinely aligned with their values. Consumers can spot "performative" activism, and influencers who jump on trending causes for the sake of profit risk alienating their audiences.

- **Corporate Social Responsibility (CSR) Integration**: Influencers will increasingly be a key part of corporate social responsibility strategies, advocating for causes and creating campaigns that bring attention to societal issues.

CHAPTER 13   THE FUTURE OF INFLUENCE: PREDICTIONS AND INSIGHTS INTO THE NEXT ERA OF INFLUENCER MARKETING

6. Influencers as Content Creators and Brand Entrepreneurs

The role of influencers will evolve beyond just being brand ambassadors. Many influencers will embrace the role of **entrepreneurs** and become the faces behind their own product lines, apps, and even agencies.

- **Brand Ownership**: Influencers will increasingly build their own brands and expand into product lines, services, or even online platforms. Their deep understanding of their audiences and established credibility make them well-positioned to create successful ventures.

- **Collaborations Beyond Traditional Ads**: Influencers will be involved in co-creating content or even entire campaigns with brands, moving from passive endorsement to active participation in product development, marketing strategies, and campaign execution.

7. Greater Scrutiny on Transparency and Ethics

As influencer marketing becomes more entrenched, issues of transparency and ethics will come to the forefront.

- **Disclosure and Compliance**: Expect stricter regulations surrounding paid partnerships and sponsored content. Influencers will be held to higher standards when it comes to clearly disclosing when content is paid for or when products are gifted.

- **Authenticity and Mental Health**: Brands and influencers will need to be more mindful of the impact that constant exposure to "idealized" lives and products can have on mental health, especially among younger audiences. Ethical marketing practices and campaigns that promote positive, inclusive, and realistic images will be a top priority.

8. The Importance of Data Privacy and Consumer Control

With increased concerns around data privacy, influencers and brands will have to adapt to new regulations and technologies designed to protect consumer data.

- **Privacy Regulations**: Stricter data privacy laws (like GDPR) will impact how influencer campaigns collect, store, and use consumer data. Transparency around data usage will become a top priority for brands and influencers.

- **Consumer-Controlled Influence**: Consumers will gain more control over how their data is used in marketing, possibly even having the option to opt in for specific influencer-driven campaigns.

The Next Era of Influence Is Data-Driven, Authentic, and Immersive

The future of influencer marketing will be shaped by a combination of technological innovation, shifting consumer preferences, and evolving platforms. Brands will increasingly turn to influencers not only as content

CHAPTER 13   THE FUTURE OF INFLUENCE: PREDICTIONS AND INSIGHTS INTO THE NEXT ERA OF INFLUENCER MARKETING

creators but as partners in creating authentic, impactful, and immersive marketing experiences. The key to success will lie in finding the right balance between creativity, data-driven insights, and maintaining a genuine connection with audiences.

As these trends unfold, both influencers and brands will need to stay agile, ethical, and open to the evolving landscape to navigate the next era of influence successfully.

The scandals that have rocked social media and the influencer industry over the past decade have provided valuable lessons for brands, influencers, and consumers alike. From issues of transparency and authenticity to the power dynamics between influencers and their audiences, these scandals have shaped the way we view online influence, marketing, and ethics. Here's what we've learned.

1. The Importance of Authenticity and Transparency

One of the key takeaways from various scandals is the critical importance of **authenticity** in influencer marketing. When influencers are caught engaging in misleading or deceptive practices, such as promoting products they don't genuinely use or endorsing fraudulent claims, trust erodes quickly.

- **Transparency in Sponsored Content**: The #Ad or #Sponsored disclosure has become standard in influencer marketing to ensure consumers know when content is a paid endorsement. However, scandals such as influencers promoting products without proper disclosure (or even using vague hashtags like #partner or #collaboration) have shown that audiences are sensitive to any perception of dishonesty. In some cases, influencers have faced backlash and lost followers after failing to disclose partnerships clearly.

- **Mismatched Values**: Consumers are increasingly drawn to influencers who align with their own values. When influencers promote products or services that conflict with their stated beliefs or engage in behaviors that contradict their public personas, it can lead to "cancel culture" or a loss of credibility. Authenticity and consistency are non-negotiable.

2. The Consequences of Overselling and Misleading Claims

Several scandals have arisen from influencers overselling products or services, particularly in categories like health and wellness, financial advice, and beauty. For instance, influencers have faced backlash for promoting unproven medical treatments, diet pills, or financial schemes, sometimes to disastrous effect.

- **Legal Implications and Accountability**: Lawsuits, fines, and regulatory crackdowns have highlighted the legal risks of making misleading claims. In some cases, influencers and brands have faced consequences for promoting unsafe or unapproved products. This has led to greater scrutiny by regulatory bodies like the Federal Trade Commission (FTC) in the United States and similar organizations worldwide, as well as growing demand for more stringent industry standards.

- **Consumer Protection**: The scandals involving misleading claims have heightened awareness about consumer protection. Influencers and brands now face increasing pressure to ensure that the products they promote are safe, legitimate, and backed by evidence. As a result, we're likely to see more rigorous vetting processes before partnerships are made and stricter policies around health claims.

3. The Power of Cancel Culture and Consumer Backlash

One of the most significant lessons learned from influencer scandals is the **power of public opinion** in the age of social media. Scandals—whether related to controversial statements, unethical behavior, or misrepresentation—can lead to swift and widespread backlash.

- **Reputation Can Be Made or Broken in Hours**: Social media has given consumers the power to hold influencers and brands accountable in real time. A single tweet or Instagram post can go viral, prompting calls for boycotts or "canceling" influencers who engage in behavior deemed inappropriate or unethical. This has forced influencers and brands to be far more cautious about their actions and messaging.

- **Public Apologies Aren't Always Enough**: In many cases, influencers who have faced controversy or scandal have tried to make amends with public apologies. However, consumers are increasingly skeptical of apologies that seem insincere or are perceived as a response to backlash rather than genuine remorse. The lesson here is that accountability and transparency must be built into the brand's and influencer's ethos, rather than serving as a reaction to public outcry.

4. The Impact of Mental Health on Influencers

Several high-profile scandals have underscored the pressures of social media fame on influencers' **mental health**. Issues like burnout, anxiety, and depression have been widely discussed, with influencers revealing how the constant pressure to maintain a curated image can take a toll.

- **The Human Side of Influence**: The realization that influencers are not immune to mental health struggles has reshaped how audiences view their online personas. In some cases, influencers who have been open about their mental health challenges have gained even more respect and support from their followers. It has led to greater empathy for the pressures of public life and increased awareness of the need for mental health support in the industry.

- **The Need for Boundaries and Self-Care**: Influencers have learned the importance of setting personal boundaries and prioritizing self-care. This includes limiting social media engagement, taking breaks from content creation, and being mindful of their mental health. For brands, this means supporting influencers in creating content in a healthy and sustainable way and encouraging transparency about the challenges influencers face.

5. Ethical Concerns Around Sponsored Content and Brand Ambassadorships

A recurring theme in scandals is the blurred line between **sponsored content** and organic recommendations. When influencers fail to disclose paid partnerships or misrepresent their experiences with products, it can lead to consumer distrust.

- **The Need for Ethical Standards**: The lack of ethical standards around influencer marketing has led to calls for more structured regulations and industry guidelines. Influencers and brands alike have learned that ethical marketing practices are not just a legal requirement but are essential for long-term success and credibility.

- **The Role of Brands in Ethical Marketing**: Brands that work with influencers must also take responsibility for ensuring their campaigns are ethical. This means thoroughly vetting influencers, being transparent about product claims, and working to avoid any form of exploitation or deception.

6. The Limits of Social Media Influence and "Influencer Fatigue"

As influencer marketing has grown, there's been increasing concern over **influencer fatigue**—the growing cynicism that consumers feel toward overly commercialized or inauthentic content. This has contributed to some scandals as influencers push the limits of what they're willing to promote for financial gain, causing their credibility to plummet.

- **Saturation and Consumer Trust**: As social media users are bombarded with sponsored posts and ads, the effectiveness of influencer marketing has started to wane. Audiences are becoming more discerning and skeptical of the products influencers promote, especially when they appear too frequently in ads or are inconsistent with the influencer's personal brand.

This has forced influencers and brands to reconsider their approach and focus on delivering high-quality, engaging, and authentic content that adds value to the audience.

7. The Power of Algorithms and Data Privacy Concerns

Scandals related to data privacy breaches (e.g., the Cambridge Analytica scandal) have highlighted the role of **algorithms** and **data** in shaping influencer marketing. With influencers gaining access to vast amounts of user data, concerns about privacy, data security, and how this information is used have become a critical issue.

- **Consumer Awareness and Consent**: There is a growing need for consumers to have greater control over their personal data and how it's used by influencers and brands. Transparency around how data is collected and used in influencer campaigns is now a top priority for brands and platforms, especially in light of privacy laws like GDPR.

- **Algorithmic Manipulation**: The role of social media algorithms in determining what content gets seen—and by whom—has been a hot topic in influencer scandals. There are concerns that influencers and brands may manipulate algorithms (e.g., through fake engagement or paid "likes") to artificially inflate their reach and influence, which can be misleading to consumers. This has led to a push for more accountability in how algorithms are designed and monitored.

CHAPTER 13   THE FUTURE OF INFLUENCE: PREDICTIONS AND INSIGHTS INTO THE NEXT ERA
             OF INFLUENCER MARKETING

The Path Forward

Scandals in social media and influencer marketing have underscored the importance of trust, transparency, and authenticity in the digital age. They have taught us that

- Influencers and brands must be transparent and responsible in their marketing practices.
- Audiences are increasingly discerning and will hold influencers accountable for unethical behavior.
- Mental health, ethical standards, and data privacy must be prioritized as the industry continues to evolve.

The future of influencer marketing will likely be shaped by these lessons, as both influencers and brands strive to foster more ethical, authentic, and consumer-centric marketing practices. As we move forward, learning from these scandals will be crucial to maintaining the integrity and trust that drives successful influencer marketing.

Index

A
Adler, Lindsay, 93–95
Alexandria Ocasio-Cortez (AOC), 217, 218
Algorithm management
    analytics tools, 226
    block/mute haters, 234
    blogs/resources, 224, 225
    case studies, 227
    content/posting strategies, 225
    creators/communities, 225
    crisis, 239
    delete comments/posts, 230
    educate/advocate, 238
    experience, 232
    experiment, 224
    features, 224
    hateful/abusive comment, 234
    haters thrive, 233
    high road and remain professional, 231
    humor, 230
    industry experts, 227
    insecurities/frustrations, 233
    learning, 232
    long-term goals, 238
    mental health, 232
    misunderstanding/misinformation, 236
    newsletters, 226
    online courses and tutorials, 227
    positive support, 236
    professional support, 237
    reflect and recharge, 236
    reporting abuse, 235
    set boundaries, 237
    stay adaptable, 223
    stay calm, 228
    supportive community, 231
    third-party tools, 226
    transparency and professionalism, 229
    trolls thrive, 228
Alighieri, Dante, 18
Armstrong, Archibald, 17
Artificial intelligence (AI), 23, 253, 280
Augmented reality (AR), 251, 257, 270, 282
Authenticity, 205
    Alexandria Ocasio-Cortez (AOC), 217, 218
    audience, 211

INDEX

Authenticity (*cont.*)
   brands, 207
   brands/posting content, 210
   Chamberlain, Emma, 214, 215
   consistency, 208, 212
   counts, 206
   engagement, 208
   evolution, 213
   leverages, 214
   long-term connection, 206
   partnerships, 209
   patient, 213
   personal brand, 209, 213
   products, 206
   promote products/services, 210, 211
   promotional content, 208
   reputation, 206
   set boundaries, 212
   sharing personal stories, 212
   sponsored content, 210
   strategies, 214
   tone/style, 208
   transparent, 207
   Zoe Sugg (Zoella), 215, 216

B

Ballerina Farm
   community, 140
   content optimization/algorithm insights, 145
   homesteading, 140
   influencer model, 143
   key values/goals, 141
   leveraging platforms, 143
   platform-specific strategies, 146
   social media platforms, 141, 142
   strategic vulnerability and connection, 142
Barrymore, Drew, 134–137
Bondone, Giotto di, 18
Burnout management, 222, 223, 245

C

Casey, Kate, 155
Chamberlain, Emma, 214, 215
Chaucer, Geoffrey, 18
Chick-fil-A, 3, 4
Content creation
   Adler, Lindsay, 93–95
   agility, 92
   audience, 41
   authentic connections, 91
   backlighting, 96
   calendar, 119–122
   call to action (CTA), 115
   camera app, 97
   camera movements, 102
   checklist, 39
   competitors, 40
   composition techniques, 97
   consistency, 116
   consistent style, 101
   continued learning, 110
   current assets, 41

elements, 115
Facebook, 123
formats, 92
golden hour, 95
high-profile influencers, 91
influencer creation process, 116
    brainstorming ideas, 117
    editing process, 118
    filming/shooting, 117
    planning/ideation, 116
    promotion/engagement, 119
    research/planning, 117
    scripting, 117
    testing/optimization, 118
Instagram, 122
instructional content, 93
key considerations, 124
keyword optimization, 115
keyword research, 40
leading lines and framing, 98, 99
lens flares, 97
leverage feedback/data, 40
lighting techniques, 94
motion/speed ramping, 102
partnerships, 41
personality, 38
photo, 103
post-production, 102
practice/patience, 109
production, 37–39
props and textured backgrounds, 101
sharp focus and depth, 99, 100
silhouettes, 97
social media posts, 110–113
social media strategies, 91
strategic tool outlines, 119–122
TikTok, 122
trends and community, 91
trial and error, 110
videography, 101, 102
visual identification, 100, 101
visual medium, 113, 114
YouTube, 124
Corporate social responsibility (CSR), 272, 283
Crisis management
    accountability, 240
    comments, 239
    cyberbullying, 239
    key strategies, 243
    long-term actions, 242
    public acknowledgment, 240
    public perception, 244
    reaffirming values, 242
    reflection and public education, 241
    responsibility, 241
Criticism management, 222, 244

D

Deeper Dive
    citizen journalism, 150
    communication/social interaction, 149
    e-commerce/consumer culture, 152

INDEX

Deeper Dive (*cont.*)
    entertainment/
        pop culture, 150
    news and misinformation, 150
    online shopping, 152
    political engagement, 151
    political polarization, 151
    social movements, 151
    streaming services, 151
Digital influencers, 27–29

E

Ethical considerations, 52
    accountability, 56
    commercial side, 51
    conflict of interest, 61, 63
    face subtle/direct
        pressure, 59
    FTC guidelines/legal
        requirements, 59, 60
    libel and slander, 53–55
    long-term success, 61, 62
    private information/
        NDA, 55, 56
    review units/products, 58, 59
    sponsored trips, 57
    transparency, 56, 57
    trips/brand perks, 57, 58
    trust and authenticity, 51
    trust/leaks/confidential
        information, 60
    YouTuber Trevor Jacob, 52
Eyck, Jan van, 18

F, G

Facebook, 123, 133
    Ballerina Farm, 146
    hashtags strategies, 160
    influencers, 12
Federal Trade Commission (FTC), 24, 59, 60, 287
Financial reports, 3
Forleo, Marie, 86

H

Hill, Jaclyn, 34

I

Increasing followers/engagement
    audience/data analysis
        tools, 130
    community building, 133
    community initiatives, 139
    content creation/
        optimization, 131
    data analysis tools, 131
    direct engagement, 130
    hashtag optimization, 133
    influential community, 134–137
    Instagram/TikTok, 133
    live streams/Q&A sessions, 138
    paid advertising
        platforms, 134
    personal brand, 138
    strategies, 132

INDEX

transition, 138
value-driven content, 138
Industry, 247
Influencer life, 165
    attention economy, 165
    availability, 174
    breaks/disconnect, 176
    communication channels, 175
    consuming content, 165
    continuous evaluation/
        adjustment, 176
    daily time schedule, 167, 168
    digital detox, 172–174
    healthy boundaries, 174
    mindfulness practices, 174
    physical health, 174
    projects/campaigns, 169
    self-reflection, 177
    strategies, 167
    structured routines, 167
    support systems, 176
    tasks/delegate, 175
    time blocking
        techniques, 169–171
Influencers, 2
    authenticity, 10, 11
    content creation, 37–39
    criticism, 36
    ethics, 51
    information/media literacy, 13
    knowledge/skill, 36
    marketing, 15
    metrics, 7, 8
    niche, 35, 42
    passion, 36
    pop culture trendsetters, 8–10
    responsibility, 11–13
    traditional media, 6
Instagram, 23, 53, 122, 133
    Ballerina Farm, 146
    hashtags strategies, 158
    influencers, 12

J

Jiangao, Shen, 17
Johns, Kristin, 199
    ad revenue, 200
    affiliate marketing, 200
    aspiring influencers, 202
    brand sponsorships/
        collaborations, 199
    exclusive content, 202
    monetization, 202
    Patreon, 202
    selling digital products/
        services, 201
    sponsored YouTube videos, 201
    YouTube, 200

K

Kardashian, Kim, 92, 165
Kattan, Huda, 46
    beauty blogger, 46
    community, 47
    content expansion, 47
    global phenomenon, 47

Kattan, Huda (*cont.*)
   lash line, 47
   product creation, 46
Khare, Michelle, 87

L

Less edited contents
   community boundaries, 80
      accessibility, 83
      active listening, 82
      community members, 83
      differences, 81
      direct messages (DMs), 82
      engagement representation, 80
      high-quality images and videos, 84
      messaging information, 85, 87
      model inclusive behavior, 82
      positive interactions, 82
      safe/supportive environment, 81
      trends/developments, 84
   creation, 78
   imperfection, 78
   post-production, 79
   risks, 79
   vulnerability, 79
Libel and slander, 53–55
LinkedIn
   Ballerina Farm, 146
   hashtags strategies, 160
   influencers, 12

M

Marketing, 279
   AI-driven takes, 280
   algorithms/data, 291
   authenticity, 16, 283, 286
   boycotts/canceling, 288
   celebrity endorsements, 18, 19
   collaborations, 284
   consumer behavior, 24, 283
   consumer protection, 287
   consumers, 285
   data-driven insights, 286
   data privacy laws, 285
   digital influencers, 27–29
   digital revolution, 21, 22
   entrepreneurs, 284
   ethical standards, 290
   evolution, 16, 23
   globalization, 25
   historic influencer, 25–29
   immersive marketing, 286
   influencer fatigue, 290
   Lauder, Estée, 26
   livestreaming, 283
   long-term partnerships, 24
   mass media, 20
   medieval courts, 17
   mental health, 289
   metaverse, 282
   micro-and nano-influencers, 280, 281
   mismatched values, 287
   niche creation, 23

overselling products/services, 287
personalized content, 280
platform expansion, 23
platforms/technologies, 282
political influencers, 29–31
predictive analytics, 280
professionalism, 24
public apologies, 288
regulation and transparency, 24
saturation and consumer trust, 290
short-form video, 283
soap opera, 16
social commerce, 282
sponsored content, 289
transparency, 284, 286
trust, transparency, and authenticity, 292
virtual influencers, 24, 281, 282
Monetization methods
  ad revenue, 182
  affiliate links, 180
  classifications
    audience size, 183, 184
    niche influencers, 186
  compensation, 183, 197–199
    affiliate marketing, 187
    cost per engagement (CPE), 186, 187
    exclusive content, 189
    flat rate, 186
    long-term partnerships, 188
    paid appearances, 189
    performance-based compensation, 187
    product/service, 188
    revenue share, 189
  consulting/coaching services, 183
  crowdfunding/donations, 181
  digital offerings, 181
  entertainment and brands, 179
  factors compensation, 190, 191
  intellectual property (IP), 183
  Johns, Kristin, 199–203
  licensing content, 182
  macro-influencers, 194, 195
  mega-influencers, 196, 197
  merchandise, 181
  micro-influencers, 192, 193
  mid-tier influencers, 193, 194
  nano-influencers, 191, 192
  sell physical products, 182
  speaking/appearance fee, 182
  sponsored content, 180
Musk, Elon, 143

N

Nano-influencers
  characteristics, 191
  compensation, 192
  monetization, 192
Natural language processing (NLP), 72

INDEX

Netflix, 2
Niche
    authenticity, 34
    content creation/consistency, 45
    factors, 34
    gap identification, 42
    history, 33
    leveraging personal brand, 42
    market research/analysis, 44
    passion/expertise, 42
    self-discovery/passion, 43
    specialization, 44
    unusual areas, 45
Non-disclosure agreements (NDAs), 55, 56, 60

O

OnlyFans models, 21

P

Patagonia, 11
Personal branding
    definition, 65
    Forleo, Marie, 86
    Khare, Michelle, 87
    less edited content, 78–88
    quality content, 66–78
    Vaynerchuk, Gary, 85
Persuasion, 6
Photoshop application
    adjustments menu, 103
    auto settings, 104
    brightness/contrast, 103
    burn tool, 108
    color balance, 104, 105
    crop and straighten, 109
    curves, 104
    dodge tool, 108
    filter menu, 105
    gradient map, 108
    healing brush, 107
    hue/saturation, 104
    layers, 106, 107
    levels, 104
    lookup adjustment layers, 108
    quick selection tool, 108
    select and mask, 108
    sharpen image, 105, 106
    vibrance and saturation, 104
Picasso, Pablo, 20
Political influencers, 29–31
Presley, Elvis, 20

Q

Quality content production
    authenticity, 67, 70
    beliefs and principles, 69
    collaborations, 76, 77
    comments/messages, 73
    comments/questions, 69
    community building, 78
    consistent tone/style, 68
    contests and challenges, 70
    conversations, 69
    definition, 66

Eventbrite/Facebook Events, 76
gathering direct feedback, 75
Hashtag monitoring, 72
high-quality content, 67
inclusive language, 70
in-person interactions, 76
key method, 74
keyword-based searches, 72
metrics, 74
one-on-one interactions, 76
participation, 75
relationships, 78
sentiment analysis, 72
share personal experiences, 67
social listening, 71
social media tracking tools, 71
strategies, 67
strong community, 69
transparency, 77
trends, 74
user-generated content, 71
viral challenges, 75

R

Return on investment (ROI), 28, 258
Rogan, Joe, 155

S

Sharing animations, 1
Social media, 4, 138
    digital revolution, 21, 22
    Instagram, 122

TikTok, 122
visual and copywriting
    guide, 110–113
Social media influencers
    accounts/engage interest,
        157, 158
    active engagement, 128
    algorithms, 223
    audience, 153
    authenticity, 128
    Ballerina Farm, 141–147
    boundaries, 130
    build relationships, 154
    built-in advantage, 152
    community building, 127, 129
    cultural landscape, 146–149
        communication/
            interaction, 147
        E-commerce/consumer
            culture, 148
        entertainment and pop
            culture, 147
        news/information
            consumption, 147
        politics/movements, 148
    deeper dive, 149–152
    different platforms, 154
    diversity and inclusion, 129
    hashtags strategies, 158
        collaboration, 161
        contests, 162
        Facebook, 160
        features, 162
        Instagram, 158

INDEX

Social media influencers (*cont.*)
    LinkedIn, 160
    performance analysis, 162
    quality content, 160
    research relevant, 161
    TikTok, 159
    Twitter, 159
  hashtag strategies, 128
  high-quality content consistent, 153
  key strategies, 128
  mindful promotion, 129
  niche down, 152
  patient/persistent, 154–156
  platforms/online content creators, 5
  techniques, 130
  valuable content, 129

T

Teigen, Chrissy, 239–244
TikTok, 122, 133
  Ballerina Farm, 146
  hashtags strategies, 159
  influencers, 13
  monetization methods, 182
  short-form video domination, 247
Traditional media
  creator's community, 7
  democratization, 7
  newspapers, 6
  non-digital channels, 5

Trends/opportunities
  AI/data analytics, 253
  AI integration, 256
  AR and VR technologies, 251
  AR-Driven Shopping, 257
  authentic content, 255
  authentic endorsements, 269
  authenticity, 249, 255, 262
  brands/influencers/audiences, 261
  business-to-business (B2B), 260
  campaign goals, 263
  cause marketing, 266
  clubhouse/BeReal/substack, 248
  co-creation, 271
  consistency, 262
  consistent messaging, 256
  consumer behavior, 269, 276
  creator-owned businesses, 251
  crowd-influenced purchasing, 271
  crowdsourced content, 264, 271
  crowdsource endorsements, 267
  data-driven, 258
  data privacy concerns, 268
  data security, 268
  demand access, 262
  diverse industries, 260
  ecommerce integration, 258
  ethical practices, 266
  ethics and values-driven consumption, 272
  future, 254

genuine engagement, 269
hyper-personalization, 275
interactive and participatory content, 263
interactive/immersive brand, 270
long-term partnerships, 261, 262
long-term relationships, 252, 256
marketing platforms/data tracking, 254
metaverse, 257
micro-and nano-influencers, 252
monetization options, 250
narrative-based campaigns, 267
niche communities, 255
one-off campaigns, 252, 256
peer reviews/testimonials, 266
performance metrics, 259
personalization, 259, 269
personalized content, 264
personalized recommendations, 270
platforms/digital spaces, 247
predictive analytics, 265, 275
privacy and data security, 274
purpose-driven campaigns, 265
purpose-driven influencers, 259
real-time customization, 275
seamless integration, 273
shared values, 263
social commerce, 258
social consciousness, 269
storytelling and content, 267
sustainability/ethics/social responsibility, 265
technology-driven, 261
TikTok, 247
tracking and feedback, 265
transparency, 268
transparent brand relationships, 262
two-way conversations, 263
user-generated reviews, 266
value-driven content, 267
virtual/digital influencers, 274
virtual events, 257
virtual influencers, 256
Twitter, 123, 133
  Ballerina Farm, 146
  hashtags strategies, 159
  influencers, 12
  niche, 43

U

Unique selling proposition (USP), 42, 44
User-generated content (UGC), 264

V

Vaynerchuk, Gary, 85, 137
Virtual reality (VR), 23, 251, 270
Visuals, 113, 114

INDEX

W
Wedgwood, Josiah, 15
Witherspoon, Reese, 135

X
X (formerly Twitter), 123

Y
YouTube, 124, 137, 182

Z
Zoe Sugg (Zoella), 215, 216

GPSR Compliance

The European Union's (EU) General Product Safety Regulation (GPSR) is a set of rules that requires consumer products to be safe and our obligations to ensure this.

If you have any concerns about our products, you can contact us on

ProductSafety@springernature.com

In case Publisher is established outside the EU, the EU authorized representative is:

Springer Nature Customer Service Center GmbH
Europaplatz 3
69115 Heidelberg, Germany

www.ingramcontent.com/pod-product-compliance
Lightning Source LLC
LaVergne TN
LVHW010337260326
834688LV00036B/749